Not[illegible]

Ultimat[illegible]
Saltwater Fishing [illegible]

Larry V. Notley

Artwork by Larry V. Notley

FAP
FRANK AMATO PUBLICATIONS

All inquiries should be addressed to:

Frank Amato Publications, Inc.

P.O. Box 82112, Portland, Oregon 97282

503.653.8108 • www.amatobooks.com

Illustrations by Larry V. Notley

Book: Kathy Johnson

Cover Design: Tony Amato

Printed in China

Softbound ISBN-13: 978-1-57188-482-4 • UPC: 0-81127-00324-2

1 3 5 7 9 10 8 6 4 2

Dedication

Dedicated to my wife Louise who encouraged me and unselfishly stood beside me through the many months of work that took valuable time from her.

Contents

Chapter 1 • General Information

Chapter 2 • Knots

Chapter 3 • Rigs and Tackle

Chapter 4 • Fly-Fishing Leaders and Rigs

Introduction

While standing in my booth at a fly fishing conclave a distinguished gentleman walked up and proceeded to pick up and thumb the pages of *Guide to Fly Fishing Knots,* my second book. As he did he had a smile that stretched ear to ear as the pages turned. He went as far as to read the Foreword written by Flip Pallot. After completing his journey through the book he placed it back in its original spot on the table.

Still smiling he asked, "Why should I buy this book when I can find the same information in other books and magazines?"

Returning the smile and in a humble voice I replied, "Yes, sir you can. But may I ask, do you remember which magazines or books the information is in, where you left them and how big a hurry you're in for the information?"

The gentleman picked the book back up, handed me payment for the book and replied with two simple words, "Point made."

As a sport fisherman I have become a teacher of the knots and rigs I have learned over the past three decades. The majority of you that page through this book do not care or have time to continually look through stacks of magazines and books for information you need and want now. This book is for beginners to advanced fishermen and in a clear, illustrated format that guides you through an array of information, knots, and rigs. I would like to offer these pages as a solid informational base for general information, knots, and rigs.

It's your job to work and enjoy your time fishing, the job of this book is to save you research time so you can do what you do best.

Tight knots, good rigs and happy fishing,

Larry V. Notley,

Galactic War Lord and Mad Dog Fisherman

Chapter I
General Information

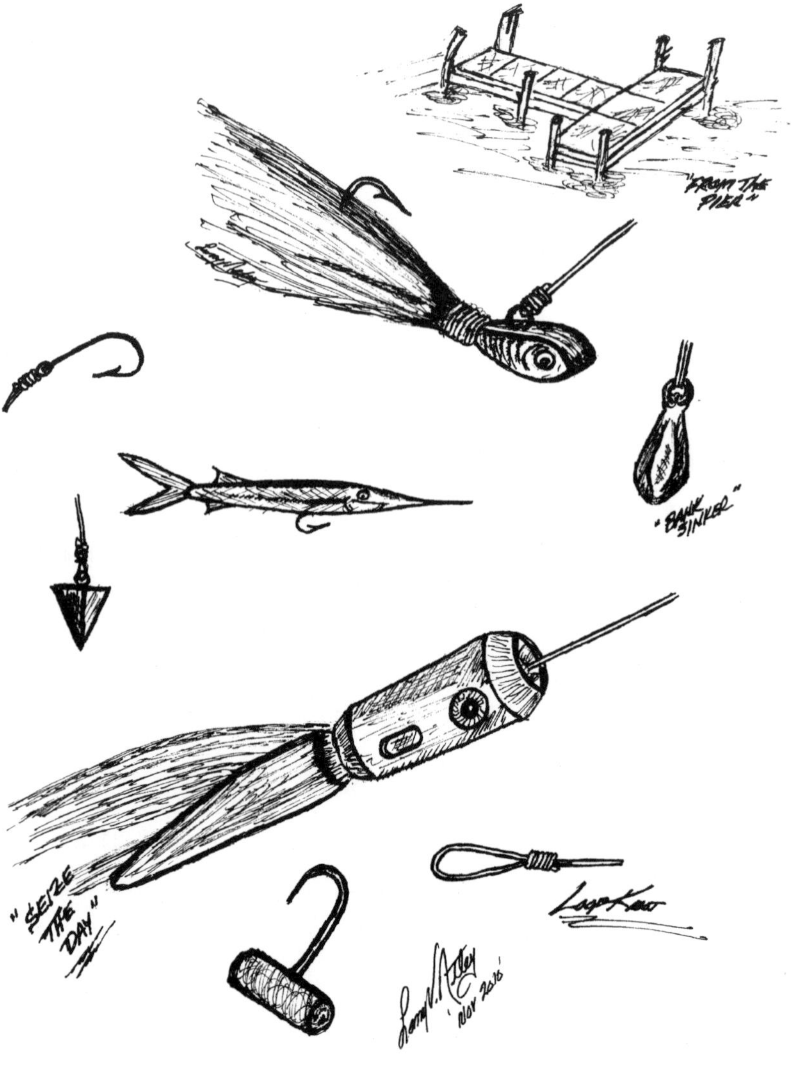

Anatomy of a Hook

A hook is not just a hook, there is a variety of sizes, shapes and styles and each has its time and place. It's important to use the right hook at the right time. Contact your local tackle shops for advice on the best hook for your destination.

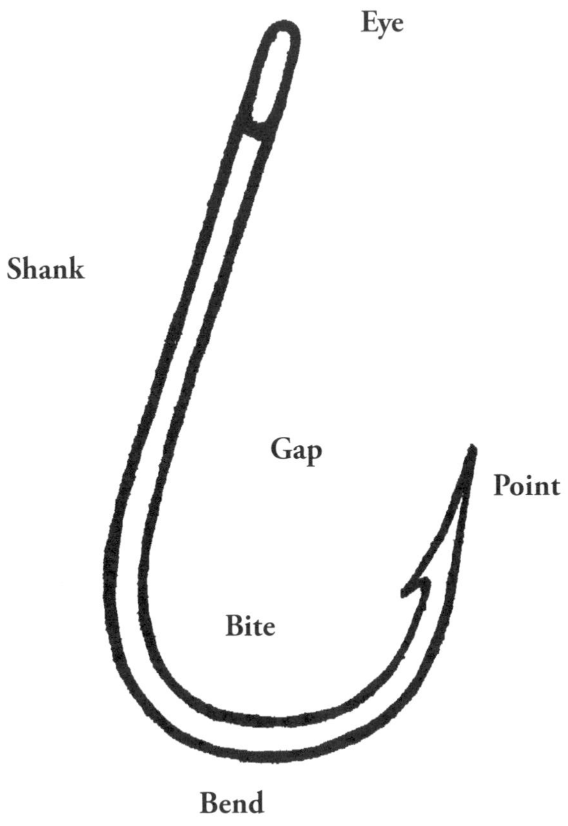

Bait Buckets

When visiting an area for several days, use a bait bucket. A five-gallon bucket with a lid that seals shut and an inexpensive 50-foot rope attached to it works well when tethered off a pier. Drill several holes several inches above the bottom so water can enter and exit when lowered and raised, keeping your bait alive and fresh. Drill several holes near the bottom to drain the bucket.

A commercial bait bucket works just as well. Just a suggestion, if you do not take the bait bucket home give it to a youngster on the pier and make his/her day.

Making a Bait Bucket

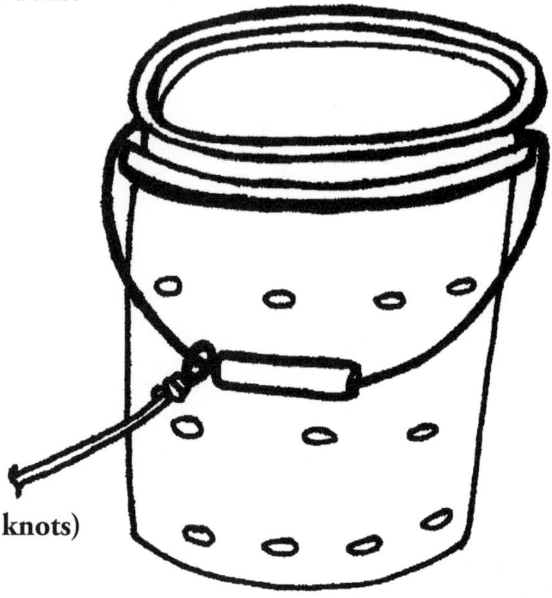

Ballyhoo Hook Size

Ballyhoo lengths range from about 6 inches to 12 inches, with an average size of about 10 inches.

Small bait: 5/0 or 6/0 hook

Medium bait: 7/0 or 8/0

Large bait: 9/o or 10/0

Note: ***Experiment with your line, hooks and weight to suit your fishing style.***

Building a Bomb

There is nothing like making your own jigs to add to the satisfaction of the catch. It doesn't take much; in fact you more than likely have all the materials at home. Pick your colors for clear and overcast days. Also get your kids involved.

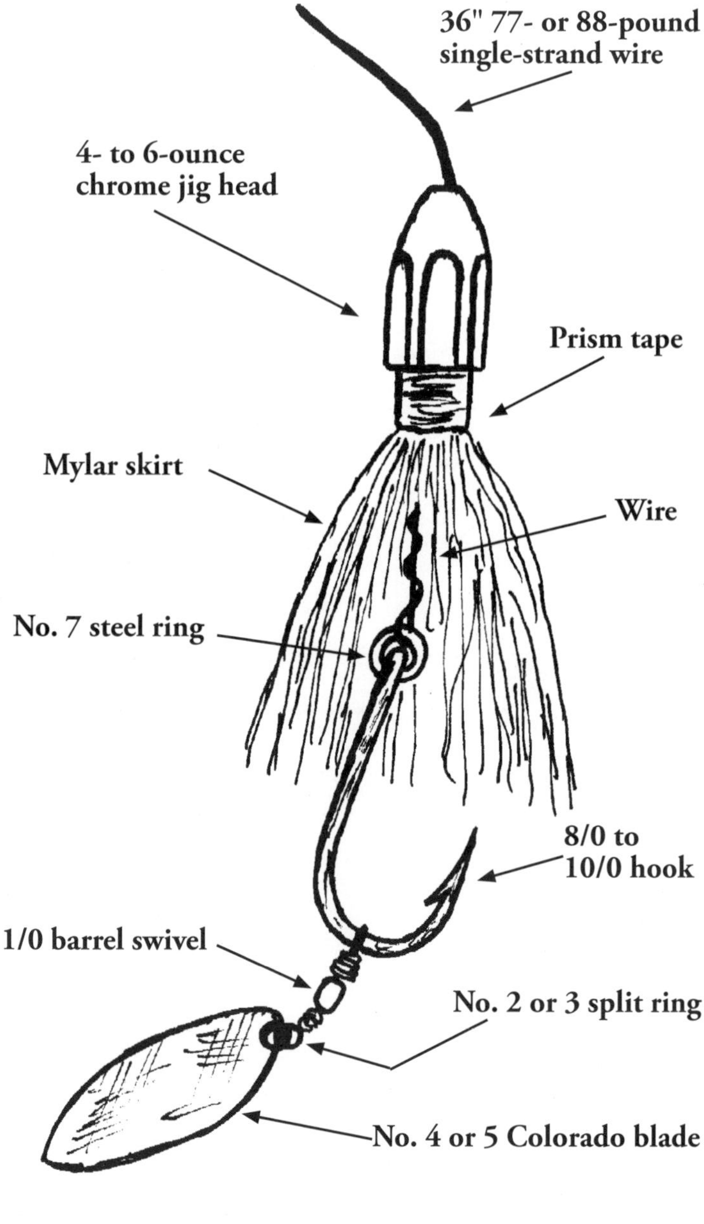

Chum Chucker

Chum chucker, think tennis-ball chucker for dogs. This device helps keep your hands clean and puts your chum where you want it. It's great for use in a boat, off a pier or jetty.

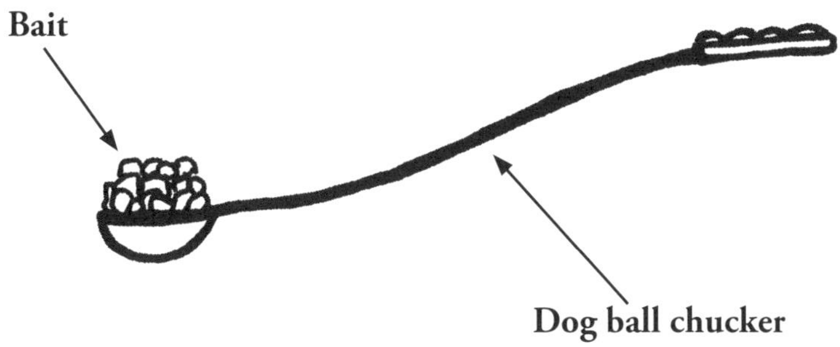

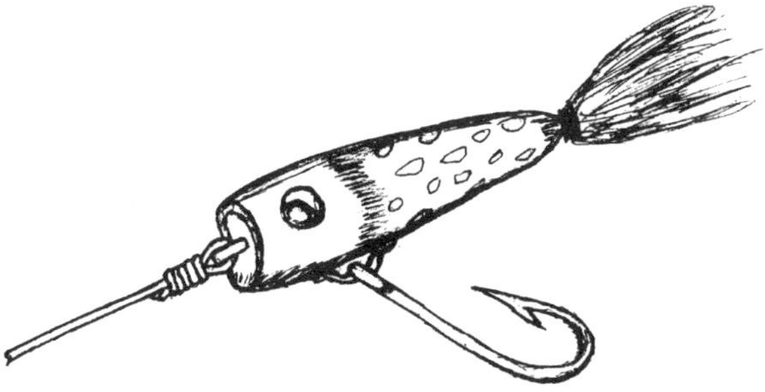

Circle Hooks

- ▶ Wide-gap hooks are good when using large bait. You do not have to go up a hook size.
- ▶ Circle hooks are particularly good for hook-ups without a violent hook-set and for reduced fish mortality.
- ▶ Diamond point hooks are very sharp. Use them when you don't sharpen yourself; however, they are very hard to sharpen once they become dull.

Circle hooks are showing more and more advantage over the more typical hooks. Circle hooks offer the following advantages:

- ▶ Circle hooks lower fish mortality from being deep hooked. They are as much as 10 times better than standard hooks.
- ▶ Circle hooks nearly eliminate foul-hooking a fish in most circumstances.
- ▶ Circle hooks are great for hooking fish and keeping them hooked. In some circumstances they are twice as efficient at bringing in fish as the standard hook.
- ▶ Circle hooks are easier to set on less aggressive fish because the circle hook's natural tendency to twist in a fish's mouth once bitten.

Common Hook Placements

Hook mullet through top lip or back

Small-mouth fish hook side to side near mouth

Hook under tail for more depth

Pilchard hook through eye-socket or nostril

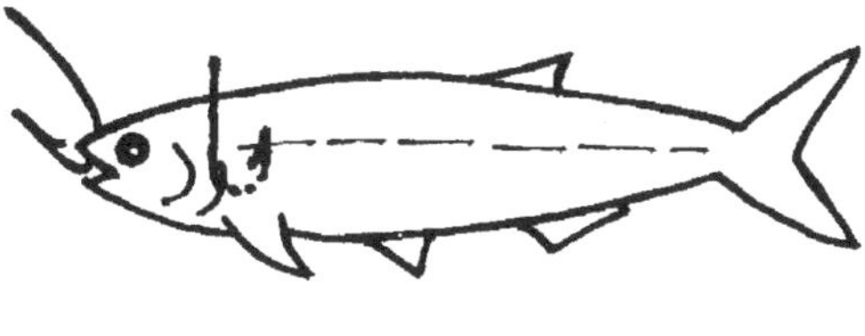

Hook anchovy through nose or gill collar

Cut-Bait Rigs

Six methods for hooking cut baits primarily for casting and bottom fishing.

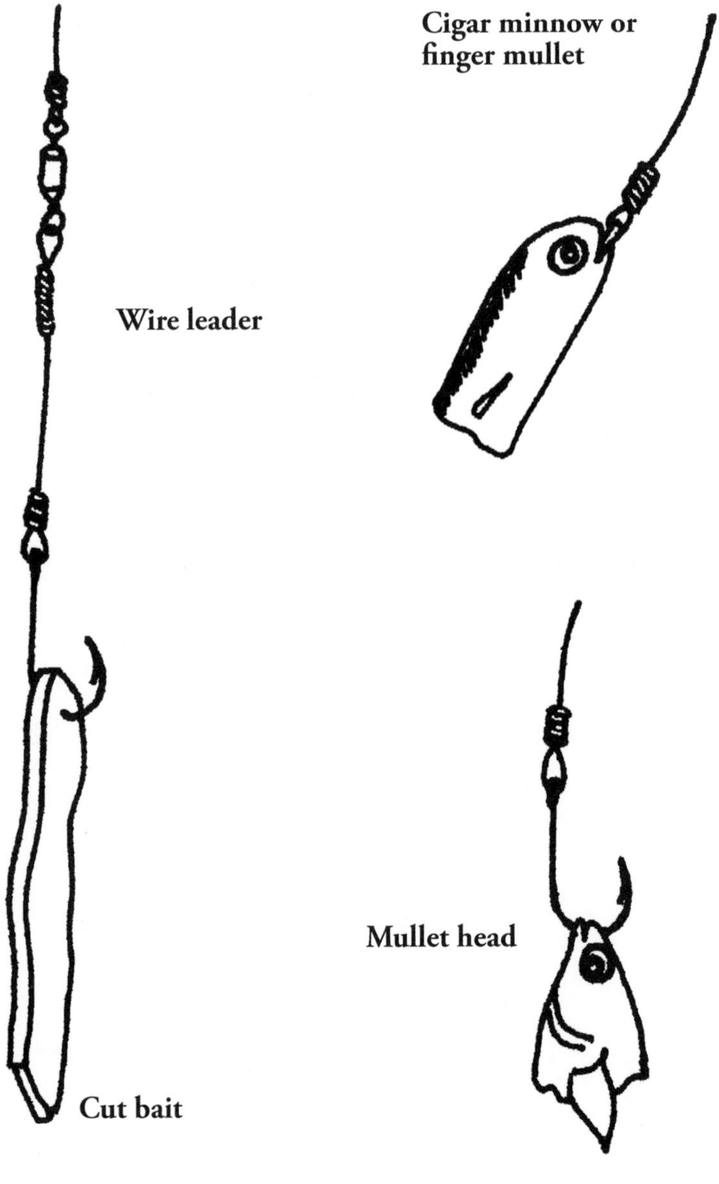

Cutting Bait

There are right and wrong ways to cut bait. The diagram shows six methods for cutting bait and hooking bunker chunks.

Cube

Split

Chunk

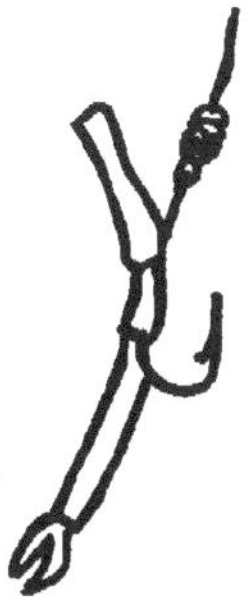

Crab leg

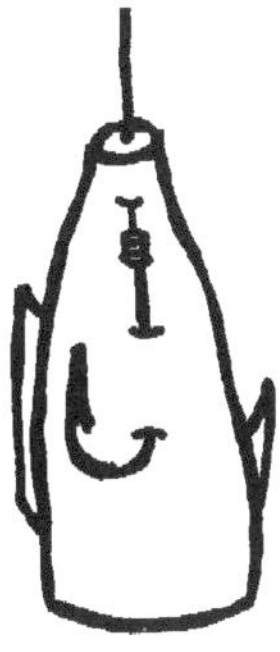

Half bait

Strip bait

Cutting Braided Line

If you have had trouble cutting braided line try using this simple but efficient letter opener. They're inexpensive and easy to use.

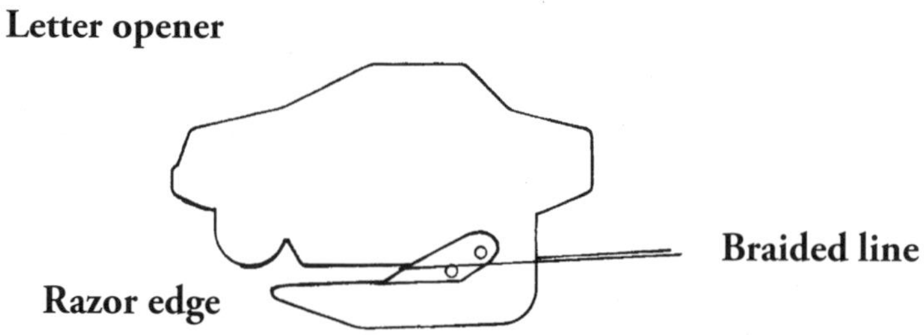

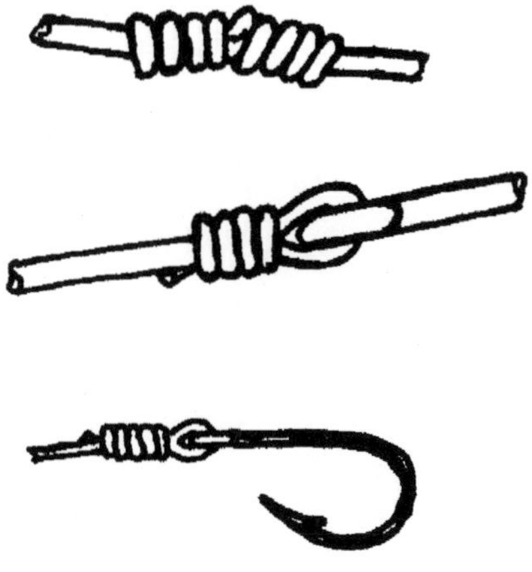

Fish by the Moon

New Moon

The new moon phase reflects no light, creates powerful tides and is recognized as the most promising time to go fishing.

First Quarter

The first quarter moon phase is also known as a half moon. This phase offer little light and the weakest tides of the month.

Full Moon

The few days before and few days after the full moon phase are recognized to be the best days to go fishing.

Third Quarter

The third quarter moon phase also known as the last quarter is similar to the first quarter provides little light and weak tides.

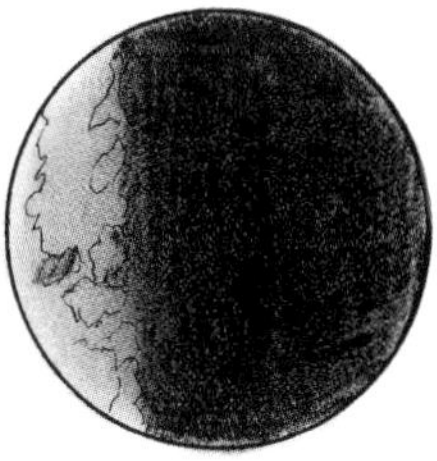

Five Bait Chunking Tips

Think Fresh, Fresh, Fresh!
Fresh bait is a must for a good day on the water.

1. **Fresh Bait:** Always use fresh bait. If you can, carry live bait then cut it up on site. Remember, the smell of slime is your ticket to attracting more fish. Handle bait only when necessary.
2. **Prime Cut Bait:** Try to cut your bait on the spot for freshness. Attract larger fish by removing the head and tail then cutting the bait in two pieces starting around the shoulder and cutting back and down to the anus area.
3. **Terminal Tackle:** Use circle hooks whenever possible, this will help eliminate lost fish and reduces the chance of gut-hooking your catch. Always use the lightest weight possible to hold the bait on the bottom and the lightest leader possible.
4. **Jigging:** When your jig hits bottom, jig the bait up and down occasionally or give it two or three short jerks then let it come to rest for a short period of time. Repeat this action when you feel the need.
5. **Set the Hook:** Leaving the reel on free spool, the line tight and clicker on, watch the rod tip for any type of action. When the fish takes the bait remember that setting a circle hook requires a steady but firm pull.

Saltwater Fish Water Temperature Preferences

Species	Lower	Optimum	Upper
Atlantic Mackerel	40	45-55	70
Barracuda	55	72-80	86
Bigeye Tuna	52	62-74	80
Blackfin Tuna	65	70-75	82
Black Marlin	68	72-82	87
Bluefin Tuna	50	60-72	82
Bluefish	50	66-72	84
Blue Marlin	70	74-82	88
Bonefish	60	72-84	92+
Dolphin (fish)	70	72-78	82
Fluke (Summer Flounder)	56	62-66	72
Haddock	36	42-48	52
Jack Crevalle	65	70-85	90
Kelp Bass	62	64-68	72
King Mackerel	65	68-76	88
Permit	70	75-85	92
Pollock	33	40-50	60
Pompano	65	70-82	85+
Red Drum (Channel Bass)	52	70-90	90+
Red Snapper	50	55-65	70+
Sailfish	68	72-82	88
Skipjack Tuna	50	58-62	70
Snook	60	70-82	90
Spotted Seatrout	48	68-78	88
Striped Bass	50	55-65	75
Striped Marlin	61	68-76	80
Swordfish	50	60-70	80
Tarpon	70	75-90	100+
Tautog	45	50-60	76
Weakfish	45	56-68	78
White Marlin	65	68-78	80+
White Seabass	58	64-68	74
Winter Flounder	35	48-52	64
Yellowfin Tuna	64	72-82	80
Yellowtail (Pacific)	60	62-66	70

Note: Carry a thermometer to check for changes in water temperature.

Health and Safety Tips for Shore and Surf Fishing

Angling from the shore can be very hazardous. Your life is more valuable than a fish so don't make stupid decisions.

Anglers of all levels need to be very careful:

THIS MEANS YOU!

1. Never, ever fish a new area without help and advice from someone experienced and knowledgeable in the area you wish to fish.
2. Always check the tide to ensure you will be safe to access and exit your chosen area. Watch your footing.
3. If unsure about the area you are fishing, watch out for cut-off points and drop-offs. Caution is the rule, always tell someone where you are fishing or fish with a partner.
4. Check the day's weather forecast prior to fishing. Watch the weather for changes during the day.
5. Don't access closed areas for any reason, your life isn't worth catching a fish.
6. Carry some device for communication: cell phone, 2-way radio, whistle, Spot, etc.
7. ALWAYS tell one or more persons where you are going and when you intend to return. Ask them to raise the alarm should you not return.
8. Never fish heavy seas. It's very dangerous, rip tides may occur and you're wasting your time, fish do not care for rough seas.

ALWAYS THINK SAFETY FIRST!

Holding Fish

Comfort Lift: Hold center of the fish's body

Vertical Lift: Immobilize non-sharp-toothed fish by holding them by the lip.

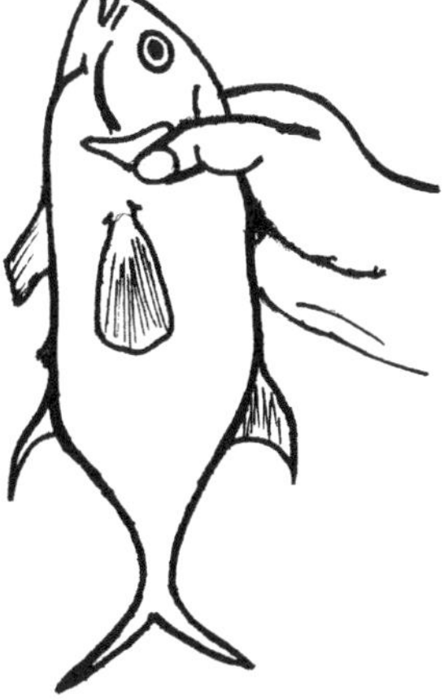

Holding Saltwater Species: Paralyze jack species without harm by gripping them across the head and pressing the first finger and thumb against the fish's body.

Hooking Live Bait #1

When you hook live bait near the base of the tail the bait swims away from the boat near the surface.

Hooking Live Bait #2

When you hook live bait near the pectoral fins the bait swims down and away from the boat.

Hooking Live Bait #3

When you hook live bait lip(s) the bait swims at the top and in a circular motion.

How to Measure A Fish

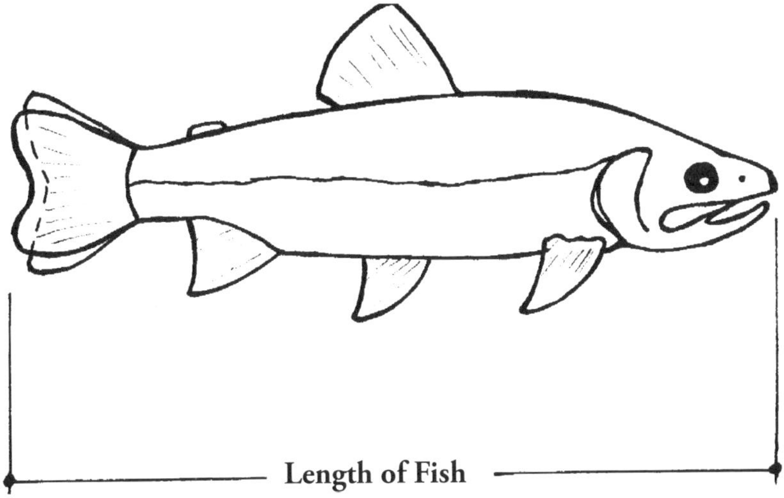

1. Lay the fish on top of or beside a flat measuring rule.
2. DO NOT lay the measuring rule over the curvature of the fish's body.
3. Close the fish's mouth and squeeze the tail lobes together.
4. Measure from the tip of the snout to the end of the tail.

Food for Thought

By using a circle hook the release of your catch will be easier and your catch will be released healthier.

How to Measure A Fish
(Continued)

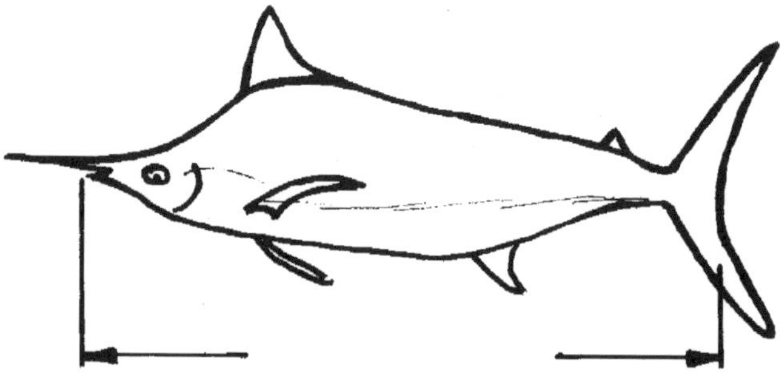

Blue Marlin

Yellowfin, Blackfin, Bluefin and Bigeye Tuna

IGFA Line Class for World Records

Pound/Kilogram Class	Maximum IGFA Test Class	(in pounds)
2	1	2.20
4	2	4.4
6	3	6.61
8	4	8.81
12	6	13.22
16	8	17.63
20	10	22.04
30	15	33.06
50	24	52.91
80	37	81.57
130	60	132.27

Table of Wet and Dry Tests

Standard Label (pound)	If Dry Test Is	Wet Test Would Be	Allowance Wet Test Is
2	2.5	2.13	2.2
4	5	4.25	4.4
8	10	8.5	8.8
12	15	12.75	13.22
16	20	17	17.6
20	25	21.3	22
30	38	32.3	33

Leader Wire Size, Single Strand

		Pound Test	
No.	Diameter	Stainless	Titanium
2	.011	28	--
3	.012	32	20
4	.013	39	--
5	.014	54	30
6	.016	61	40
7	.018	72	50
8	.020	88	70
9	.022	108	--
10	.024	127	--
12	.029	184	--
15	.035	258	--
19	.043	352	--

Jig Head Profiles

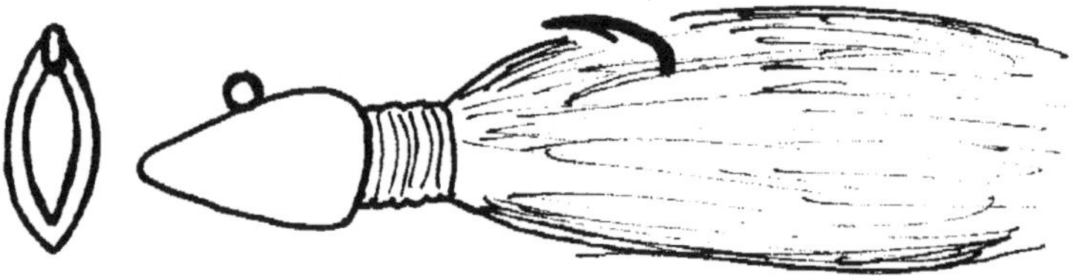

Arrowhead Jig: Popular for bottom species and open-water game fish. Its pointed head allows it to sink fast and when jigged, the head moves the jig up and down sharply.

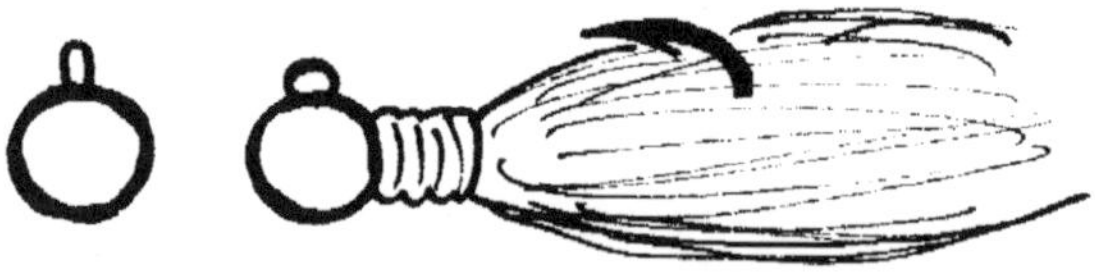

Ball Jig: Mostly used inshore when working inlet passes and shallow rips in strong currents. It has more weight in a compact package that sinks fast and tracks straight when retrieved.

Bonefish Jig: The flat-head design is balanced so the hook rides up. Since the hook rides up, the jig is virtually snag free. On retrieve and descent the jig flutters, mimicking the action of a crab.

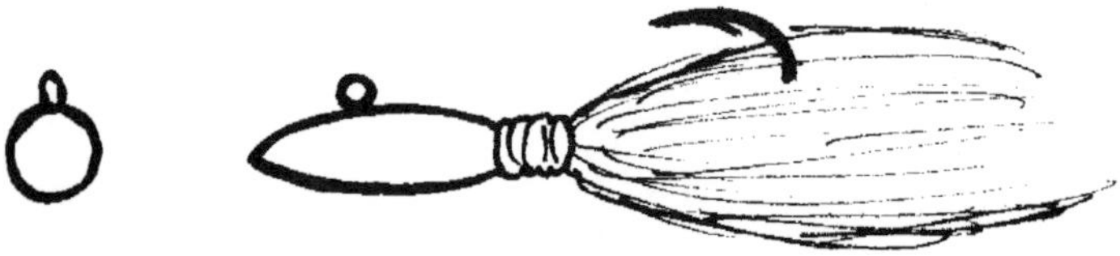

Bullet-Head Jig: A favorite jig when fishing offshore. Its streamline design allows it to cut through the water with minimum resistance.

Jig Head Profiles

(Continuted)

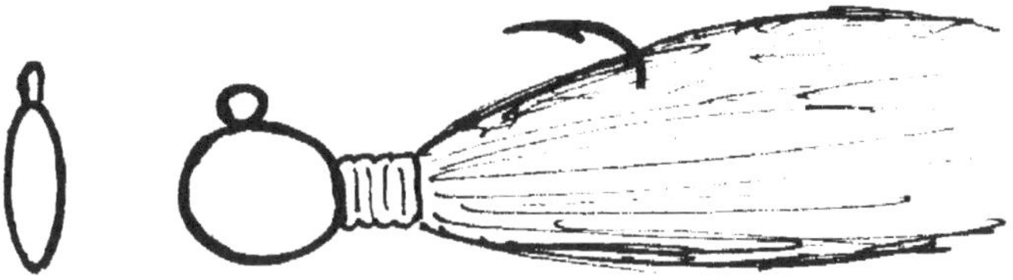

Flat-head Jig: Used primarily inshore and sometimes on schooling fish offshore. The shape makes it look like an injured baitfish or sinking piece of chum.

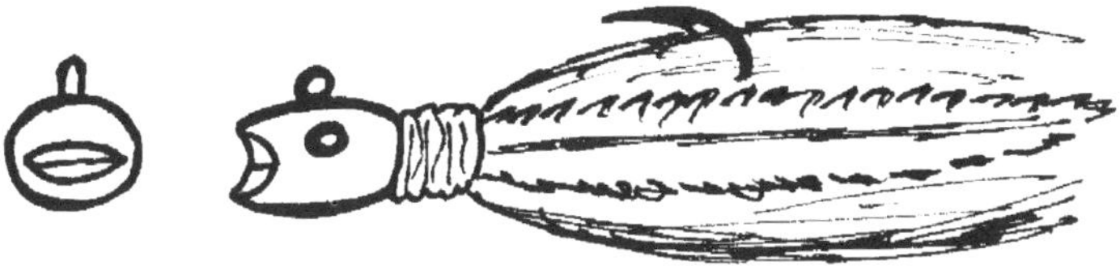

Hot Lips Jig: The pocket designed in the front sinks the jig quickly in an erratic action. Works well in shallow and swift-moving water.

Slider Jig: With its hook on top, this popular inshore jig rides up. Its primary use is skimming over shallow grass beds, oyster bars, flats and rocky passes.

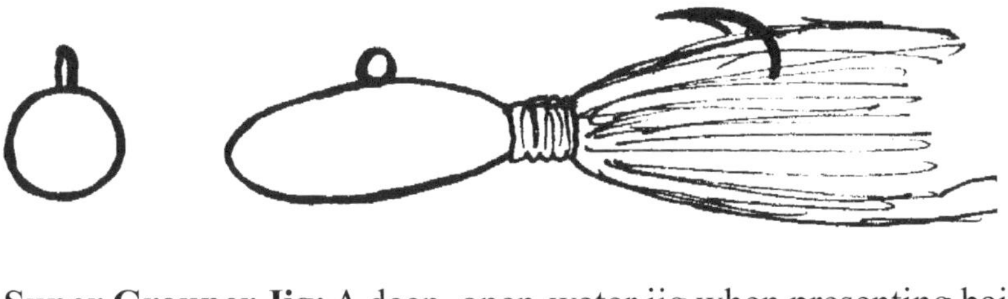

Super Grouper Jig: A deep, open-water jig when presenting bait over structure as deep as 300 feet. Also used when bouncing or hovering just off the bottom.

Leader Wire Size (Cable)

Table is for Seven Strand

Size (pound test)	Diameter
18	.011
27	.012
40	.015
60	.018
90	.024
135	.029
179	.033
250	.039

Leader Wire Size (Nylon-Coated Cable)

Sevalon

Size (pound test)	Diameter
18	.018
27	.020
40	.024
60	.034
90	.048
135	.058
179	.065
250	.075

Tyger Wire Size

Size (pound test)	Diameter
2	.006
5	.010
15	.014
30	.019
50	.024
70	.030
120	.037

Leader Wire Size (Aircraft Cable)

Size (pound test)	Diameter
175	.036
275	.042
400	.053
600	.067
800	.092

Line Twist

Line twist is common when retrieving a spoon or similar bait. To help eliminate line twist, attach a swivel to the spoon and a split ring to the swivel.

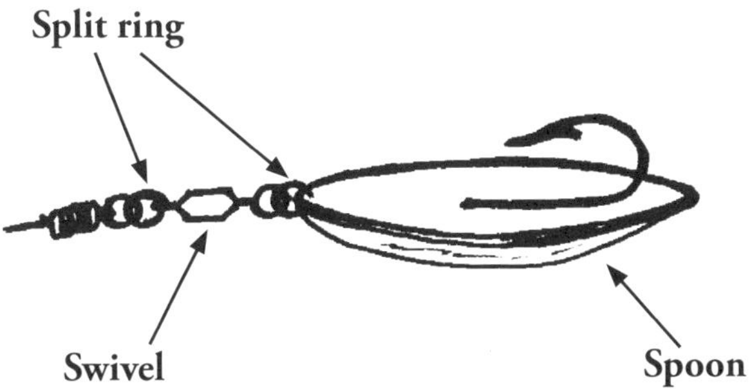

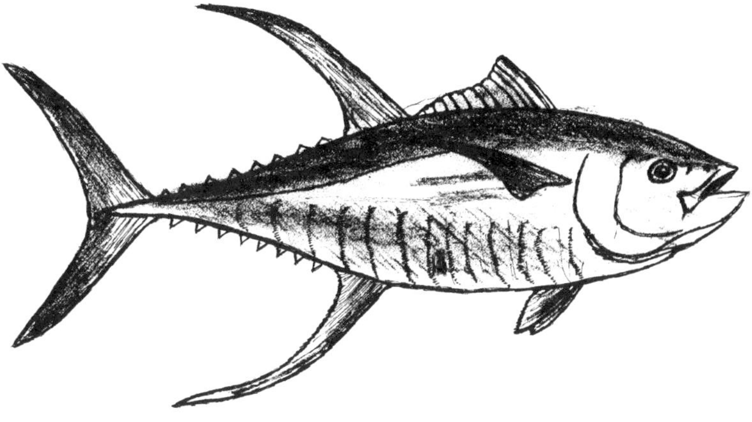

Live Bait

Below are some of the most popular live baits. These baits can be caught in inlets or channels using Sabiki rigs and/or a casting net.

Goggle Eyes	**Pilchards**	**Threadfin Herring**
Blue Runners	**Pinfish**	**Sardines**
Rainbow Runners	**Greenies**	**Cigar Minnows**

When rigging live bait for kite fishing, flat lines, or deep dropping, place the bait through the eye sockets or nostrils.

When drift fishing for kingfish, tuna, dolphin, wahoo and bass, hooking the bait just behind the head is the preferred choice of many anglers.

When slow-trolling live baits, hook the bait through the nose with a skinny hook to avoid breaking the nostrils. Set the drag as light as possible. When the fish picks up the bait, lock the drag and set the hook.

When drift fishing live baits with some degree of drag, pick up the rod, set the hook and start reeling when the fish hits the bait.

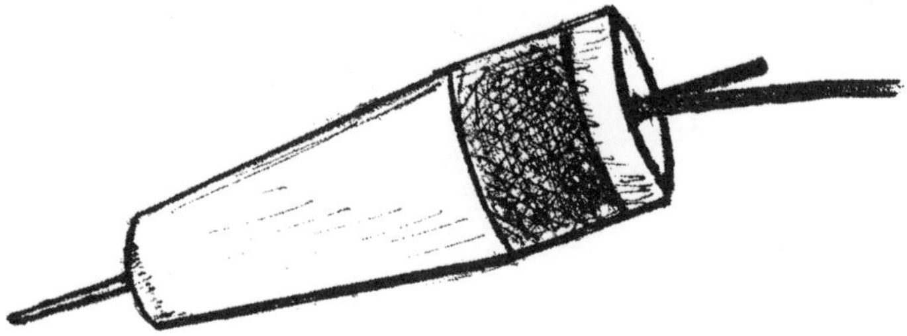

Remember:
Keep your bait as fresh as possible!

Monofilament Leader Sizes

Note: These are recommended sizes and may vary to your fishing style.

Type of Fishing	Leader Length	Leader (pound test)
General freshwater	2 to 3 foot	none to 20
General inshore	2 foot to rod length	20 to 40
Snook, tarpon	rod length	30 to 50
Deep jigging, reef or bottom fishing	rod length	50 to 60
Ocean/sea casting (surface to medium depth)	rod length	30 to 60
Ocean/sea trolling sailfish, small/average tuna, dolphin, etc.	6 to 12 feet	40 to 80
Ocean/sea trolling blue marlin, giant tuna, etc.	12 to 15 feet	80 to 300

Wire Leader Size Recommendations

Type of Fishing	Leader Length	Leader (pound test)
Inshore casting, trolling, light bottom fishing	6" to 3 feet	2 to 5
Offshore trolling and drifting sailfish, tuna, dolphin, etc.	6 to 10 feet	3 to 7
Offshore trolling sailfish, tuna, dolphin, etc.	12 to 15 feet	9 to 12
Bottom fishing, deep trolling	3 to 10 feet	7 to 9
Large shark fishing	12 to 15 feet	9 and up

Offshore and Tournament Checklist

1. Rigging needle, waxed line, ballyhoo wire and rubber bands.
2. Bait, ice, lures, teasers and salt.
3. Hooks and hook-sharpening stone or file.
4. Monofilament leaders and wire.
5. Ball-bearing swivels, snap swivels, crimps and crimping tools.
6. Knives, multi-tool, line snippers, pliers and weight scale.
7. Grease pencil, navigation chart and water temperature chart.
8. Polarizing sunglasses and eyeglass safety strap.
9. Tagging stick and tags.
10. Large flying gaff, small straight gaff and tailing rope.
11. New line on all reels.
12. Test and set drags.
13. Lubricate reels and rod rollers.
14. Inspect leaders and crimps.
15. Harness, gamble belt, gloves, etc.
16. Gloves, bill cap, short(s), tee shirt(s) and headlamp.
17. First-aid kit.
18. Rags, sponge.
19. Sunscreen.
20. Belt, for holding pliers and knife sheaths.
21. Tail rope/noose.
22. Jigs, jig heads, baits and assorted weights.
23. Sabiki rig to catch baitfish.

Basic First-Aid Kit

Adhesive strip bandages	Alcohol
Moleskin	Latex gloves
Cold pack	Scissors
Sterile bandage material	Medical tape
Aloe vera gel	Eye drops
Wire cutters for embedded hooks	Hydrogen peroxide
Iodine tincture	Gauze

Pier Fishing

Pier fishing is an exciting method of fishing for a variety of fish. I've been pier fishing from the early 80's to the present. Half of all my saltwater fishing is done from piers and surf during business trips, vacations and exploring new territories. It allows for easy access to the water when a boat is unavailable. Prior to visiting an area I'll research via the internet, other fishermen and local Chambers of Commerce.

Below are a few tips to help make your next pier outing a little easier and a lot more enjoyable:

1. A light-action 7- or 7 1/2-foot rod with 6- to 10-pound-test spinning or casting outfit works best for catching baitfish. Once you're set up on the pier the first thing is to catch some small bait, such as pilchard, pinfish or threadfin, using a Sabiki rig. For larger baitfish, such as goggle eyes and blue runners, rig with #15 Sabiki. Use a tiny piece of shrimp for catching ballyhoo.
2. Jig-fishing works great when fishing for pompano, Spanish mackerel and goofey. I find using a spinning outfit with 12- to 15-pound-test line, a medium-action 8' rod maximizes my casting distance.

   Flip your jig out and let it flutter to the bottom before retrieving with a jerking motion or bounce it on and off the bottom. Bucktails are excellent jigs with or without a bait strip.
3. I have found that fishing live bait with conventional tackle such as a 7- to 8-foot rod with a long butt section, 20- to 30-pound-test line is sufficient for medium to large sized fish.

The main reason I fish is for the enjoyment and pleasure.

Premium Mono to Braid

(Note: All dimensions are approximate and will vary by manufacturer.)

Braid (lb.)	Mono (lb)	Inches
8	1	.004
10	2	.005
15	4	.006
20	6	.008
30	8	.010
50	12	.014
80	20	.015
125	25	.021

Mono Test	Inches
20	.018
30	.022
50	.028
60	.031
80	.035
100	.039
125	.051

Fluorocarbon Test	mm.	Inches
10	.28	.011
12	.30	.012
15	.35	.014
20	.40	.016
25	.45	.018
30	.50	.020
40	.60	.024
50	.68	.027
60	.73	.029
80	1.00	.039
100	1.08	.043
120	1.20	.047
150	1.35	.053

Recommended Leader Strength

Species	Monofilament, Pound Test	Single-Strand Wire
Anchovy	2 to 15	
Ballyhoo	2 to 15	
Barracuda		2 to 8
Barramundi	50 to 80	
Bluefish		4 to 8
Boarfish	50 to 100	
Bonefish		2 to 20
Butterfish	50 to 100	
Cobia	30 to 100	
Cod	50 to 100	
Coral bream	20 to 50	
Coral trout	30 to 100	
Corvine	15 to 100	
Crocker	15 to 100	
Dogtooth tuna		4 to 15
Dorie	20 to 50	
Drum	15 to 100	
Drummers	10 to 30	
Eagle rays	50 to 100	
Emperors	20 to 50	
Filefishes, leather jack		2 to 4
Flying fish	2 to 15	
Goatfish	10 to 30	
Grouper	30 to 100	
Grunt		10 to 50
Gurnard	20 to 40	
Haddock	50 to 100	
Halfbeak	2 to 15	
Hake		50 to 100
Hammerhead shark		4 to 19
Hapuku	20 to 100	

Recommended Leader Strength (cont.)

Species	Monofilament, Pound Test	Single-Strand Wire
Herring	2 to 15	
Hogfish	10 to 100	
Houndfish		2
Hump head	10 to 100	
Ice fishe	50 to 100	
Jacks	2 to 100	
Kahawai	15 to 50	
Ladyfish	20 to 100	
Lefteye flounder	30 to 100	
Lingcod	50 to 100	
Mackerel		2 to 5
Mackerel shark		15 to 19
Mahi Mahi	30 to 80	
Maomao	8 to 15	
Margate	10 to 50	
Marlin		50 to 400
Morid cod	50 to 100	
Moonfish	100 to 300	
Morwong	30 to 50	
Mullet		2 to 20
Needlefish		2
Nurse shark	30 to 100	
Parrotfish	15 to 30	
Permit		2 to 100
Pilchard	2 to 15	
Polar cod	50 to 100	
Pollock	50 to 100	
Pomfert	30 to 100	
Pompano	2 to 100	
Porgie		20 to 50
Requiem shark		4 to 19
Right eye flounder, halibut	150 to 300	

Recommended Leader Strength (cont.)

Species	Monofilament, Pound test	Single-Strand Wire
Roosterfish	15 to 50	
Roughy	50 to 100	
Rubberfish	50 to 100	
Sea bream	20 to 50	
Sea chub	10 to 30	
Sea trout	15 to 100	
Sailfish		50 to 400
Salmon		2 to 50
Skate		30 to 80
Snapper	10 to 100	
Snook		50 to 80
Spearfish	50 to 400	
Spinecheek	20 to 50	
Spiny dogfish	30 to 50	
Stingray	30 to 100	
Stonebream	8 to 15	
Sweetlips	10 to 50	
Swordfish	300 to 400	
Tarpon		20 to 100
Temperate bass	20 to 100	
Thresher shark		15 to 19
Tiggerfish	20 to 50	
Tilefish		50 to 100
Trevally	2 to 100	
Tripletail	15 to 30	
Tropical bass	30 to 100	
Trout	2 to 50	
Trumpeter	30 to 100	
Tuna	20 to 300	
Wahoo		4 to 8
Wreckfish	20 to 100	
Wrass	10 to 100	

Saltwater Striped Bass Weight

Length vs Weight					
Age	Length	Weight	Age	Length	Weight
1	10"	0.05 lb	9	35"	16.20 lb
2	15"	2.10 lb	10	36"	19.00 lb
3	20"	3.30 lb	11	38"	20.00 lb
4	24"	4.90 lb	12	40"	22.40 lb
5	27"	6.50 lb	13	42"	27.00 lb
6	30"	8.50 lb	14	44"	35.00 lb
7	32"	12.30 lb	15	48"	42.00 lb
8	34"	14.50 lb			

Note: Measurement is taken from the tip of nose to the tip of tail. All weights are approximate.

Striped Bass Calculation

There is no substitute for an accurate scale but to estimate the weight of your striped bass, the formula is:

length x length x length/1,950

For example: A 24-inch striped bass weighs ~ 7 pounds;

24 x 24 x 24/1,950 =7 pounds.

A 32-inch striped bass weighs ~ 17 pounds;

32 x 32 x 32 / 1,950 =17 pounds

Note: To measure a striped bass properly lay the striper down flat on top of the tape measure. Do not measure a striper by measuring across the fish. Measurement is taken from the greatest length, from tip of nose to tip of tail.

All weights above are approximate.

Shark Weight

Home-Made Copper Weight

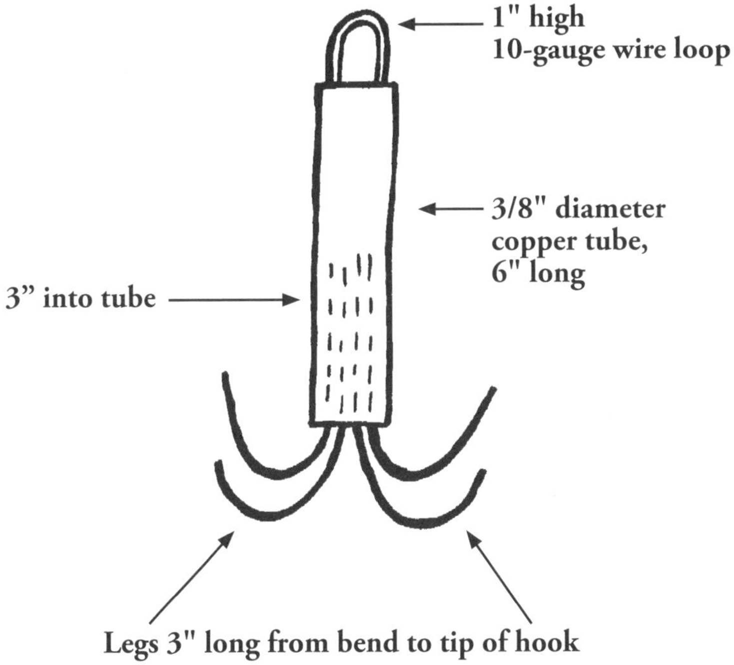

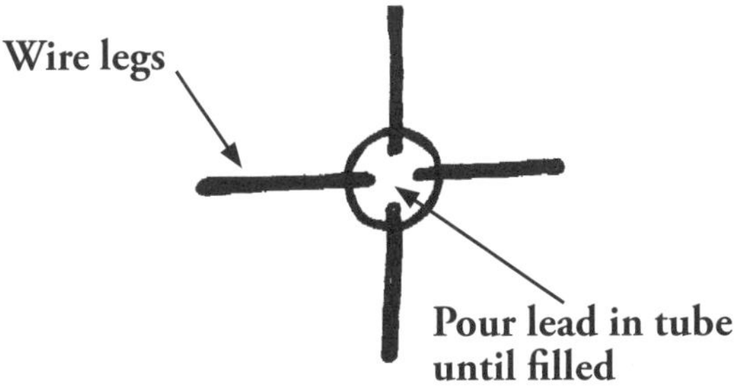

CAUTION! Lead is HOT when pouring and can cause severe burns.

Shock Absorbers

Use surgical tubing as a shock absorber. Select a piece of tubing with an I.D. (inner diameter) large enough to go over the knot of your main line and long enough to cover the full length of the knot. The egg sinker will bump against the piece of tubing instead of the knot.

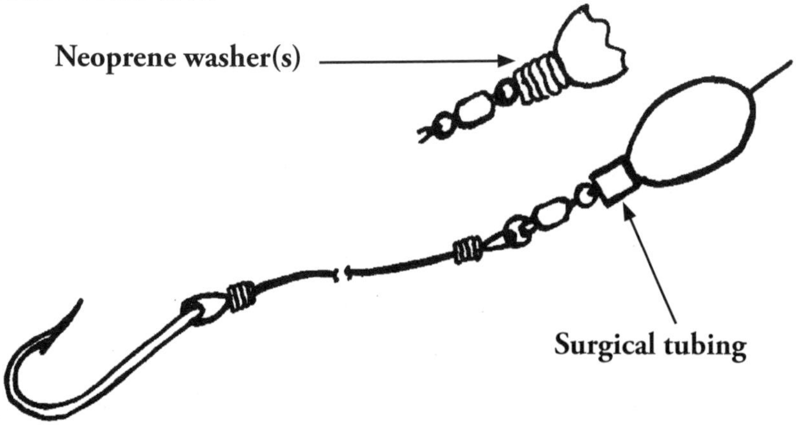

Holding Bait in Position

Use surgical tubing as a stopper. Select a piece of tubing with an I.D. that will fit snugly around the hook shank and 1/8" to 1/4" in length. Run the tubing over the bard and up the shank. After positioning your bait, move the tubing down to prevent the bait from moving up the hook shank.

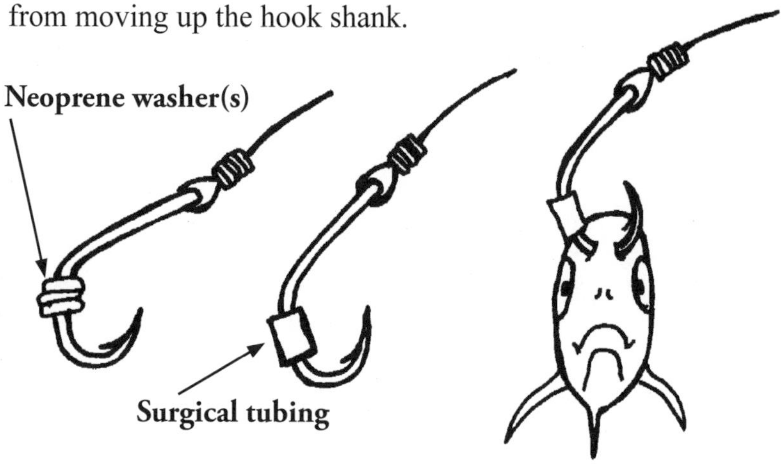

Sinkers

Sinker: A weight of lead or other metal designed for a hooked bait or lure.

Drop Casting Sinker
The swivel ensures your line won't get twisted up.

Walking Sinker
This is an improved version of a bank sinker. Drift fishing and/or rocky bottoms.

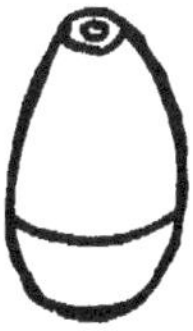

Egg Sinker
For weedless performance, a great all-around sinker.

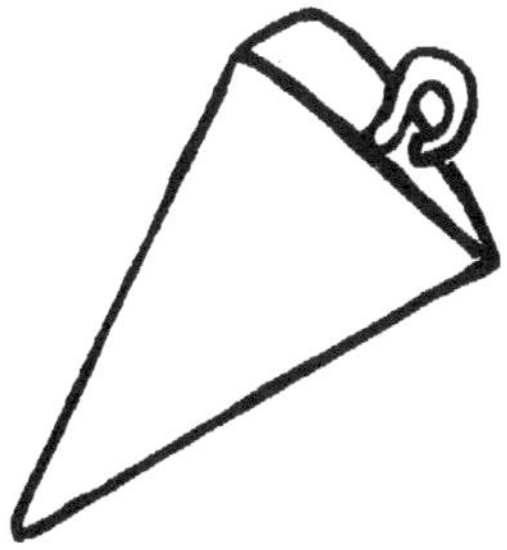

Pyramid Sinker
Primarily used for surf fishing where sandy bottoms and/or currents are present.

Bank Sinker
Used for drift fishing and/or rocky bottoms.

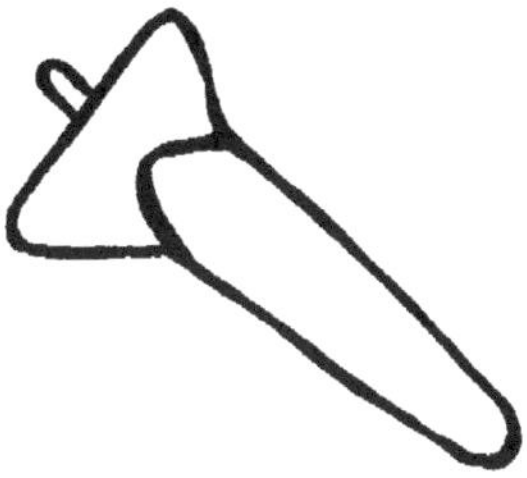

Hatteras Sinker
Primarily for surf fishing where sandy bottoms and currents are present. Better castability than a pyramid sinker.

Sinkers
(Continued)

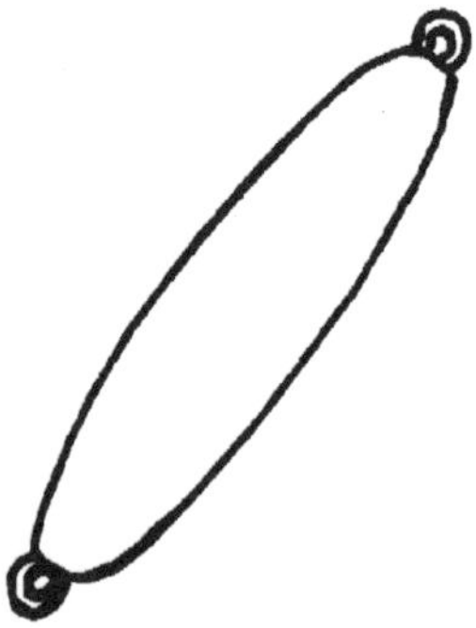

Trolling Sinker

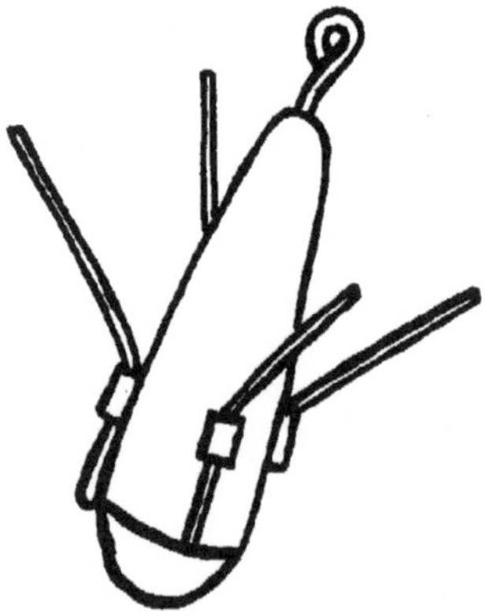

Sputnik Sinker
Primarily for surf fishing where sandy bottoms and currents are present for long-distance casting. Prongs release under pressure.

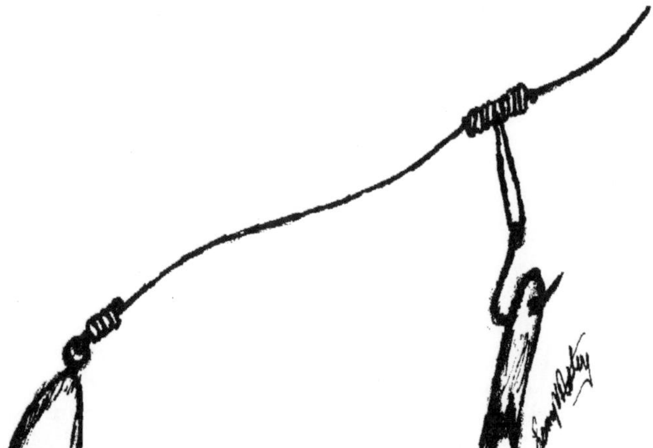

Surf Tackle

Just a few Recommendations

Heavy Surf

Spinning Outfit: Rod 11- to 12-foot, parabolic action. Spinning reel filled with 300 yards 20-pound test, capable of casting up to six-ounce sinkers plus bait.

Casting Outfit: Rod 10- to 12-foot, stiff parabolic action. Wide casting reel filled with 250 yards or more 15-pound test, capable of casting up to six-ounce sinkers plus bait.

Medium Surf

Spinning Outfit: Rod 8- to 9-foot, medium-fast action. Spinning reel filled with 300 yards of 15-pound, capable of casting up to four ounces of weight.

Casting Outfit: Rod 8- to 9-foot, medium-fast action. Wide casting reel, wide spool filled with 250 yards or more of 15-pound test.

Pier and Jetty

Spinning Outfit: Rod 8-foot, with medium-heavy action. Spinning reel filled with 200 yards of 15- to 20-pound test or the like.

Casting Outfit: Rod 8-foot, parabolic medium action. Wide casting reel filled with 200 yards or more of 15- to 20-pound test.

Quiet Surf

Spinning Outfit: Rod selection 7- to 8-foot, light action, medium to light. Spinning reel filled with 200 yards of 12- to 15-pound test, capable of casting up to two-ounce sinkers plus bait.

Casting Outfit: Rod selection 8-foot, light action. Wide casting reel filled with 200 yards or more of 12- to 15-pound test, capable of casting up to three-ounce sinkers plus bait.

All Terminal Tackle

Terminal tackle rigs such as fish finder rigs, single rigs or two-hook bottom rigs. Sinker up to six ounces: sandy bottom use a pyramid, for gravel or rock bottom use a bank sinker.

Swivels

Ball-Bearing Swivel

Crane Barrel Swivel

Barrel Swivel

Twist Brass Wire Swivel

3-Way Swivel

Note: ***To minimize line twist, add a swivel between the main line and the leader.***

Swivels
(Continued)

Duo-Lock Snap & Ball-Bearing Swivel

Duo-Lock Snap

Nylon Fish Finder Slider & Snap

Duo-Lock Snap & Barrel Swivel

Coast Lock Snap & Barrel Swivel

Trip Checklist

To make your trip or tournament more successful, here are a few checklist items and suggestions:

1. Rules and regulations from state and federal governments.
2. Rigging needle(s), waxed line, wire and rubber bands.
3. Artificial and natural baits, teasers and lures.
4. Appropriate ice chests, ice and salt.
5. Sharpened spear hooks, 7/0, 8/0 and others if you think necessary.
6. Monofilament and braided leaders (20- to 130-pound test) and additional terminal tackle.
7. Swivels, crimps and crimping tools.
8. Polarized sunglasses.
9. Navigation charts, water temperature charts, tide charts and grease pencil(s).
10. Sharp knife and knife sharpener, pliers, braided-line scissors and de-hooking tool.
11. Chum and chum bucket.
12. Inflatable life vest, fighting belt and harness.
13. New line on all reels. Lubricate reels and rod roller guides.
14. Test and set drag.
15. Check leaders, leader knots and crimps.
16. Tagging stick and tags, flying gaff, large and small gaff, gloves, tail rope, etc.
17. Several changes of clothes and footwear.

Wire-Shy Tactic

When toothy fish such as sharks and king mackerel seem to be wary of your dead bait when using a long wire leader, try this technique: Move down to a shorter length, from 6 to 8 inches, and use a strong small swivel for the connection.

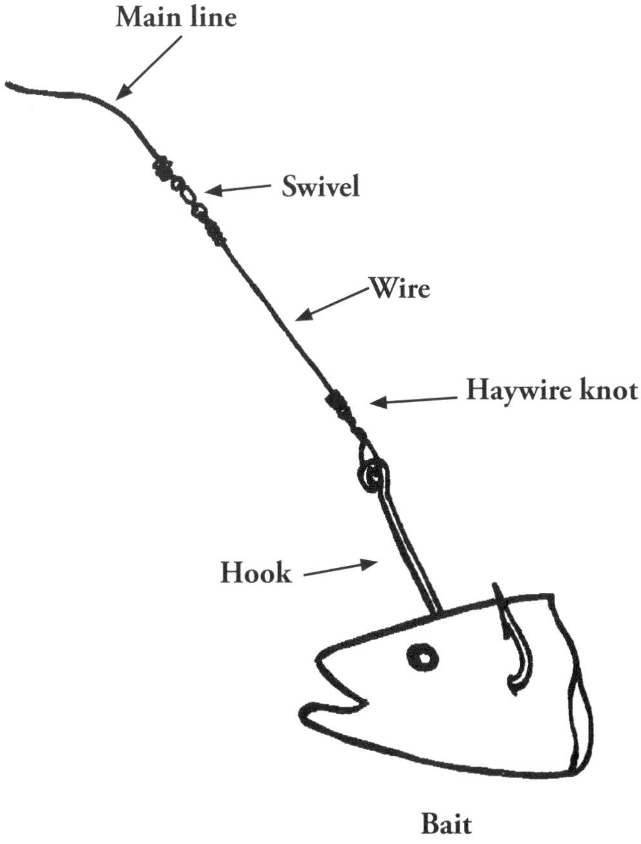

Chapter 2
Knots

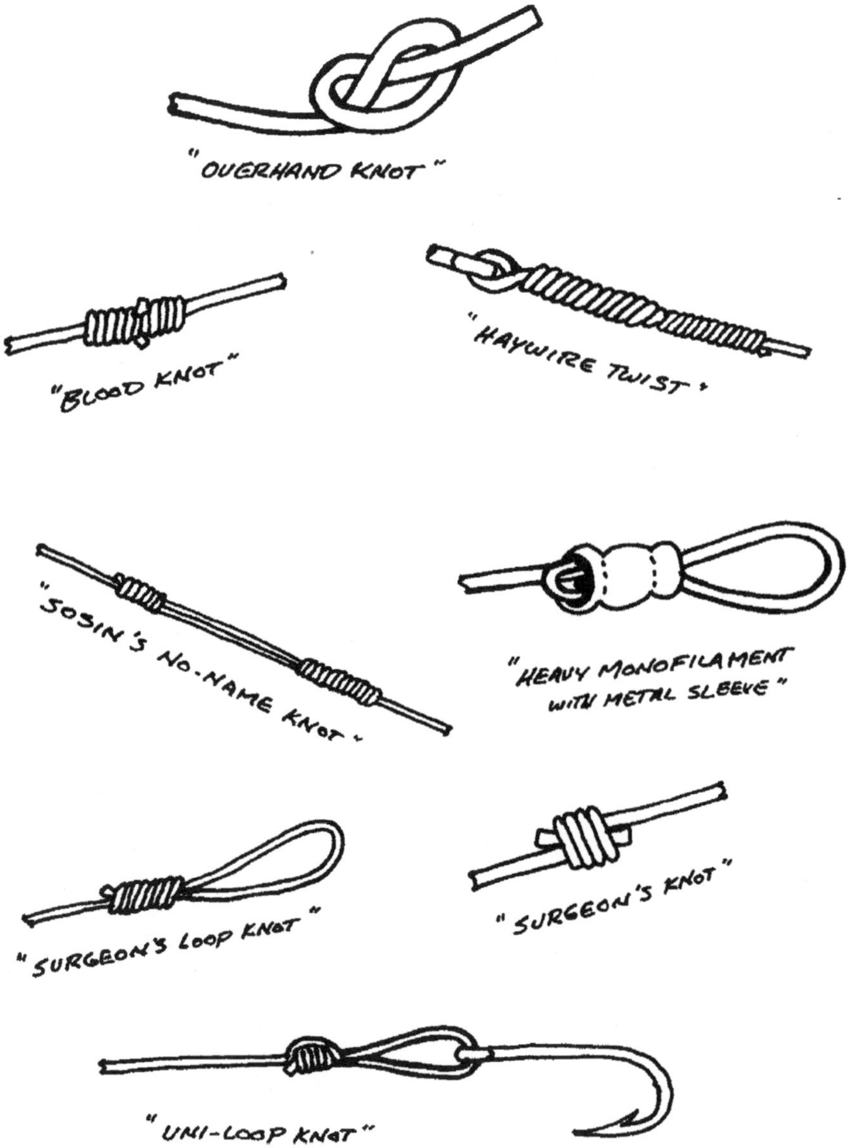
"OVERHAND KNOT"
"BLOOD KNOT"
"HAYWIRE TWIST"
"SOSIN'S NO-NAME KNOT"
"HEAVY MONOFILAMENT WITH METAL SLEEVE"
"SURGEON'S LOOP KNOT"
"SURGEON'S KNOT"
"UNI-LOOP KNOT"

Terminology

Breaking Strength: The estimated strength at which a knot will break.

Butt: The thick part of the leader. The butt of the leader is attached to the running or fly line.

Eye: A loop formed at the end of the line.

Mid Section: The section between the butt section and tippet.

Tippet: The end of the leader to which the lure, hook, or fly is attached. The tippet can be the end of a leader or an added line to the end of a leader.

Leader: The line that forms the connection between the lure, hook, or fly and the rest of the line.

Loop: The closed curved line, formed by bringing the tag end back and alongside the standing part, or a knot that creates a loop.

Overhand Knot: The foundation for many other knots.

Shock Tippet: A section of thicker line tied to the main line, used to cushion the shock of heavy-fish strikes.

Snelled: A knot tied around the shank of a hook.

Standing End: The part left after trimming a knot.

Standing Part: The main part of the line that is fixed and under tension. Such as the part of line that is on the reel.

Super Braids: Super-strong miracle fibers made from gel-spun polyethylene or agamid-fiber braided together using three to twelve carrier strands.

Tag End: The working end, the part of the line where the knot is tied.

Turns or Wraps: One complete revolution of line around another.

Working End: The part of the line used actively in tying a knot. The opposite of the standing end.

Knot-Tying Tips

Always check your lines for cracks, cuts, nicks and teeth marks. If found, replace that section.

Lubricate Knots: Before tightening a knot, lubricate it with water, saliva or a lubricant prior to drawing it tight. This will help the knot to slide and seat properly. Lubrication also decreases excessive heat which weakens monofilament.

Pull Loops Slowly: When tightening turns, wraps or loops of a knot, be sure they are pulled in a spiral. Do not let the loops/ wraps cross over each other. If loops are pulled up quickly the loops may cross over one another. This can cause the upper loops to cut the ones beneath as tension is applied.

Pull Knots Tightly: Slippage in a loosely-tied knot can cut line and cause breakage in the knot when suddenly tightened.

Seat the Knot: Tighten the knot with a slow, steady, continuous pull of the standing parts in opposite directions. Once the knot is tight, hold both standing parts of the lines close to the knot and make one, and only one, sharp pull to seat the knot.

Avoid Twisting Lines: Where a double-line knot is tied, keep the two lines parallel rather than twisting them together.

Trim Tag End: When the knot is properly snug, trim the tag end close to the knot, approximately 1/8" from the knot. Use clippers or nippers to trim the tag end. Never use heat to trim line. Heat will weaken the line.

Parts of a Line

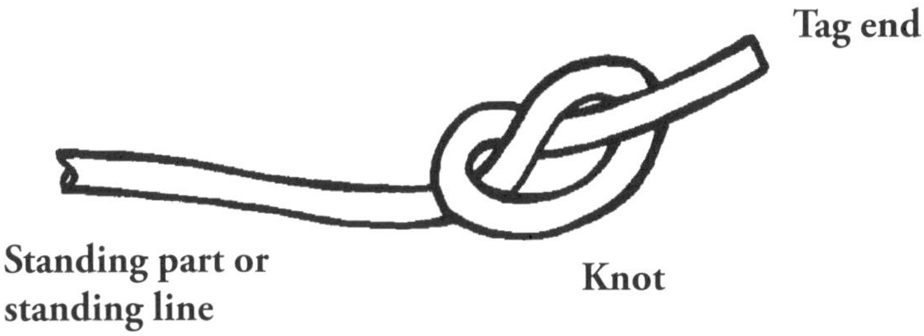

Caution: Friction generates heat that can cause a line to or break without warning. Always lubricate the line prior to drawing knot tight and tightening knots.

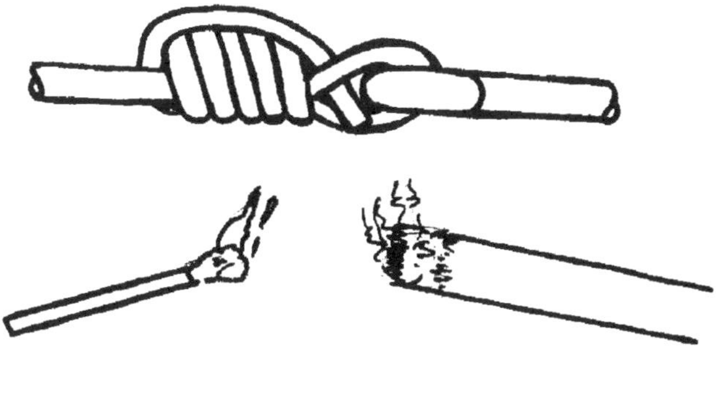

Never trim a knot or tag end with heat such as a match, cigarette, lighter or other type of device. Heat damages the line.

Albright Knot

Used to join two lines of unequal diameters or wire to monofilament. It is also good for joining fly line to leaders/backing.

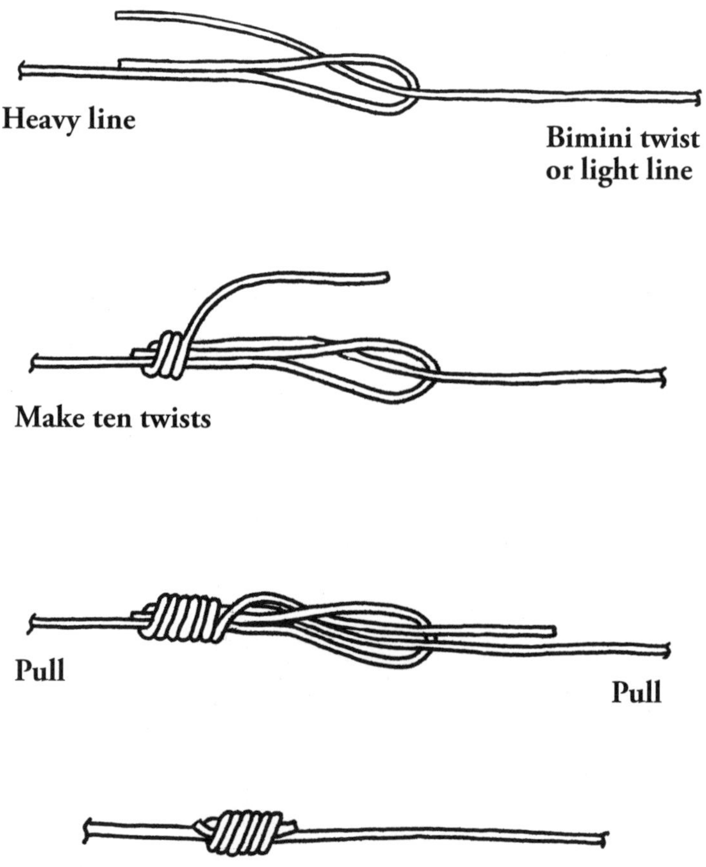

Note: Take your time when tying knots. Lubricate first, then draw the knot down slowly and evenly.

Berkley Braid Knot

Developed by Berkley for tying super braid to hooks, lures or flies. Tests show only about a 10% loss of knot strength.

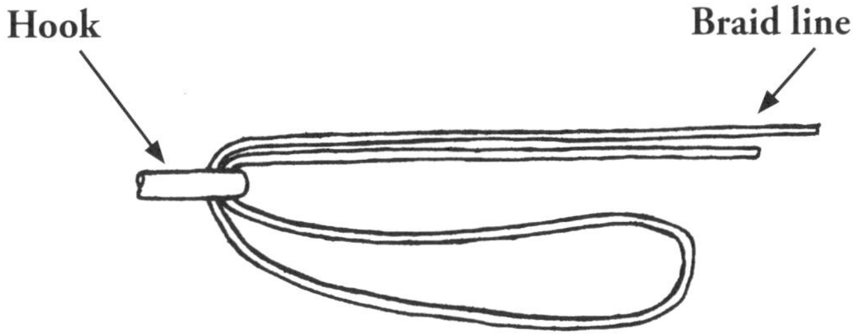

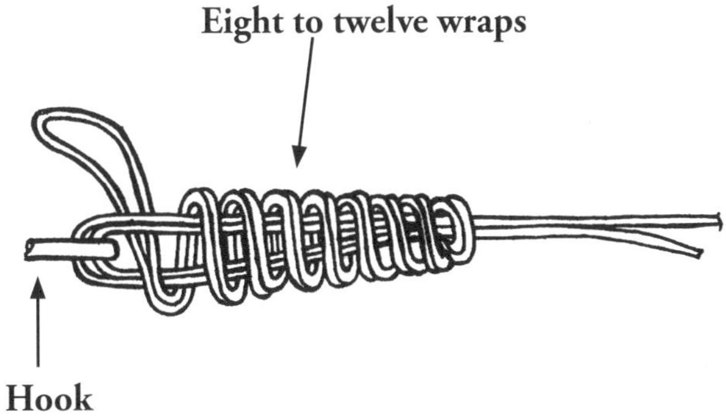

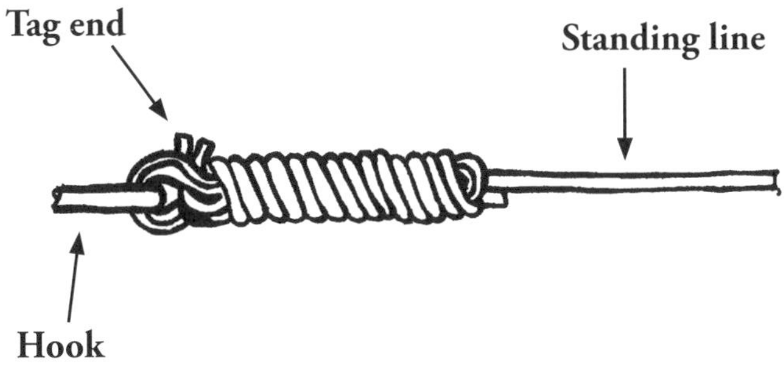

Big-Game Cable Loop Knot

Used with multi-strand aircraft cable leader, for heavy-weight bluewater fish.

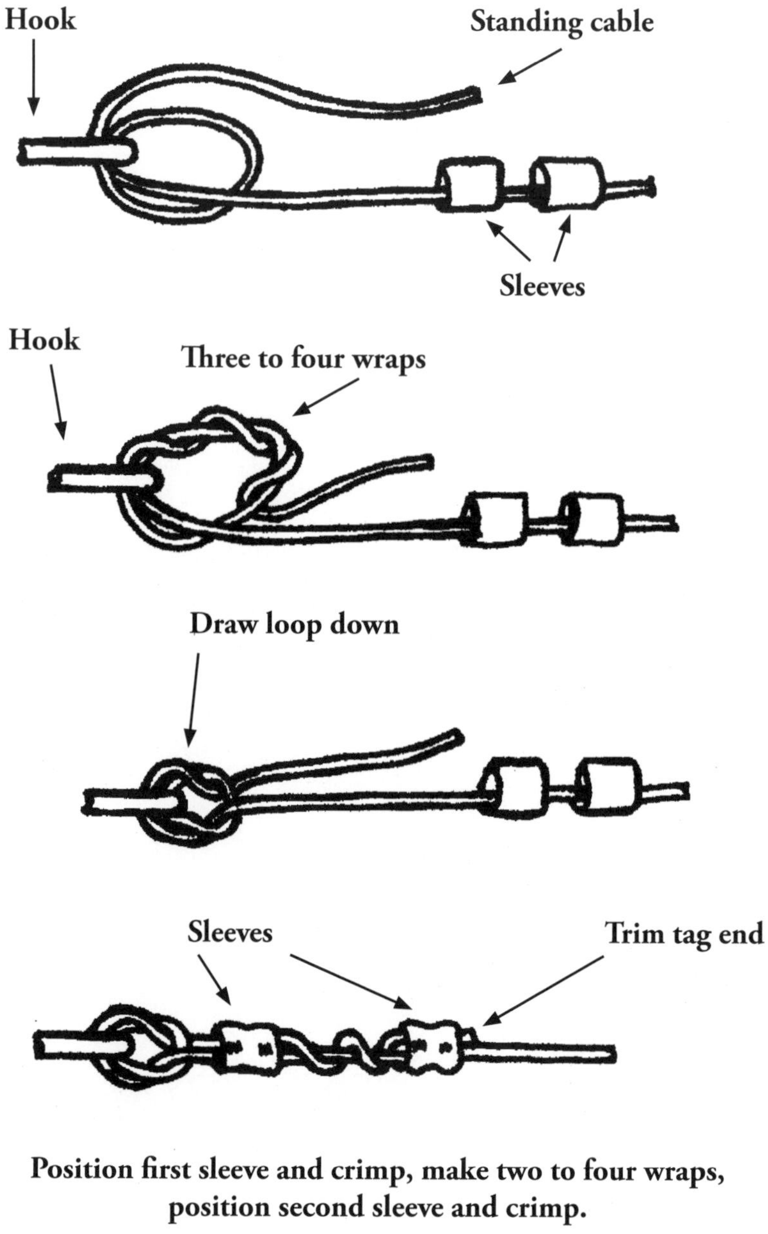

Position first sleeve and crimp, make two to four wraps, position second sleeve and crimp.

Bimini Twist

The Bimini Twist Knot is a 100% knot because it acts as a shock absorber. The standard number of twists is 20. The more twists added, the more shock the Bimini can take.

1

2

3

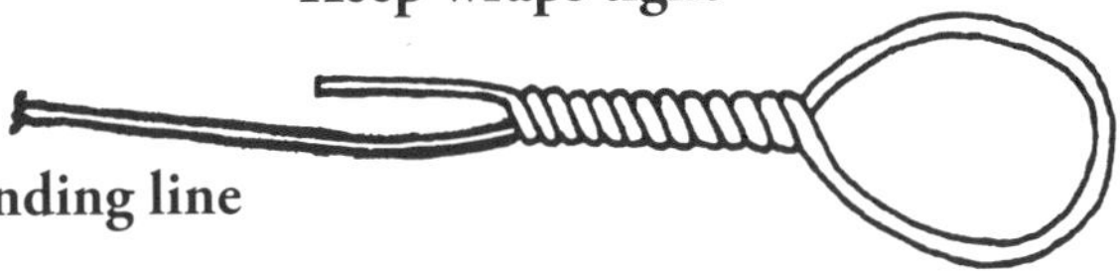

4

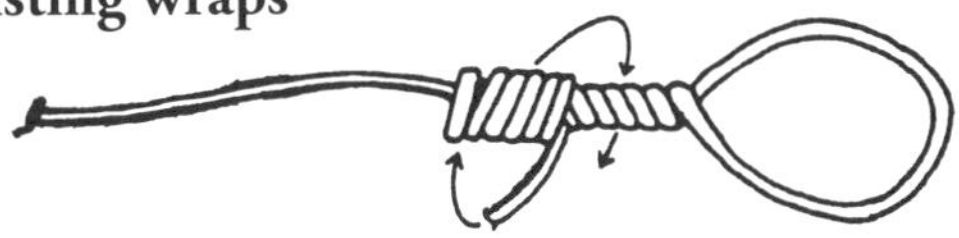

5

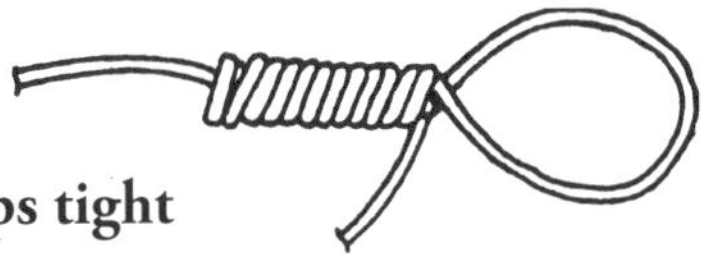

Bimini Twist
(Continued)

6 Keep wraps tight

Tie overhand knot as shown

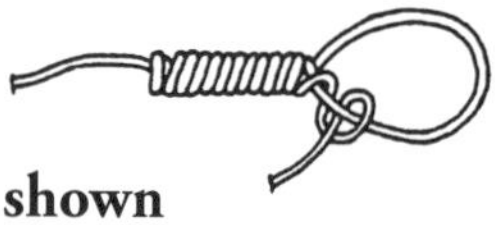

7 Draw overhand knot snug and push down toward wraps

8 With tag end, tie an open overhand knot around loop. Leave overhand knot open

9 With tag end, make two more wraps inside overhand knot as shown

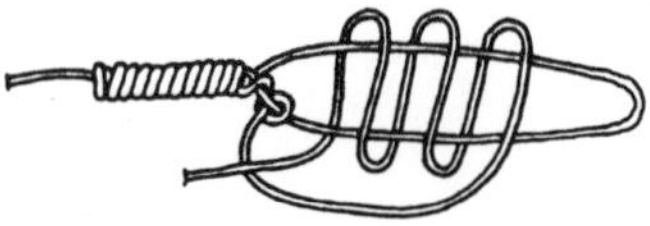

10 Draw overhand knot down, pull loop and tag end in opposite directions and draw down tight

Blood Knot

One of the strongest knots for joining two lines of equal or different diameters and for under 25-pound test. The Blood Knot is close to 100% strength.

Form an 'X' with tag end approximately 6 inches long

Make 5 turns around the standing line part

Pass tag ends through center, in opposite directions

Lubricate and draw tight

Braided Knot

An effective knot when tying braided line to a hook, lure, or fly. It's also good when tying a light line.

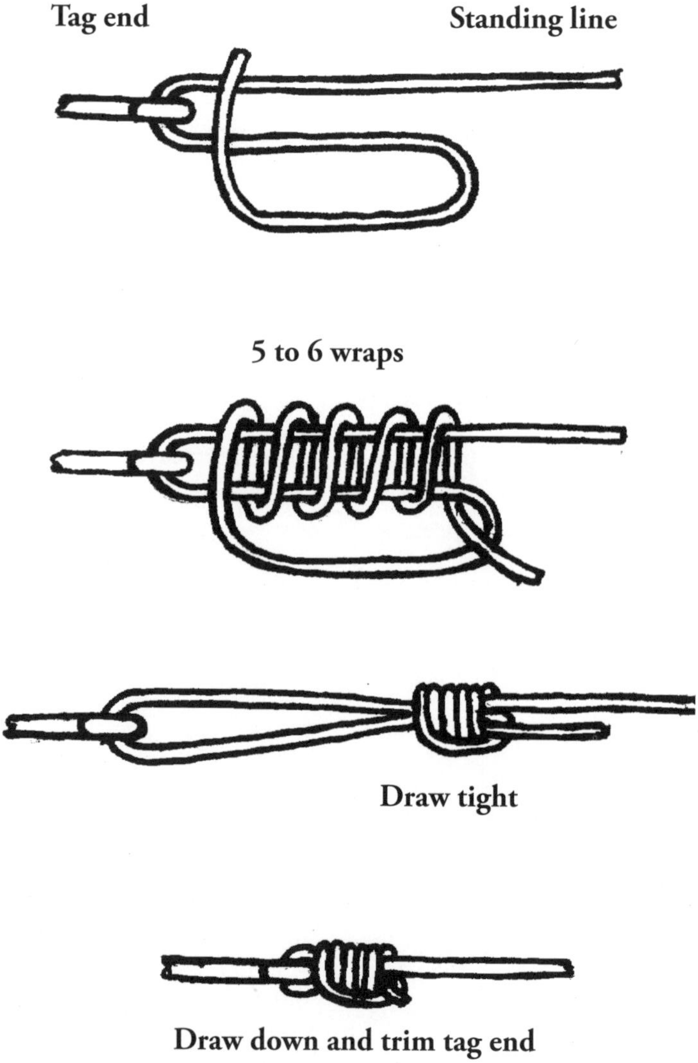

Note: Do not to allow the wraps to cross over each other.

Braided Loop Knot

Braid and Super Braid lines are slick and difficult to hold conventional knots. The Braided Loop Knot is great for making a loop at the end of the line.

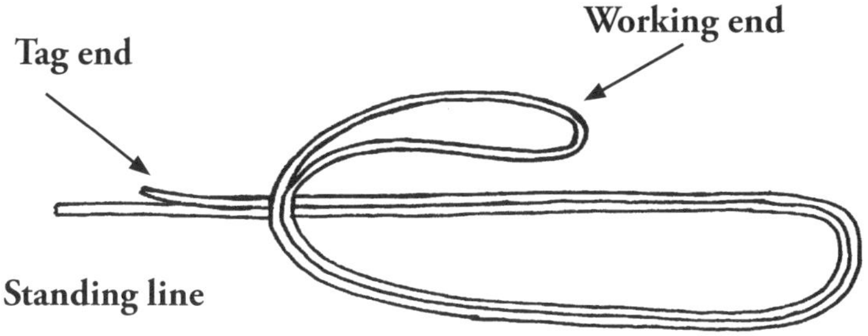

Make a double line. The working end length will determine the length of the loop.

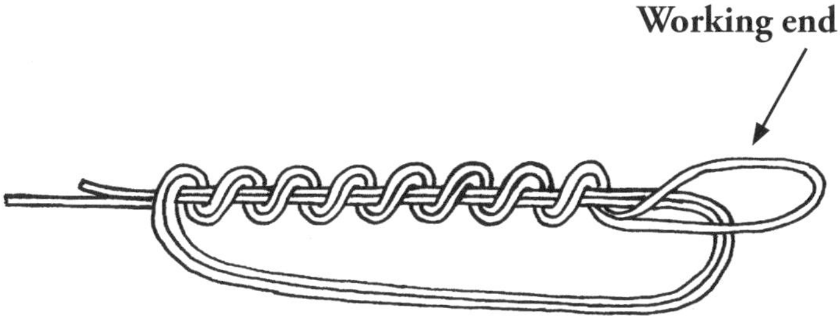

Make 6 to 8 wraps around standing part.

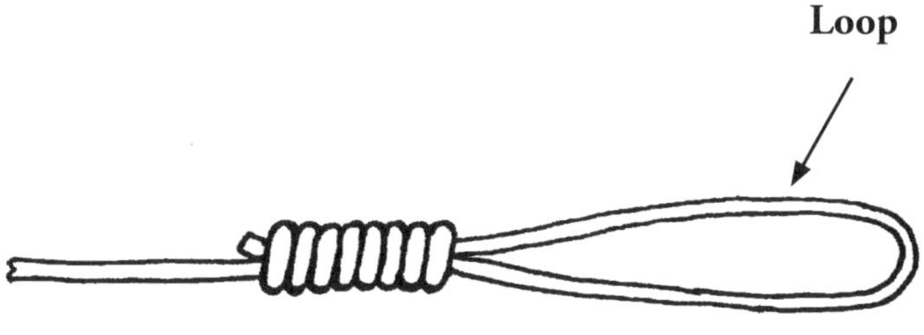

Lubricate and tighten knot.

Braided Snell

One of the strongest snells for attaching a hook to braided lines.

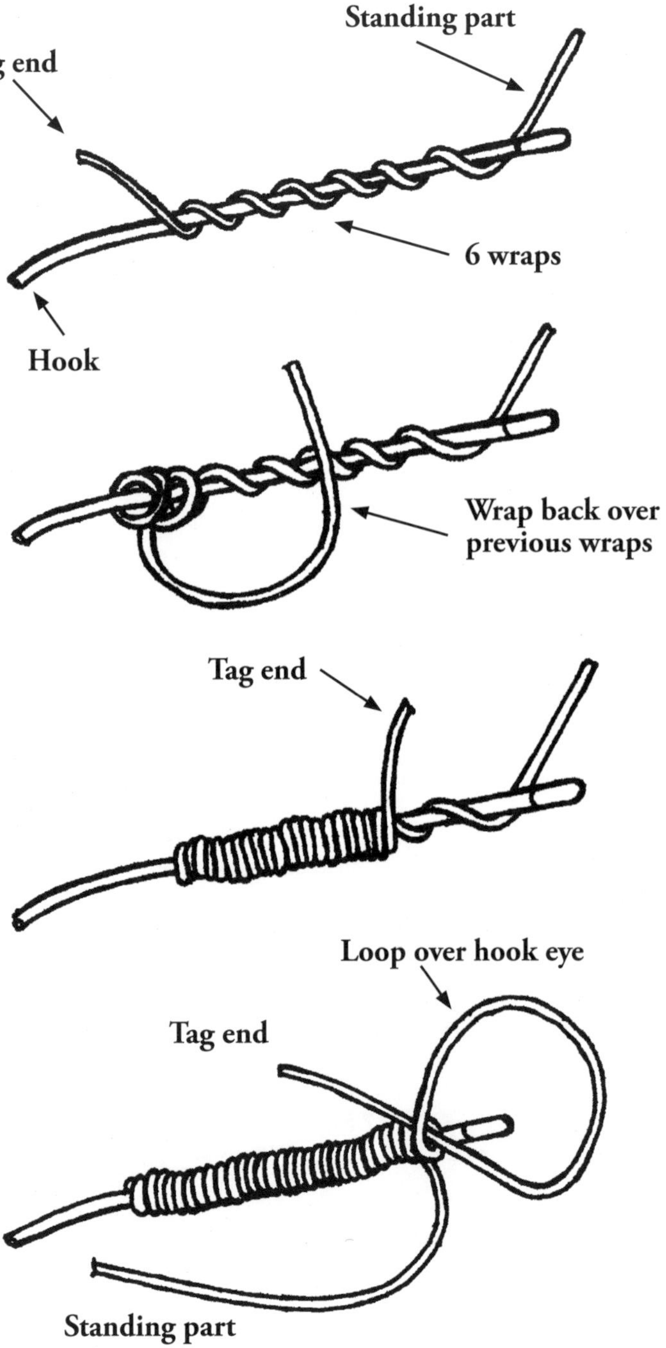

Braided Snell
(Continued)

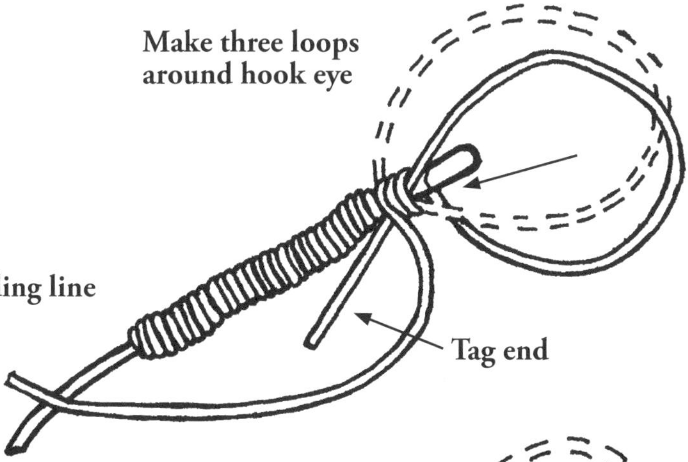

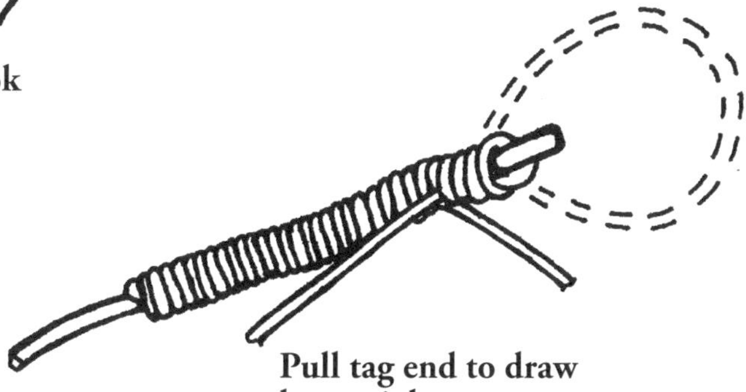

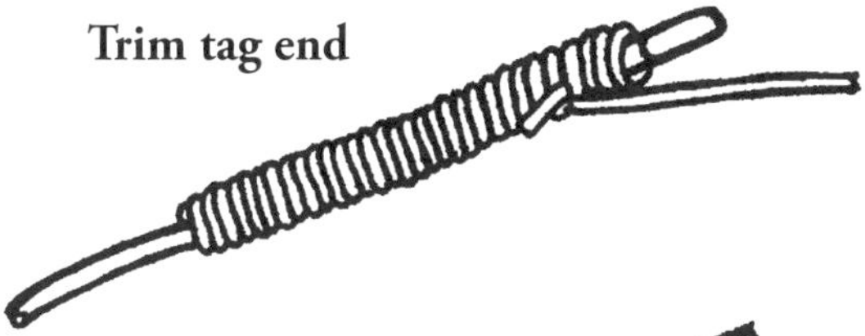

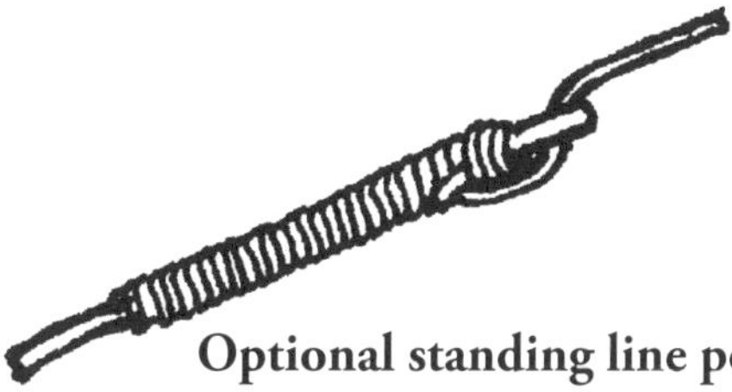

Clinch Knot, Double Improved

Braid and Super Braid lines are slick and difficult to hold a conventional knot. The Double Improved Clinch Knot offers good holding power. Make a minimum of 5 wraps around standing line. This knot works equally works on swivels, hooks or artificial baits.

Double the main line

After passing through the eye, make 5 or 6 wraps around standing line

Pass tag end through eye loop then through big loop

Lubricate and draw tight

Clinch Knot, Improved

This knot is ideal for attaching the main line (standing line) to a swivel, hook or artificial bait. It is important to make a minimum of four wraps.

Double Line Loop

A great simple Double Line Loop can be used when additional line strength is needed. It can be tied with mono or braided line and has 100% knot strength.

Make loop in line

Standing part

Bring tag end back approximately 2 feet

Make 7 to 9 wraps around the standing part

Make 7 to 9 wraps over the top of the previous wraps

Tie overhand knot

Lubricate knots and draw tight

Tie overhand knot. Lubricate knots and draw tight

Duncan Braid Loop Knot

The Duncan Braid Loop Knot is also an excellent loop knot for braid or super braid lines. It's important that all the wraps sit tightly together when drawn down.

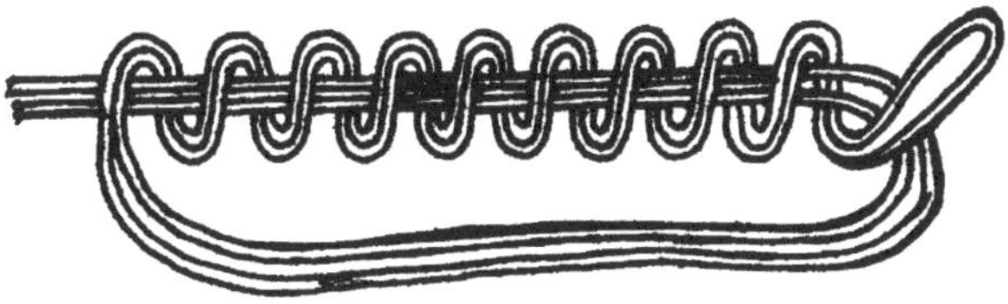

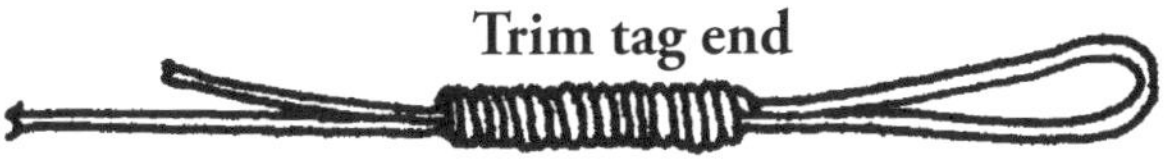

German Loop Knot

The German Loop Knot is a strong knot for tying a loop in any braid, super braid or monofilament line.

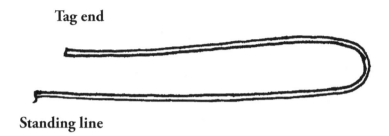

Lubricate and draw tight

Haywire Twist

for single-strand hard wire

For use with single-strand wire connecting lures or hooks to the leader.

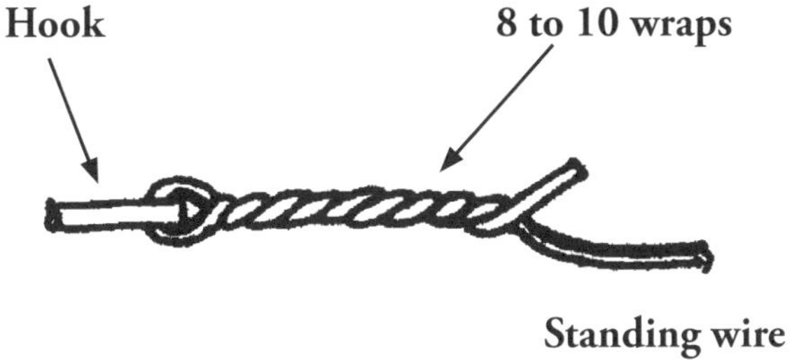

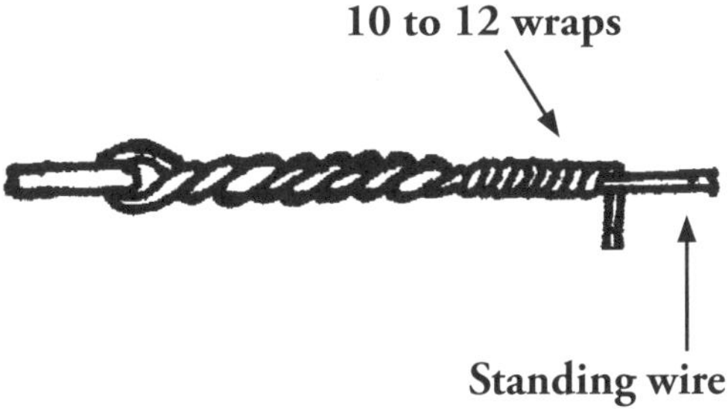

Heavy Monofilament with Metal Sleeve

Used for offshore trolling. Adjust loop size to desired size, insert tag end back in side sleeve and crimp. Select the proper size sleeve for monofilament leader.

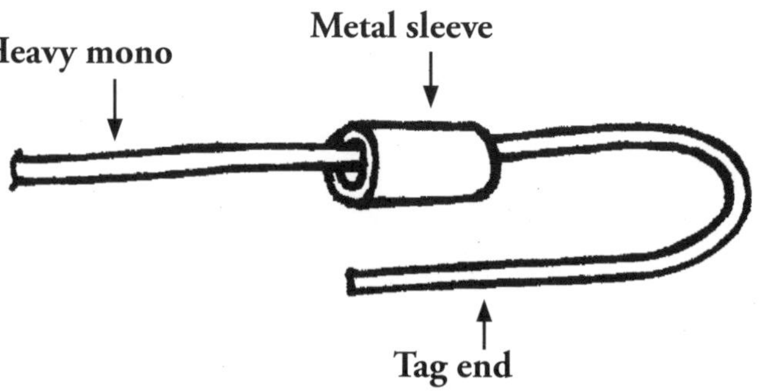

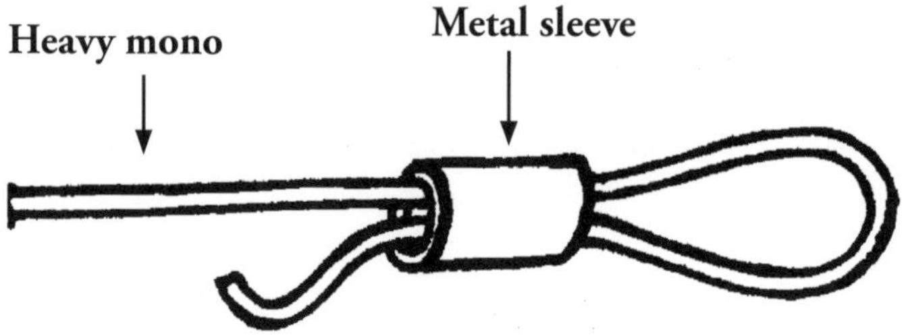

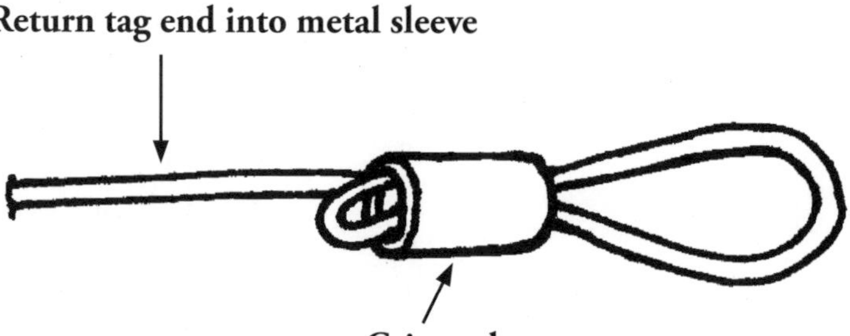

Hook or Swivel Braid Knot

A strong knot for tying super braid or monofilament to a hook and lure.

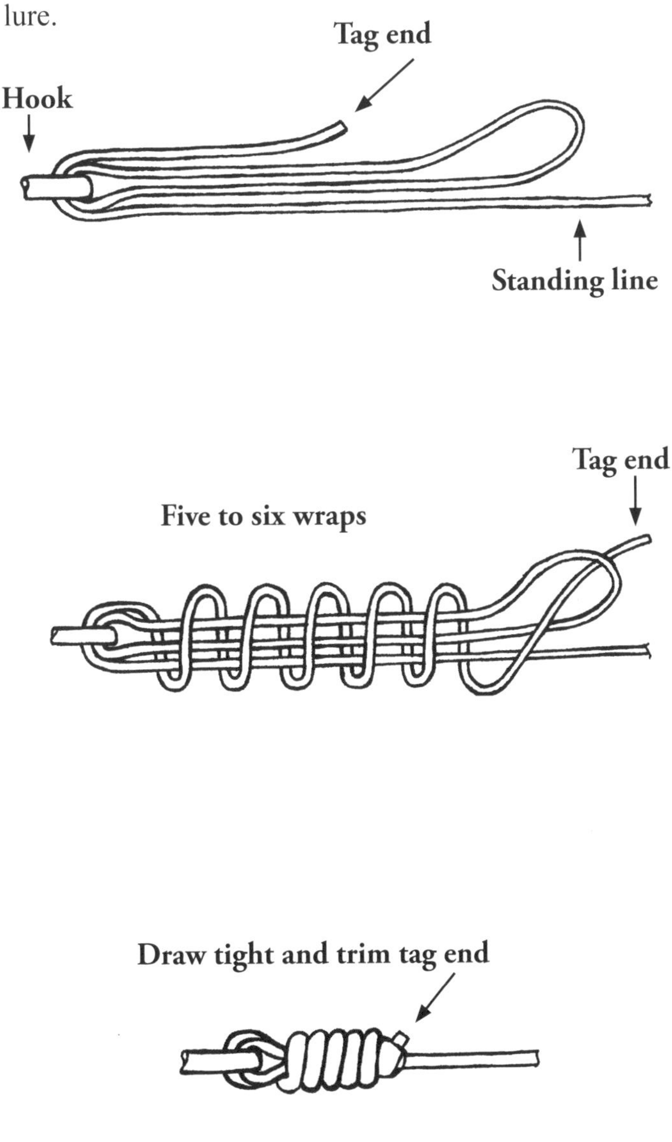

Adjust your knots and loops to the rig that you're tying. There is no one loop or knot that fits all situations.

King Sling Knot

The King Sling Knot is a fast and easy knot that creates a strong connection for attaching sinkers, hooks, and the like to heavy pound-test lines or braided line.

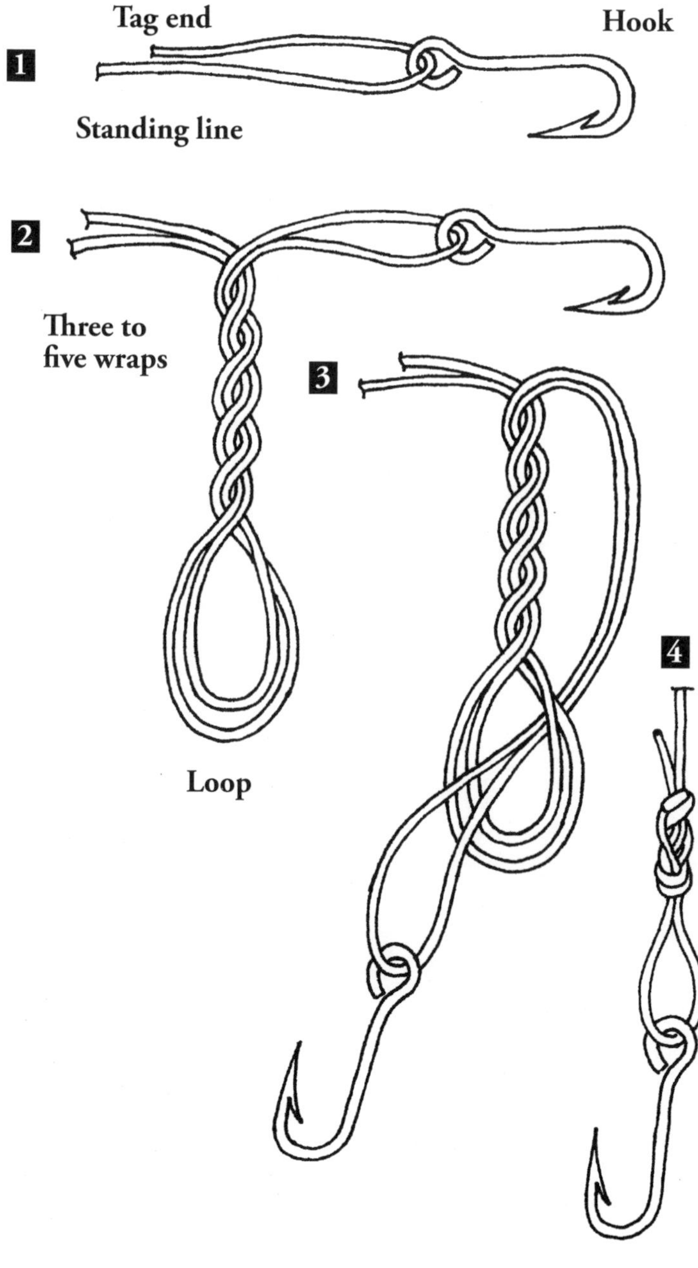

Mono to Braid Knot

An excellent knot when joining a braid or super braid line to monofilament or braid line. This knot will pass through the guides smoothly when necessary.

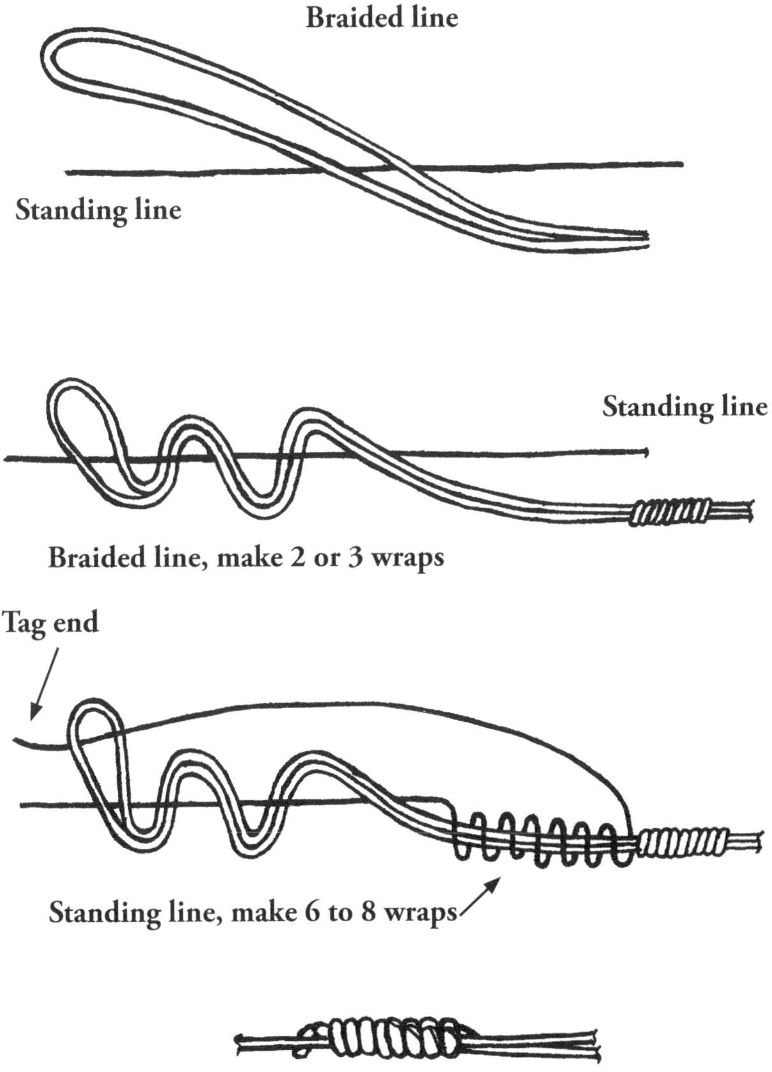

Lubricate and draw tight and trim tag end

Offshore Swivel Knot

The Offshore Swivel Knot is the best knot for attaching swivels or snaps to double-line leaders.

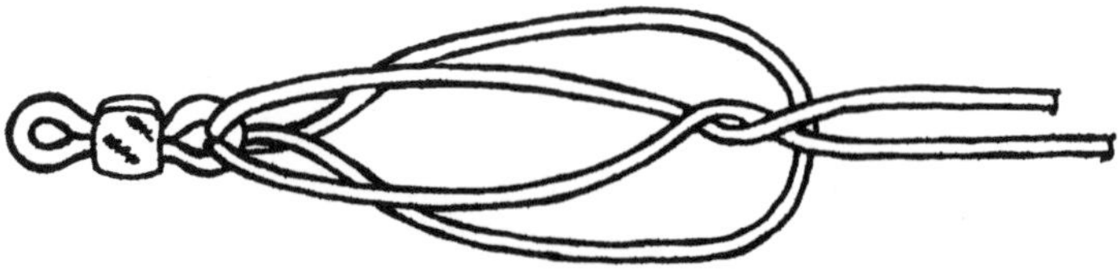

Hold swivel with one hand, pull both strands of double line with the other hand. Work knot down with fingers.

Lubricate and draw tight

Perfection Loop

Ideal for tying a loop in the end of a line. Once mastered, the Perfection Loop can be tied in seconds.

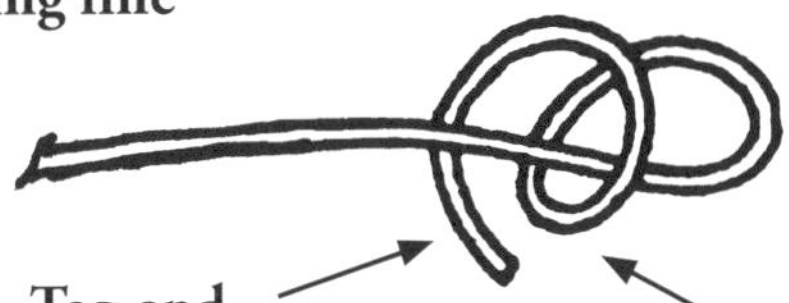

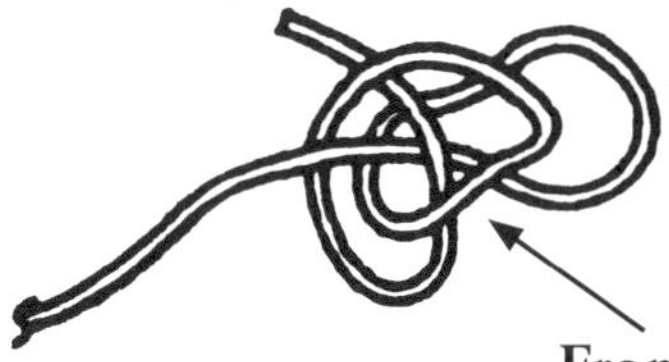

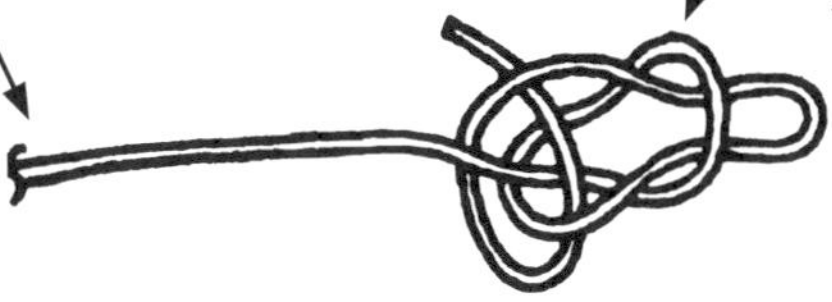

Shocker Knot

Big-Game Fish

Overhand knot in standing line

Overhand knot in leader

Draw knots tight

Make 3 to 5 wraps with leader

Lubricate and draw tight

Silly Snell

The Silly Snell is good for either monofilament or braided line.

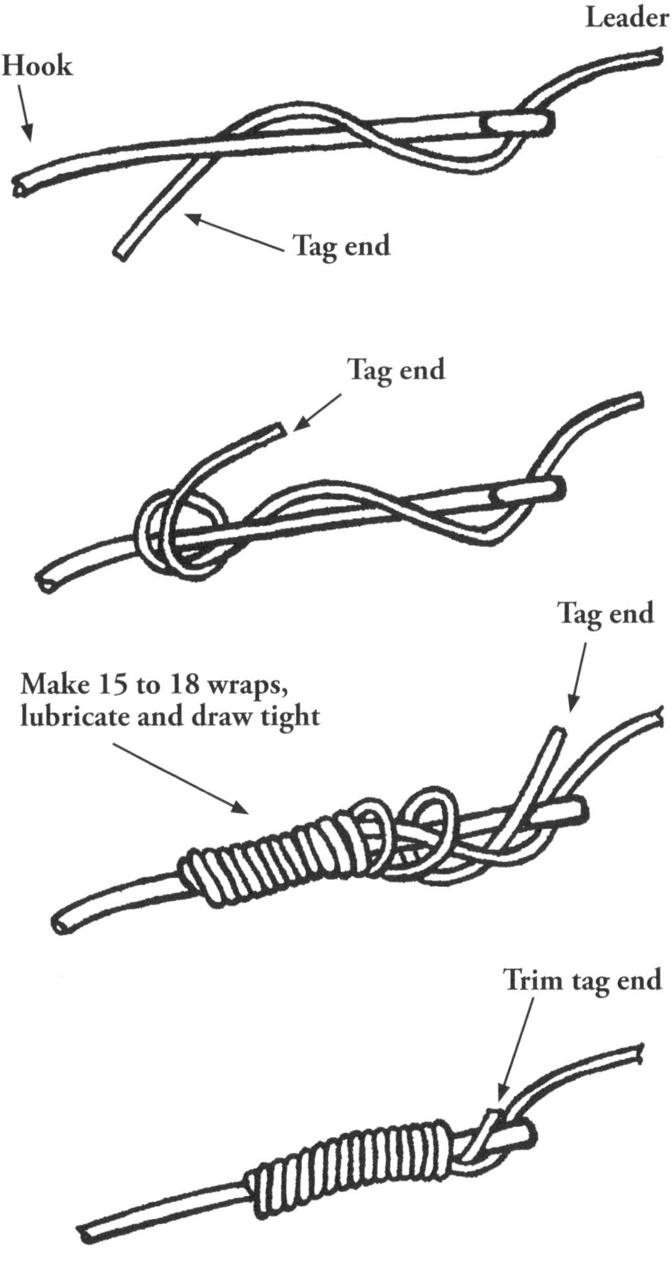

Sosin's No-Name Knot

This knot is ideal for attaching a heavy line to a lighter line. Works equally well with monofilament, braided or combination.

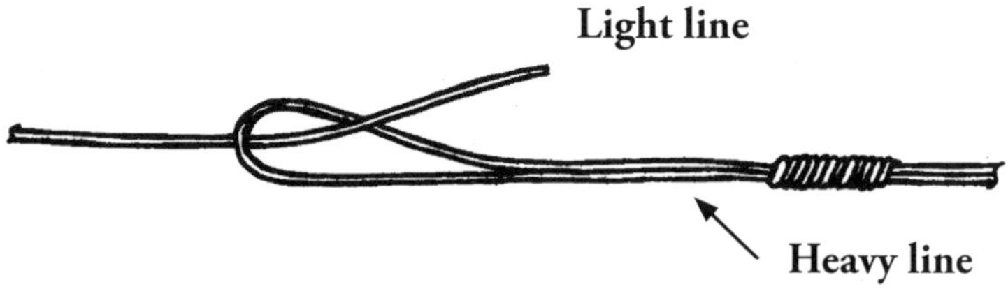

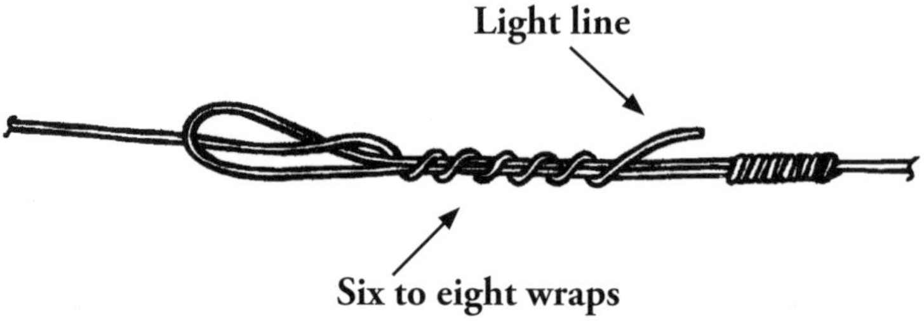

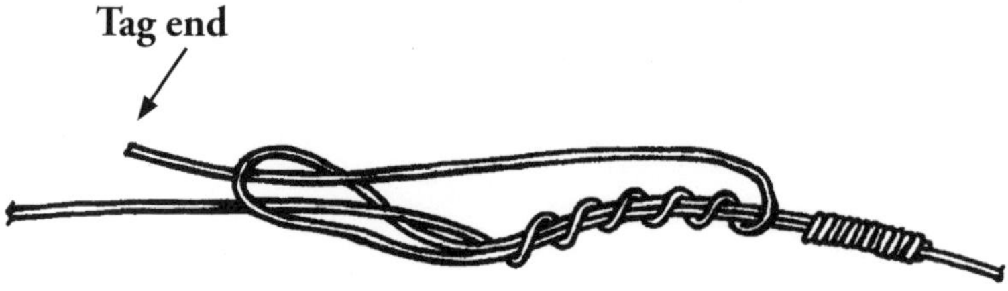

Lubricate and draw tight, trim tag end

Spider Hitch Knot

The Spider Hitch Knot is a fast and easy knot that creates a strong double-line under 30-pound test, or for attaching sinkers and the like to heavy-pound-test lines.

Standing line

Make loop in line

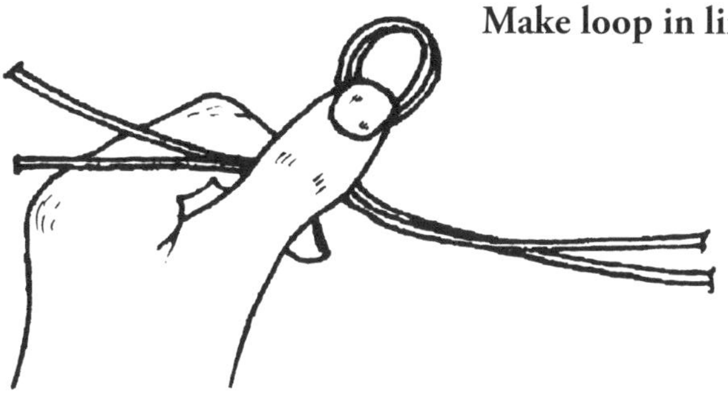

Make 5 to 6 loops around thumb and standing line

Lubricate loops and draw tight

Super Braid Knot

The Super Braid Knot is good for attaching a leader to a swivel, hooks, or artificial baits. It is a reliable general-purpose fishing knot and easy to tie.

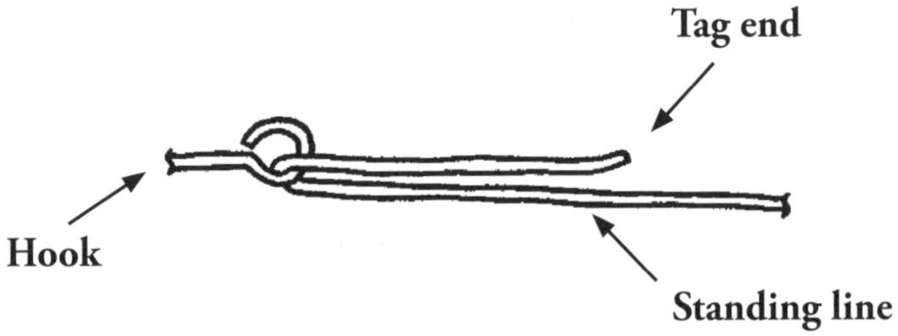

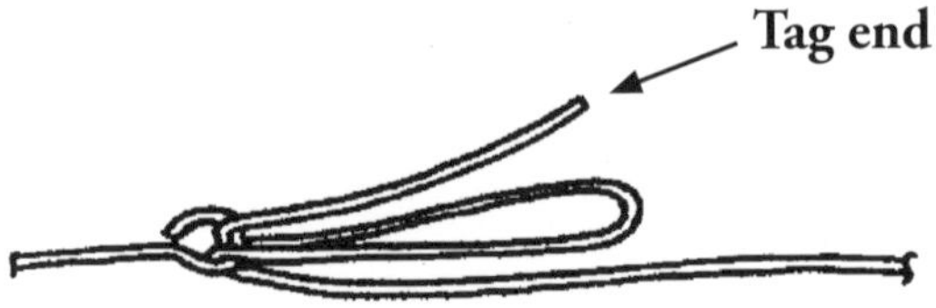

Five to six wraps

Lubricate and draw tight,
trim tag end

Surgeon's Loop Knot

One of the easiest and quickest loops to tie; retains nearly 100% of original line test. Ideal when a loop is needed quickly for a loop-to-loop connection.

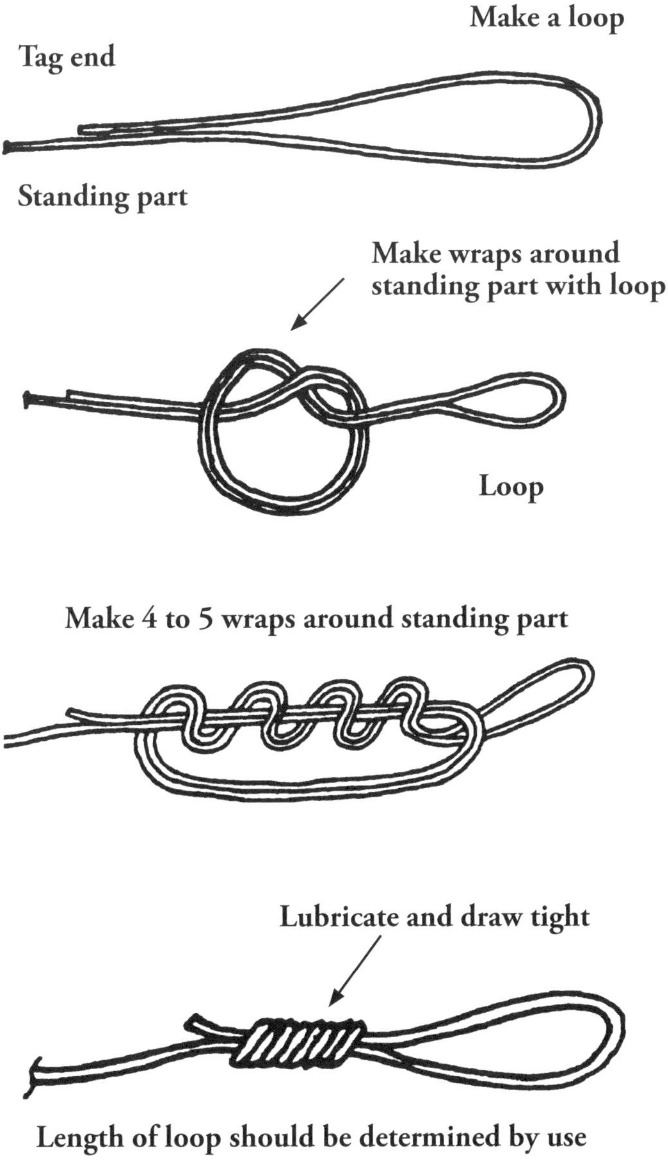
Make a loop
Tag end
Standing part
Make wraps around standing part with loop
Loop
Make 4 to 5 wraps around standing part
Lubricate and draw tight
Length of loop should be determined by use

Surgeon's Knot

Ideal for joining leader sections of equal or unequal diameter. This knot is not recommended if either section exceeds 60-pound test because the knot cannot draw tight. Properly constructed, the surgeon's knot approaches 100% efficiency.

Tie overhand knot

Make two more additional wraps

Draw loops tight

Trolling Spoon Knot

Used with medium-weight solid wire for trolling; keeps sharp-toothed fish from biting through the leader.

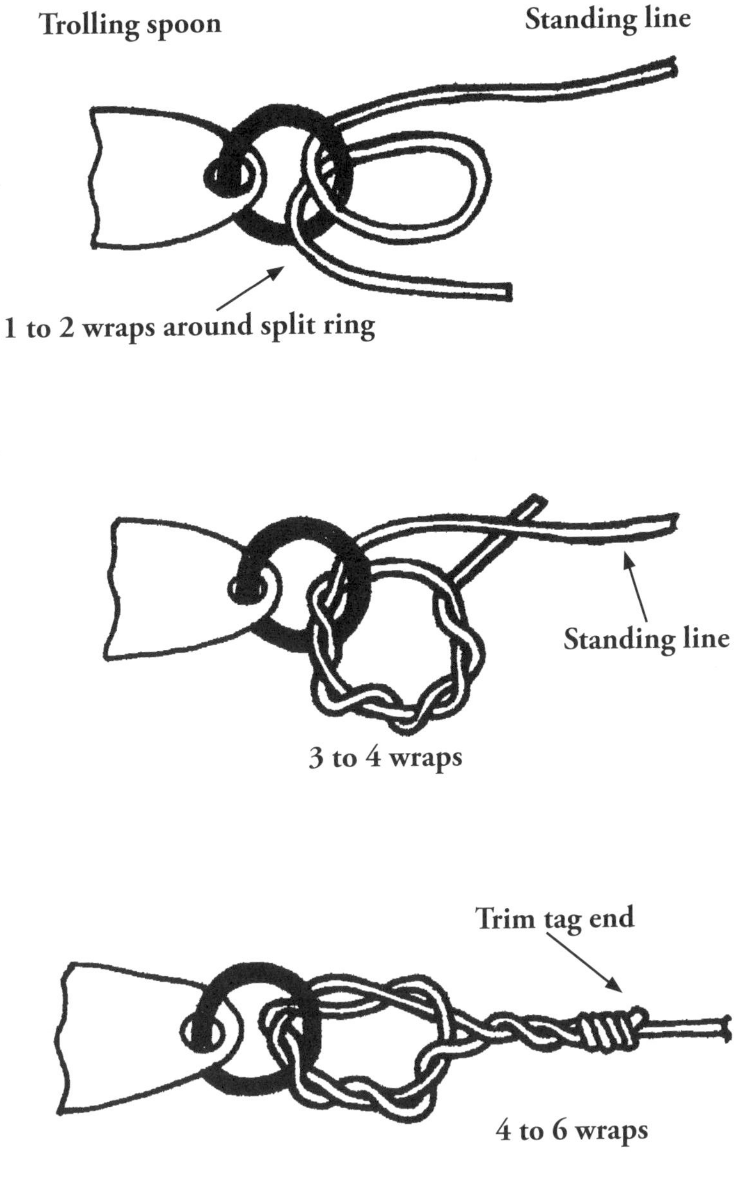

UNI-Knot

The UNI-Knot is the best fishing knot for attaching a leader to a swivel. It is a reliable general-purpose fishing knot and easy to tie.

Four to six wraps

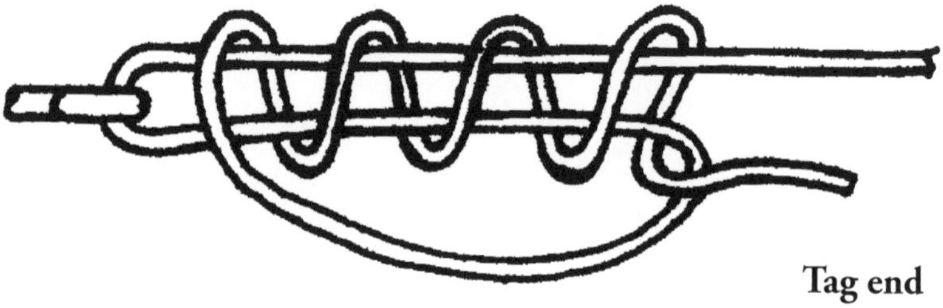

Tag end

Trim tag end

Lubricate the wraps and draw tight. Trim the tag end

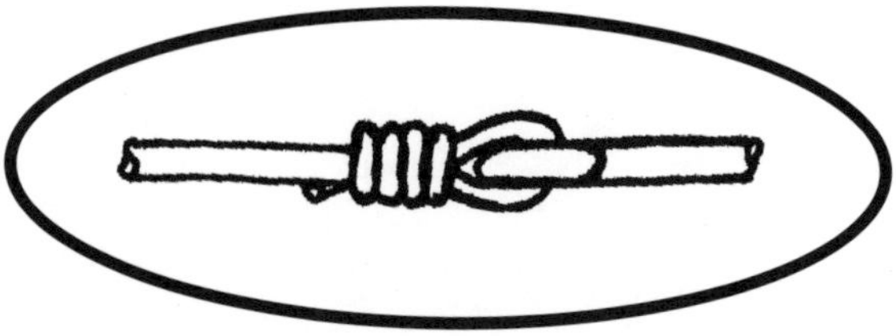

Note: Trim tag end to 1/16" no more than 1/8" using clippers, scissors or other sharp tool.

UNI-Loop Knot

The UNI-Loop Knot is a good loop knot for attaching a leader to swivels, hooks and artificial baits. It's a reliable general-purpose fishing knot and easy to tie.

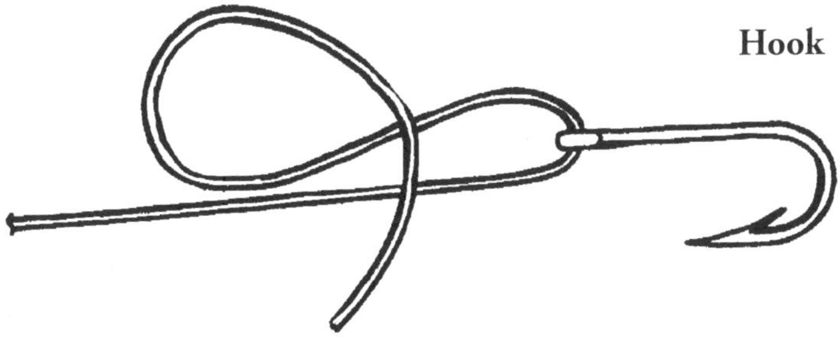

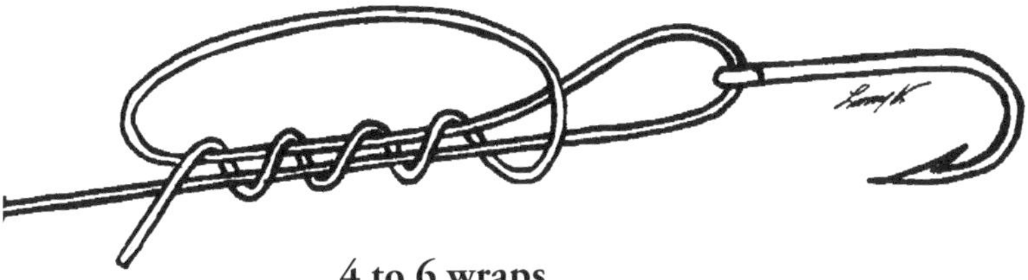

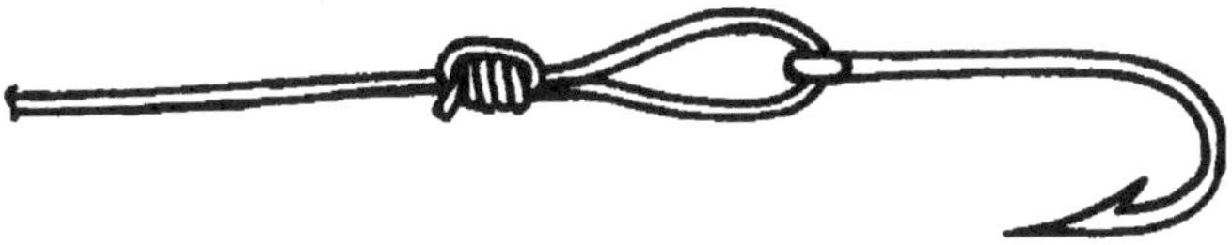

Lubricate and draw tight

World's Fair Knot

A great terminal tackle knot with monofilament or braided line.

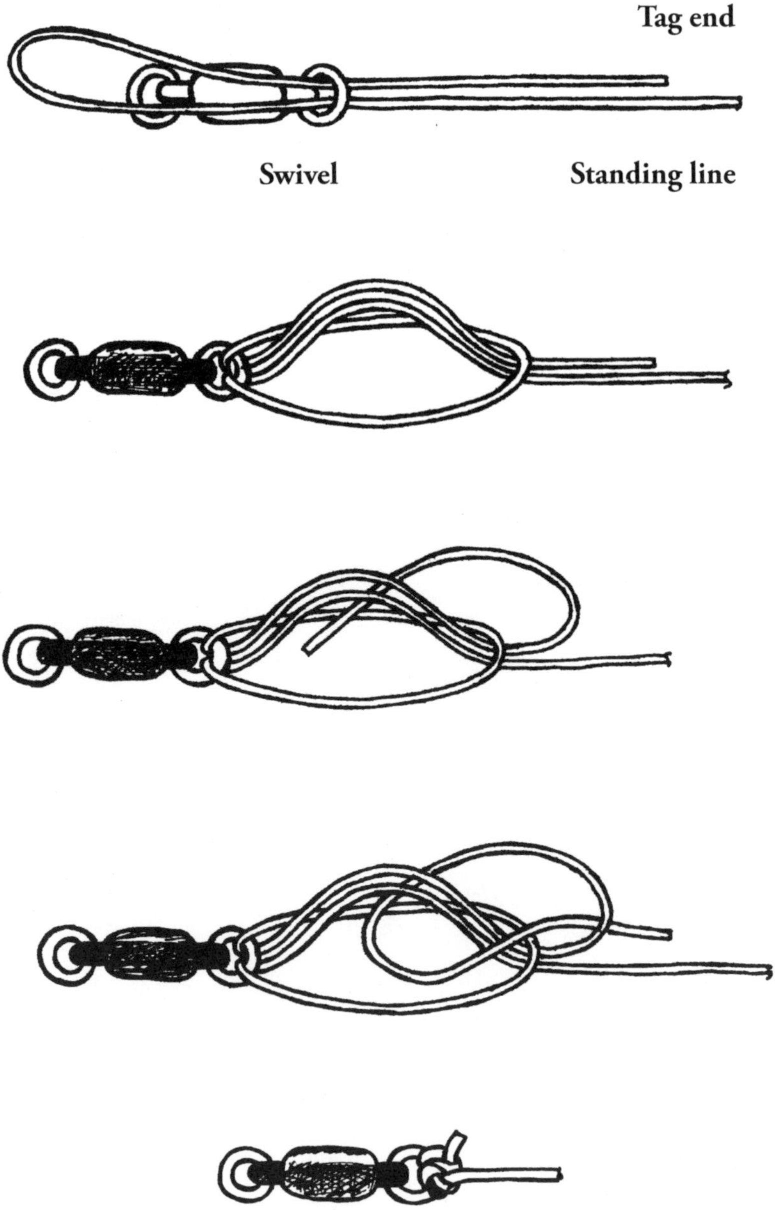

Chapter 3
Rigs and Tackle

Balloon Float Rig

One of the most inexpensive, versatile and easily carried floats is a balloon. Inflate balloon to desired size, tie a knot in the balloon lip, then tie another knot around the leader or swivel for desired depth. The fight with a fish usually pops the balloon.

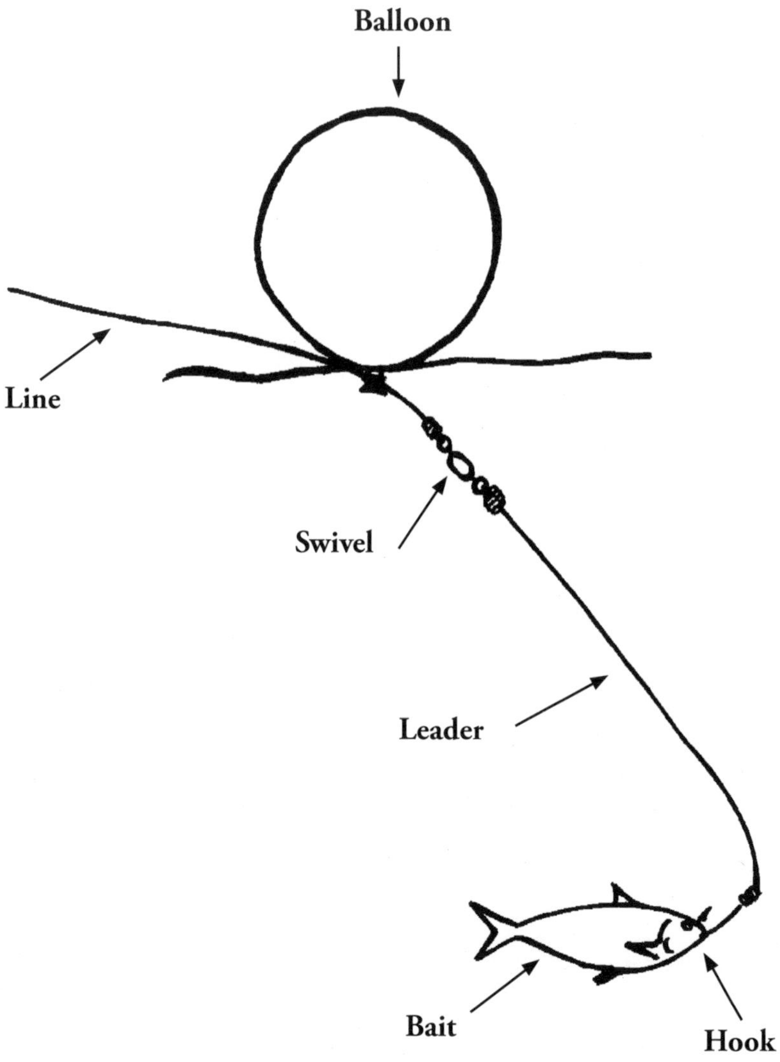

Ballyhoo Pre-Leader Construction

(for single- or double-hook rig)

To make the ballyhoo more effective in the water it's especially important to bend the ballyhoo back and forth several times to break the spine, this makes the ballyhoo flexible and enhances its swimming motion.

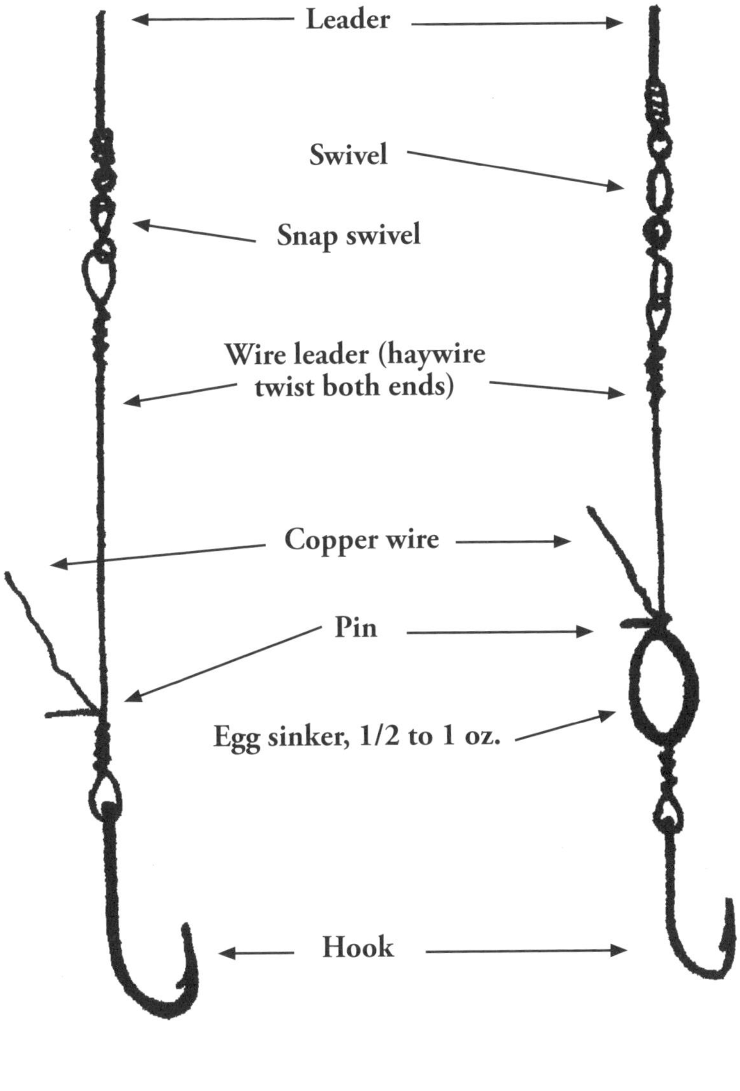

Ballyhoo Double-Hook Rig

The ballyhoo double-hook rig is primarily used for drift fishing, especially for king mackerel. This method of adding a second hook is the easiest of all double-hook rigs.

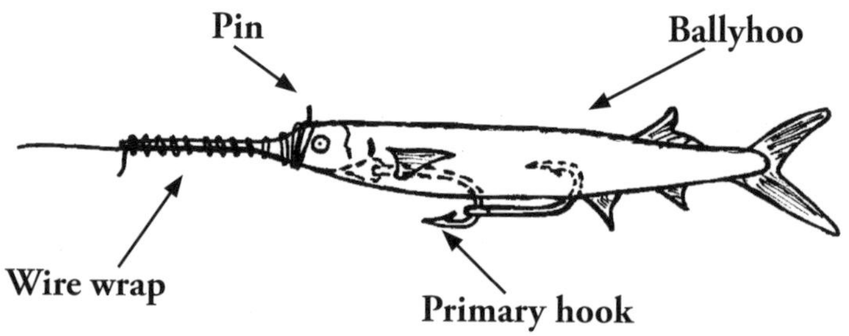

Note: The second hook is inserted AFTER the rigging is completed.

Double hook (pry open the eye of the hook, then close the eye with pliers after the second hook is in place.)

Ballyhoo Single-Hook Rig

The ballyhoo single-hook rig is primarily used for drift fishing, especially for king mackerel. Also known as a swimming leader.

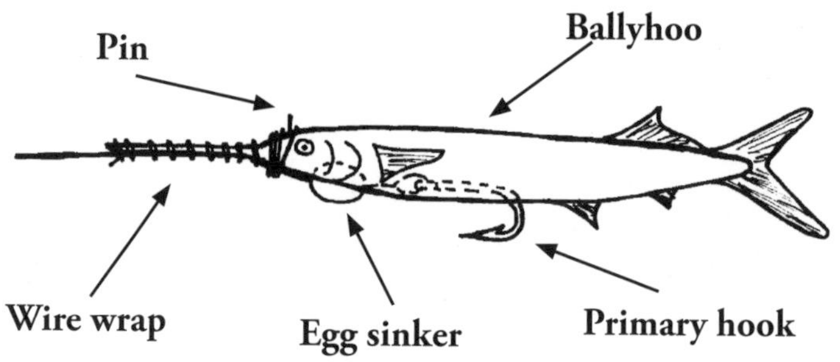

Ballyhoo Rig

(monofilament leader)

Using monofilament is the easiest and most popular way to rig ballyhoo. The one major difference between monofilament and wire is that the hook will be slightly more forward with monofilament.

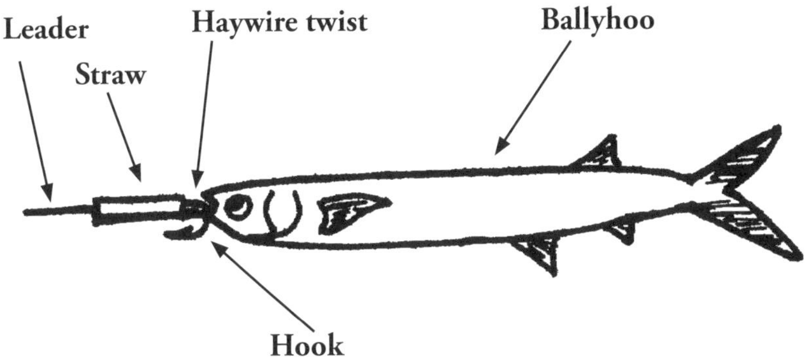

Ballyhoo Rig

(wire leader)

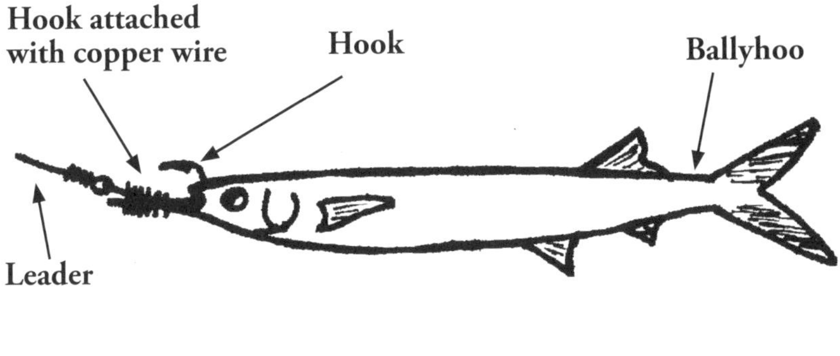

Barracuda & Marlin Rigs with Mackerel

This is a method for rigging mackerel, barracuda and other slender species. Instead of de-boning, flex the bait back and forth to break the backbone in several places, making it more flexible.

Barracuda Rig with Mackerel

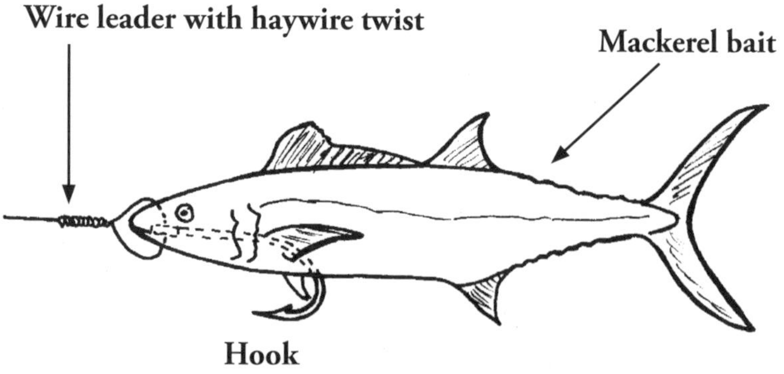

Marlin Rig with Mackerel

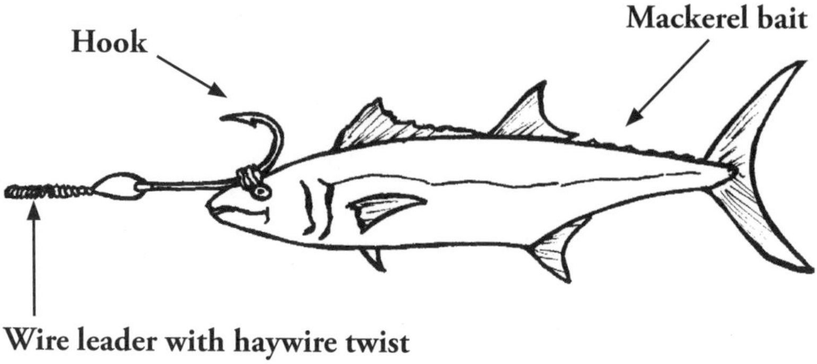

Remember: Don't try to land a fish on the downwind side of a dead-drifting boat.

Basic Stinger Rig

The Basic Stinger Rig is ideal for short strikes, generally slashing, feeding fish such as barracuda, mackerel, wahoo, etc., chop off the back of the bait. A trailer hook is used at the back of the bait to aid in the catch.

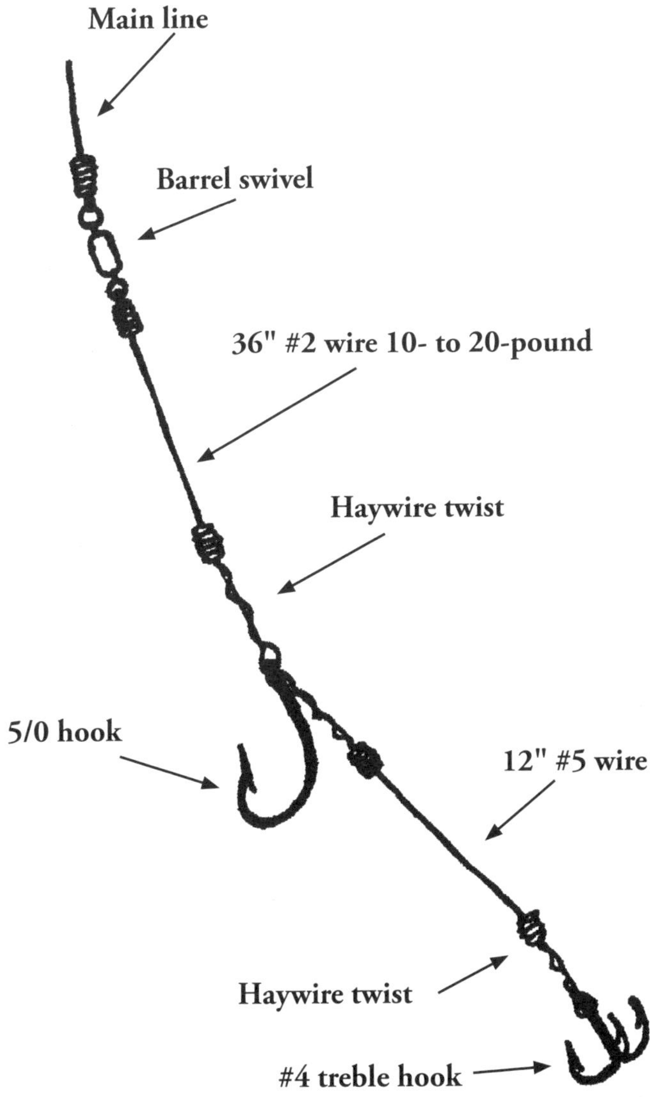

Basic Trolling Rig

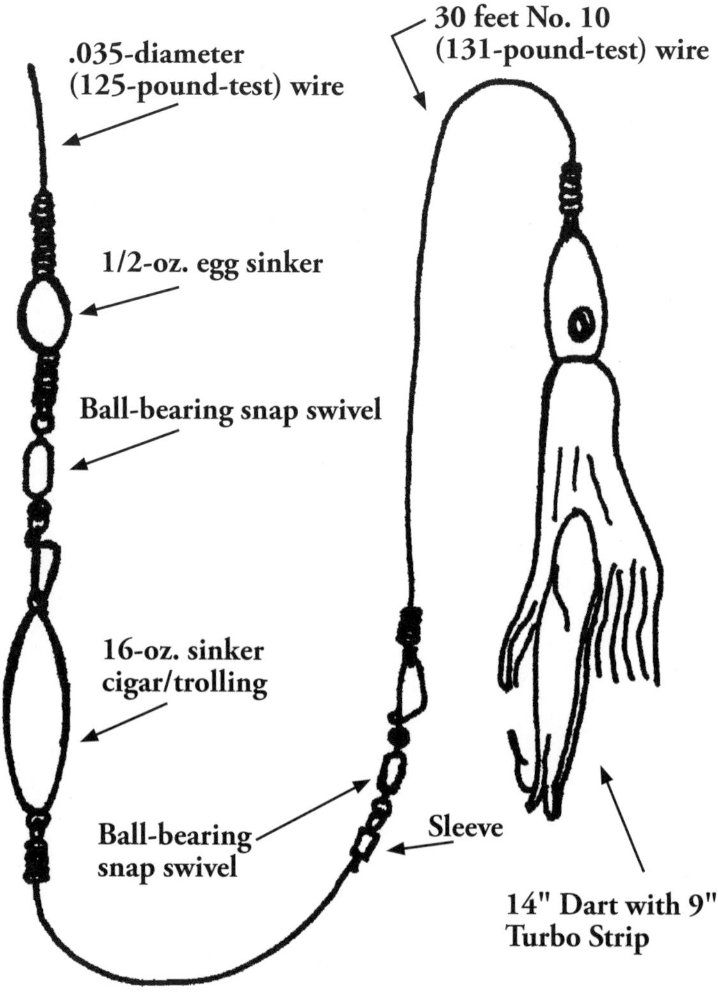

Optional Rig

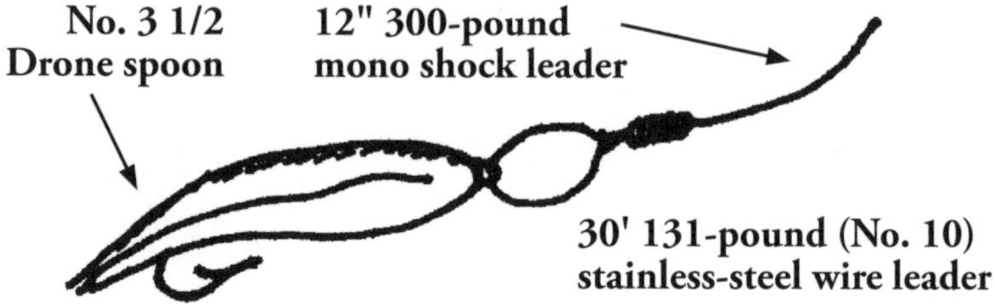

Basic Wire Outfit

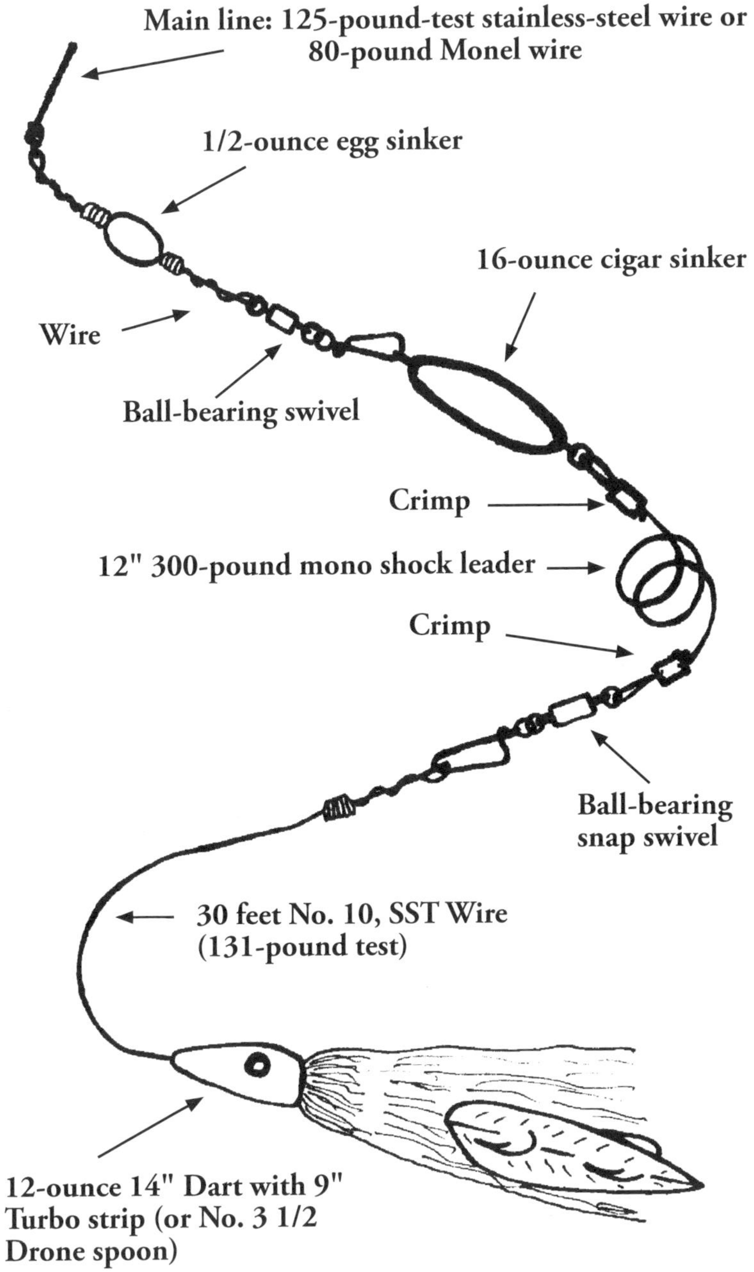
Main line: 125-pound-test stainless-steel wire or 80-pound Monel wire
1/2-ounce egg sinker
16-ounce cigar sinker
Wire
Ball-bearing swivel
Crimp
12" 300-pound mono shock leader
Crimp
Ball-bearing snap swivel
30 feet No. 10, SST Wire (131-pound test)
12-ounce 14" Dart with 9" Turbo strip (or No. 3 1/2 Drone spoon)

Blue Crab Rig

Live blue crabs are deadly bait for a variety of fish such as cobia, red and black drum, snook, reef and bottom fish like grouper and snapper. Use smaller crabs for shallow fish and larger crabs for deep-bottom fishing.

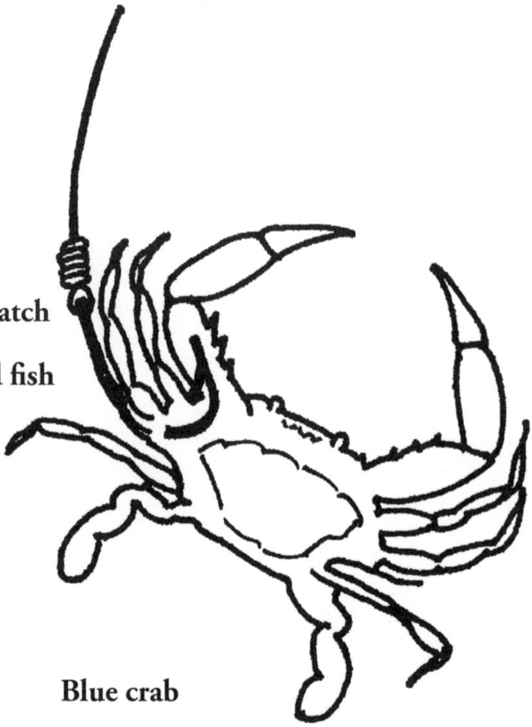

Note: For personal safety remove large claws from crabs.

Bluefish Rig, Basic

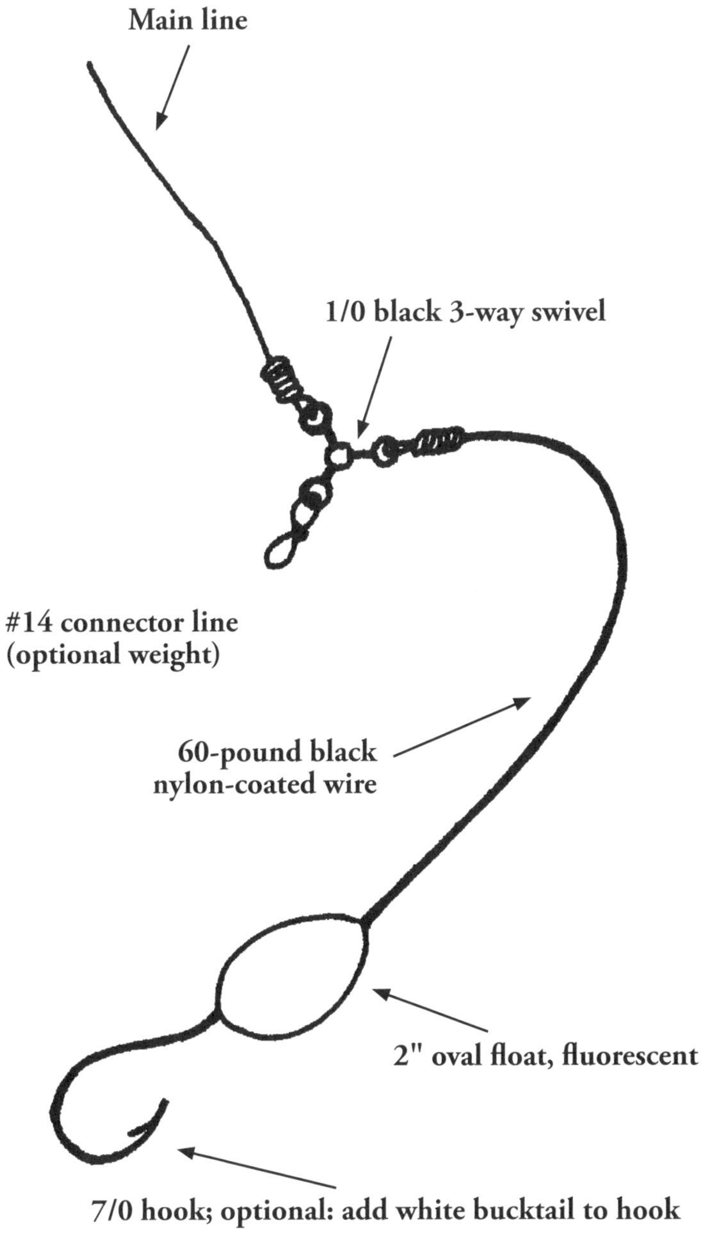

Blue Shark Rig

This is an easy and economical way to make shark leader that will perform well on medium to large blues, makos or similar sharks.

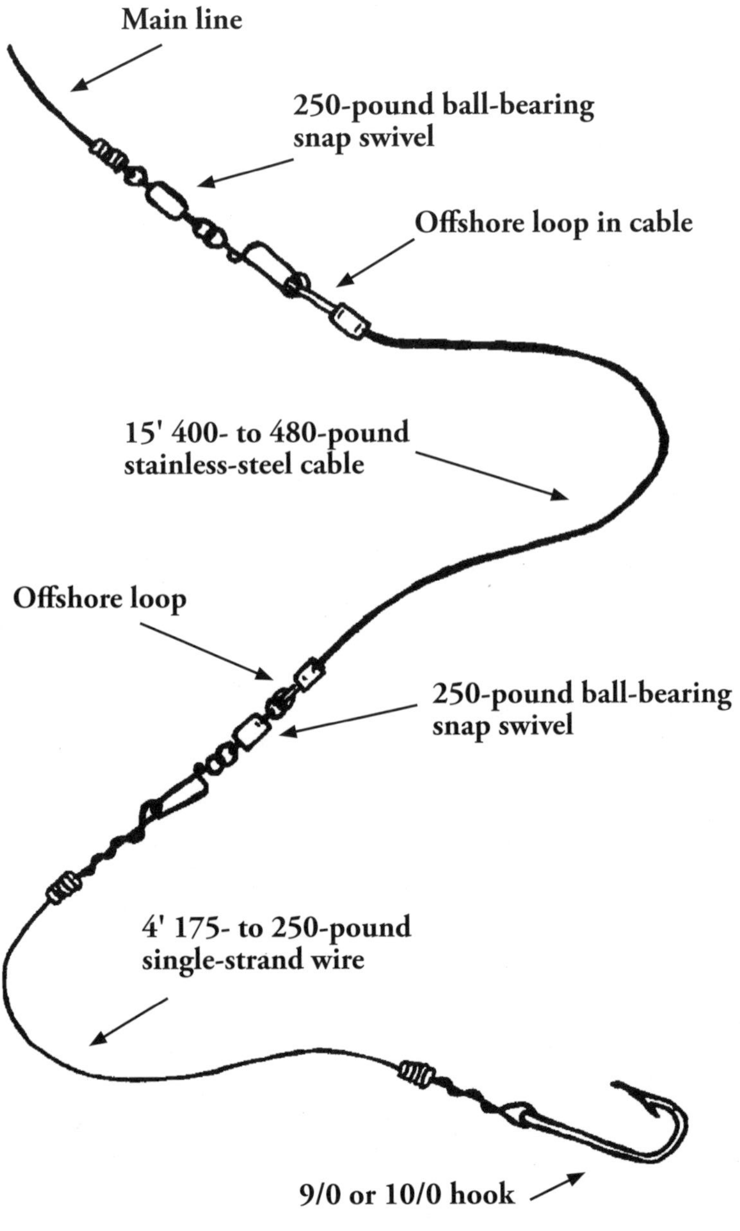

Bluefish Rig

This is a simple but effective rig for bluefish and similar fish, with or without the stinger hook.

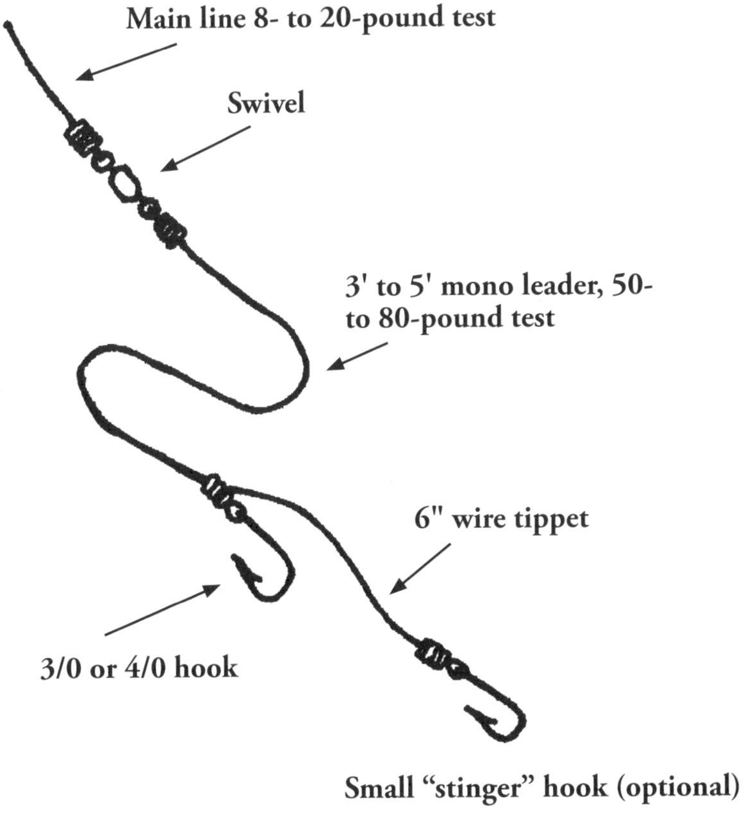

Bluefin Tuna Rig

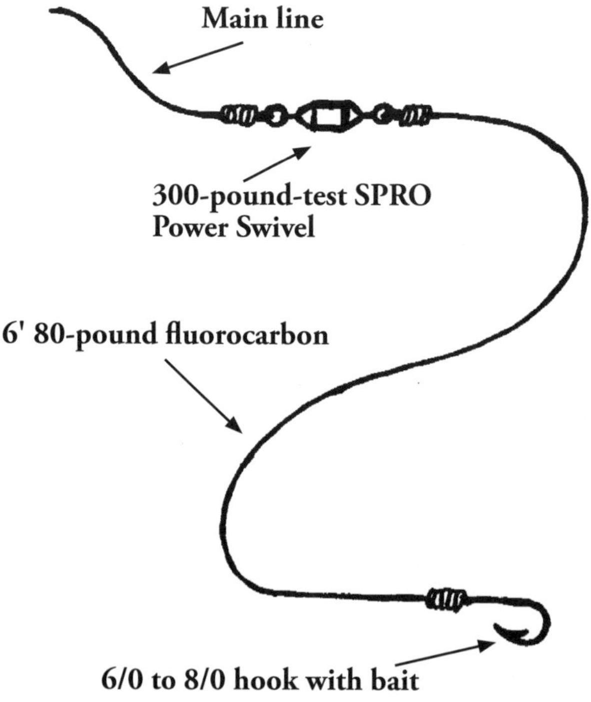

Bluefin Tuna Ballyhoo Rig

use an 8/0 to 10/0 hook

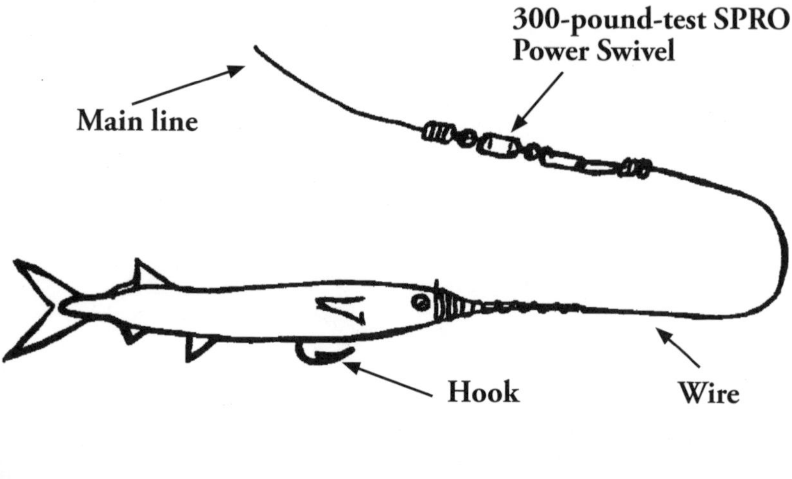

Bonito Rig, Live Bait

Bonito is one of the best all-around baits for offshore trolling. For sailfish, a bonito 12" or smaller is best for tackle up to 50-pound test. Bonito over 12" work well on marlin and tackle over 50-pound test.

Thread line through eye socket then secure with a figure-eight twist (twist wire two or three times).

Thread line through eye socket then attach to a metal fastener using a figure-eight twist (twist wire two or three times).

Hook note: Always use the proper-sized hook for the game fish you are after.

Bottom-Bouncing Rig

Dual-lure rig

Since rockfish spend most of their time on the bottom, this rig needs to bounce off the bottom to be effective.

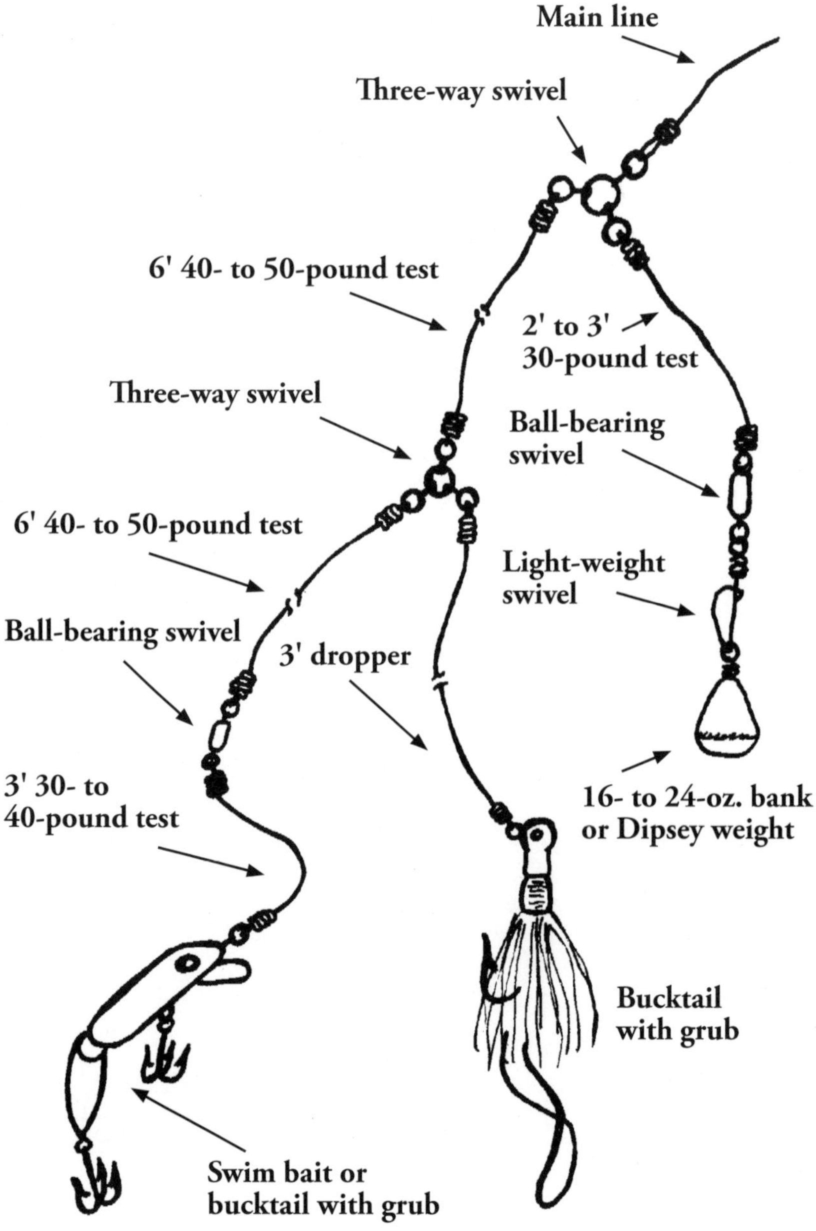

Bottom-Bouncing Rig

Standard trolling rig

Since rockfish spend most of their time on the bottom, this rig needs to bounce off the bottom to be effective.

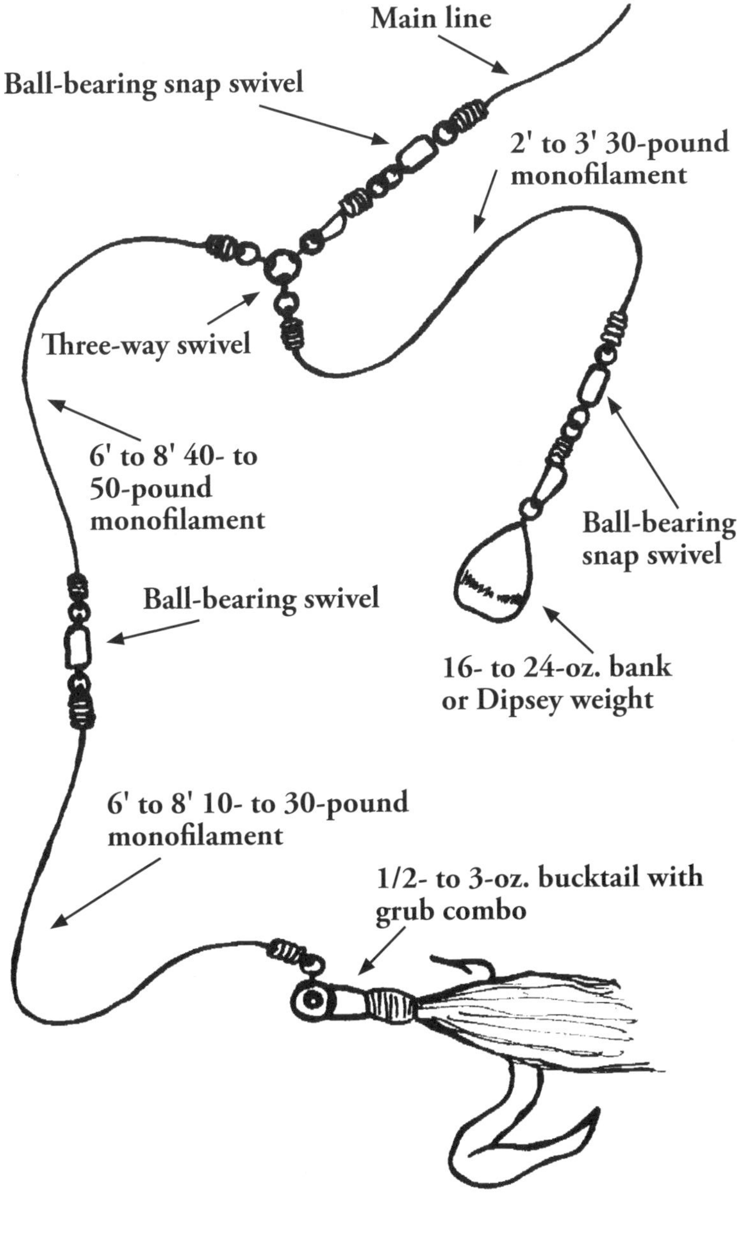

Bottom-Fishing Rig

with chunks and strips

A good all-around bait rig when dead-drifting around fishing piers, shore, jetties and other stationary platforms.

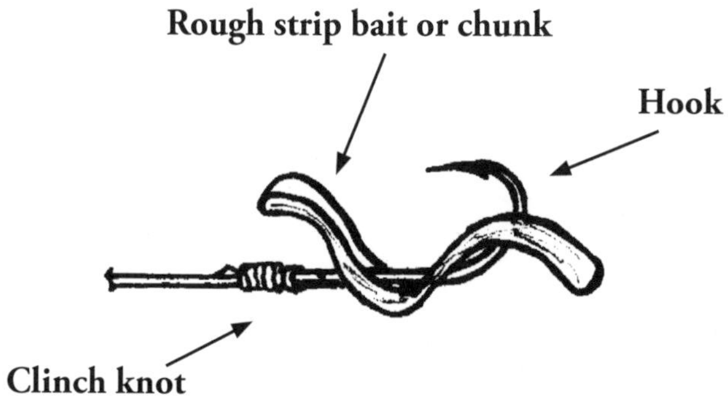

Note: Run the hook through the bait twice, three times with larger bait.

Food for Thought

When the sea floor is flat look for a hump on the bottom, also known as a profile or relief. These areas attract a variety of fish.

Breakaway Sinker

The Breakaway Sinker Rig is used to get the bait down to a specific depth. After a fish is hooked the soft wire lets go (breaks) and the weight falls free. You can now fight the fish freely.

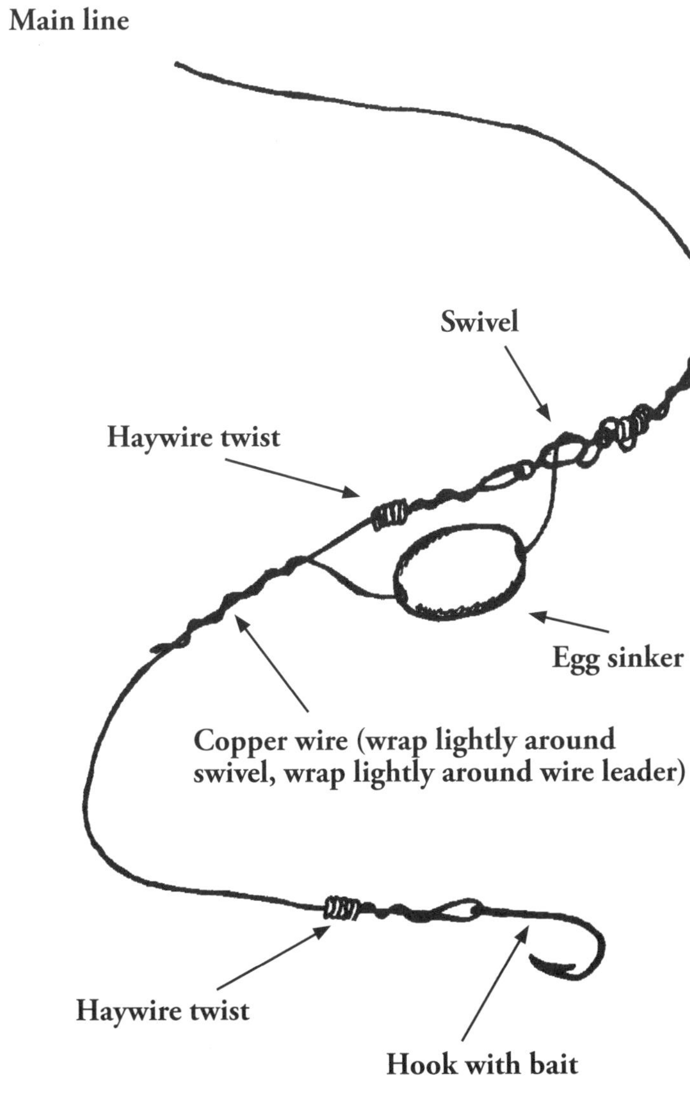

Catch-All Live-Bait Rig

Ideal for when you're using small bait fishing for mackerel and other fish that make short strikes.

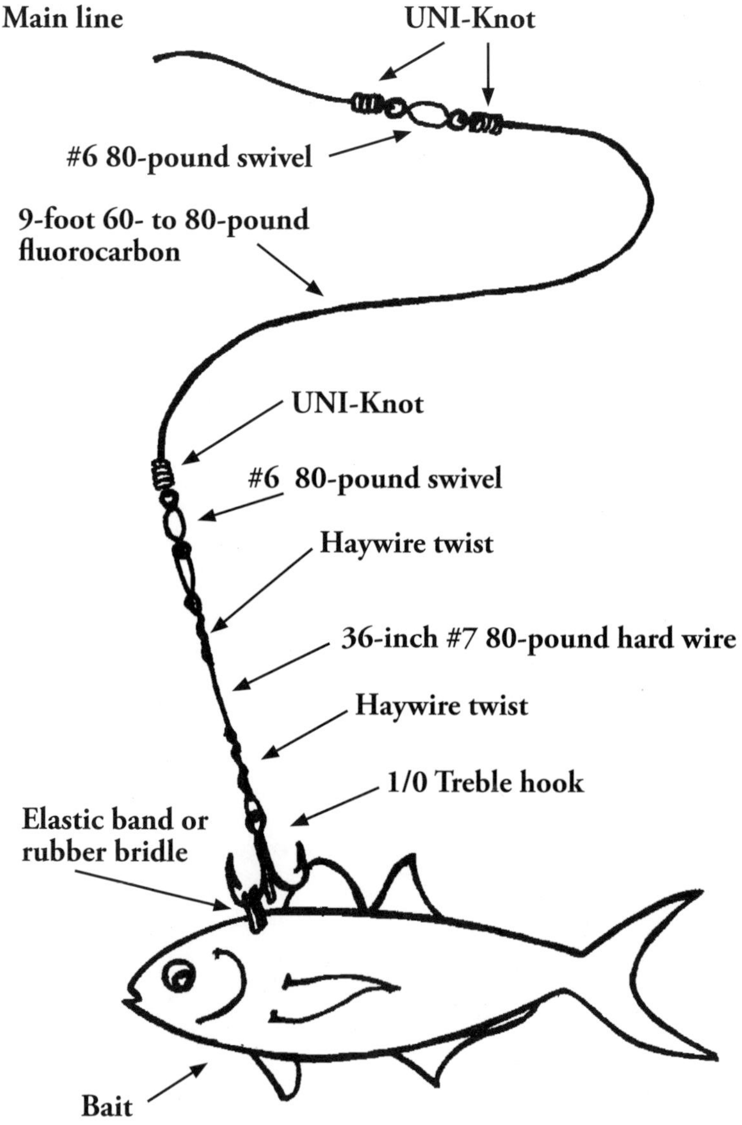

Cigar-Style Trolling Sinker Rig

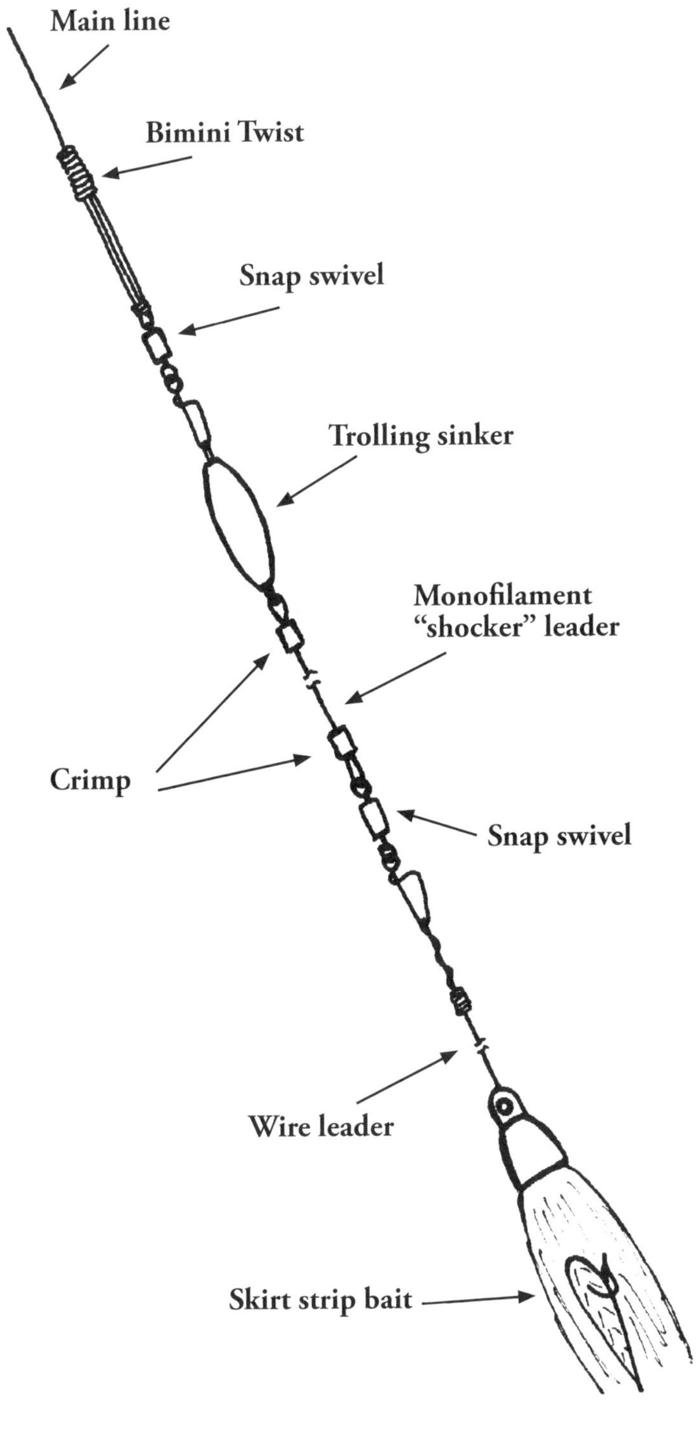

Cobia Bait/Lure Rig

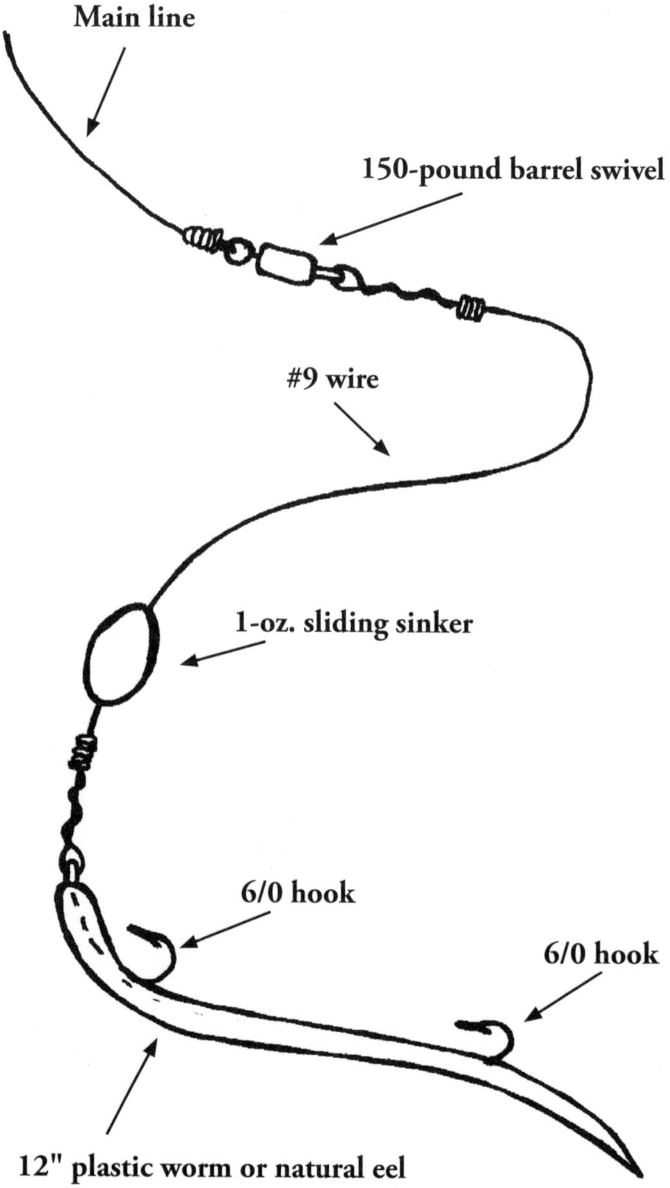

Cobia Jig Rig, Basic

This rig is best used with light-tackle and a medium-action spinning rod.

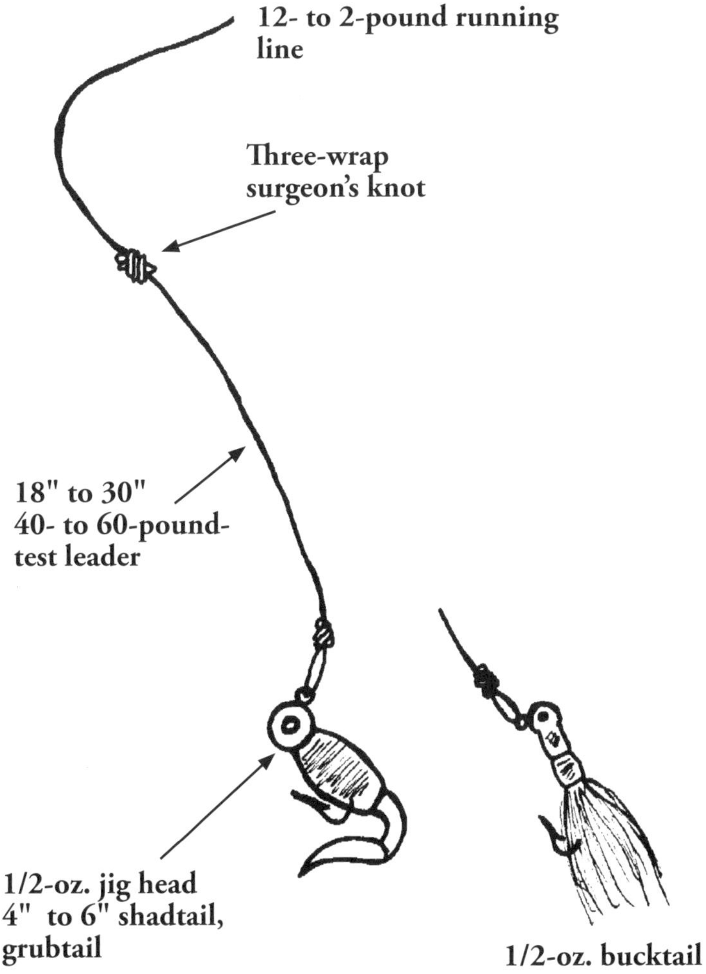

Cobia Jig or Fly Rig

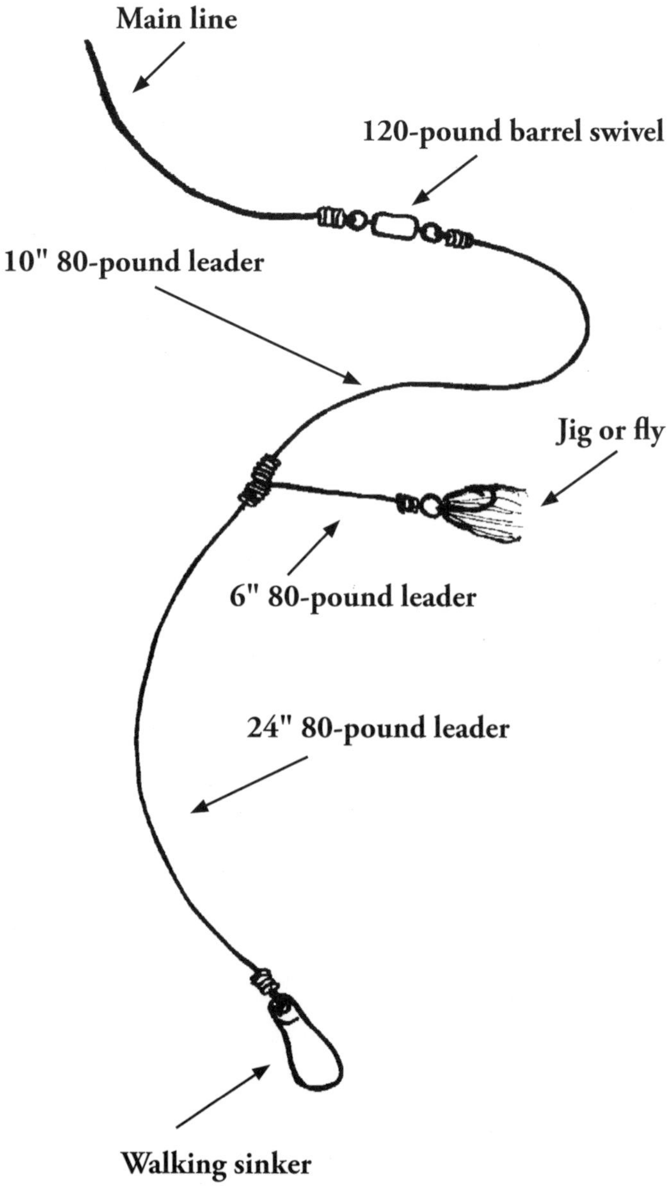

Cod Rig, Basic

Cast out the bait and let the line go straight to the bottom, then raise and lower it to draw a strike.

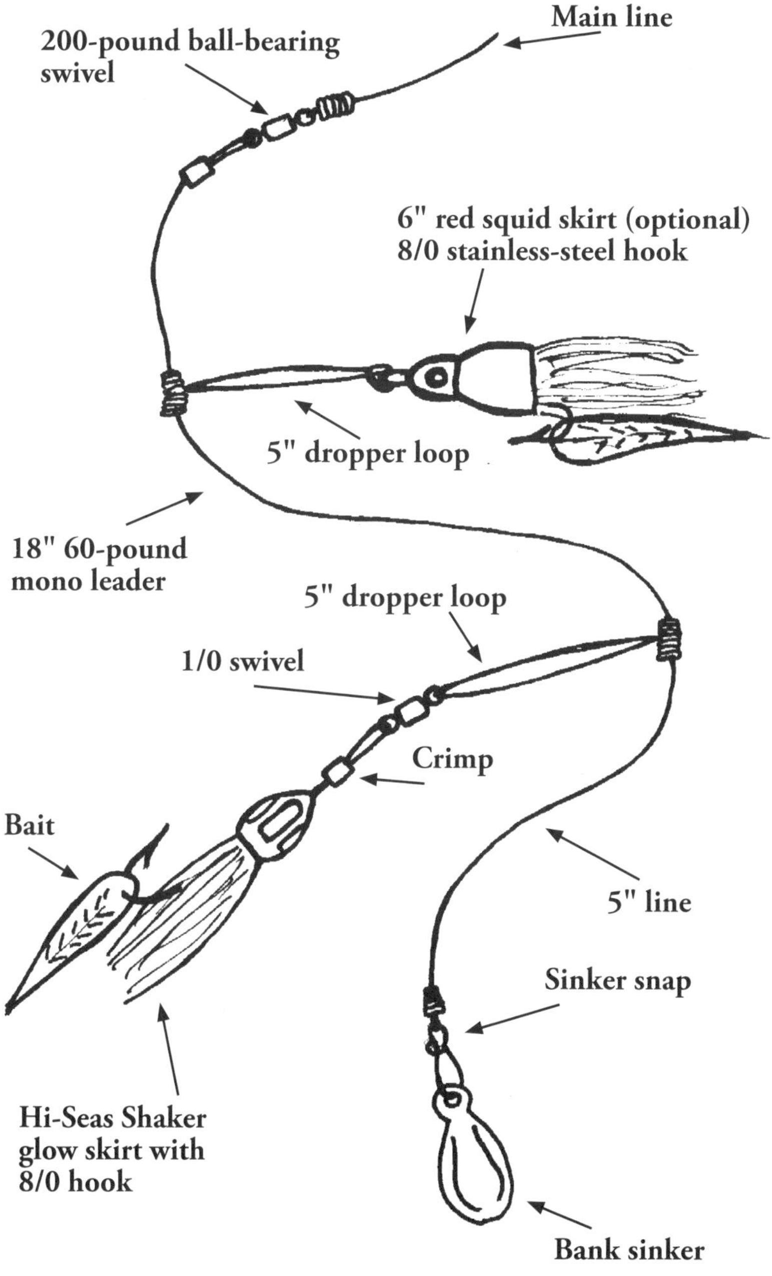

Cod and Seabass Pully Rig

This super-cast rig is design especially for cod and sea bass when surf fishing.

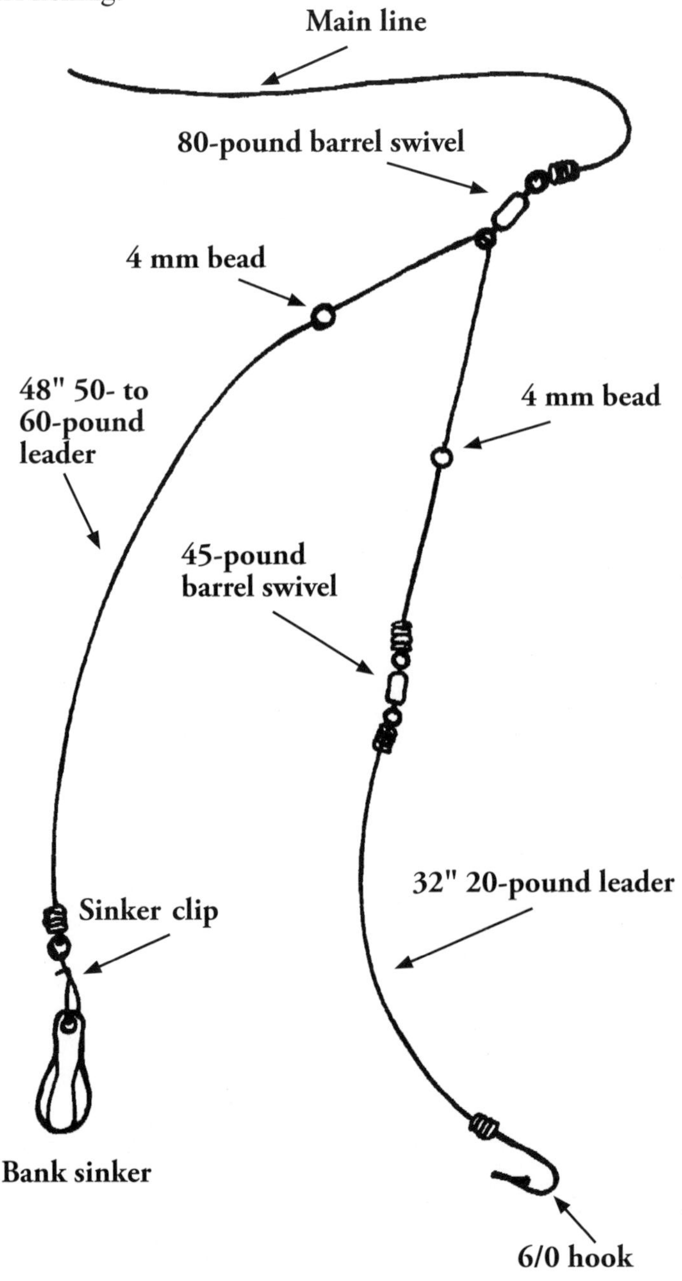

Cut-Plug Bait Rig

The Cut-Plug Bait Rig is popular with salmon fishermen. The hook size should reflect the size of the bait. The bait is slow-trolled letting the current give it an erratic, wobbling and spinning motion. It can be fished weightless, but is generally fished using a downrigger or in combination with a trolling sinker to obtain desired depth.

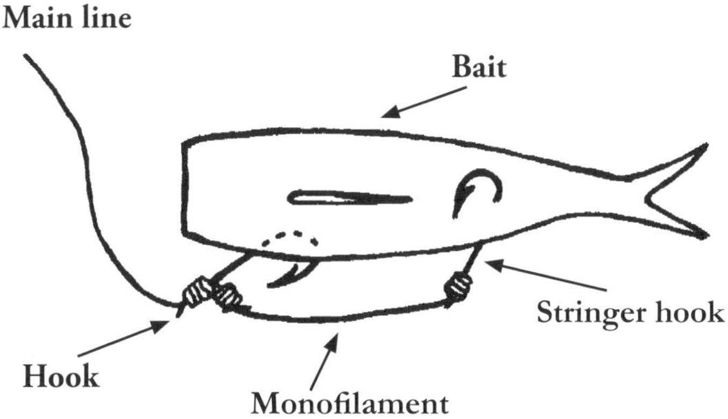

Mullet-Head Rig

An excellent bait for grouper and snapper when reef fishing and inshore fishing for goliath grouper, snook, and tarpon. Mullet heads are the bait of choice, but others work as well.

Bait hook. Run hook through lower lip, then up and through upper lip

Dancing Stinger Rig

Attaches the dancing stinger hooks to the eye of a jig, which greatly increases the hooking power. Because of the flexibility the fish can no longer leverage the hook and jig out of its mouth.

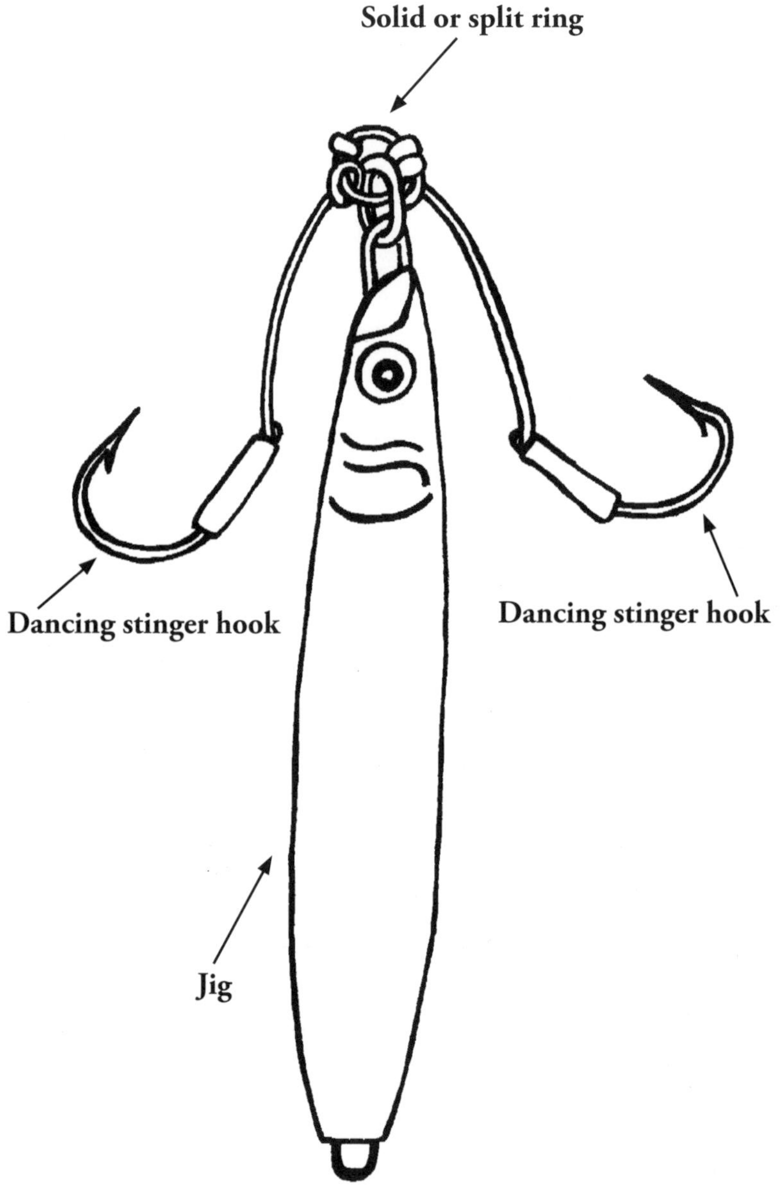

Dead Flying Fish

1. The Dead Flying Fish is generally used when kite-fishing, but is also effective when fishing dead bait.

2. Bimini Twist 12-foot-long double line is tied to the end of the main line then run through the upside down, weighted popping cork.

3. When the cork is upside down the movement of the bait causes the float to give a popping sound and vibration.

4. A UNI-Knot attaches the Bimini Twist to the #3 (60-pound) snap swivel.

5. A 36-inch leader of #7 (80-pound) hard wire is attached to the swivel with a Haywire Twist.

6. At the other end of the hard wire, use a Haywire Twist to attach a 4/0 live-bait hook.

7. A #7 (80-pound) hard wire is attached to the 4/0 hook eye and then to a 1/0 treble hook with a Haywire Twist.

8. The 1/0 treble hook is held to the tail of the fish with an elastic band.

9. The wings of the flying fish are held open with copper rigging wire. The center part of the copper wire is run through the mouth of the fish. Push the copper wire through the wing then make a couple wraps to hold it in place.

Dead Flying Fish

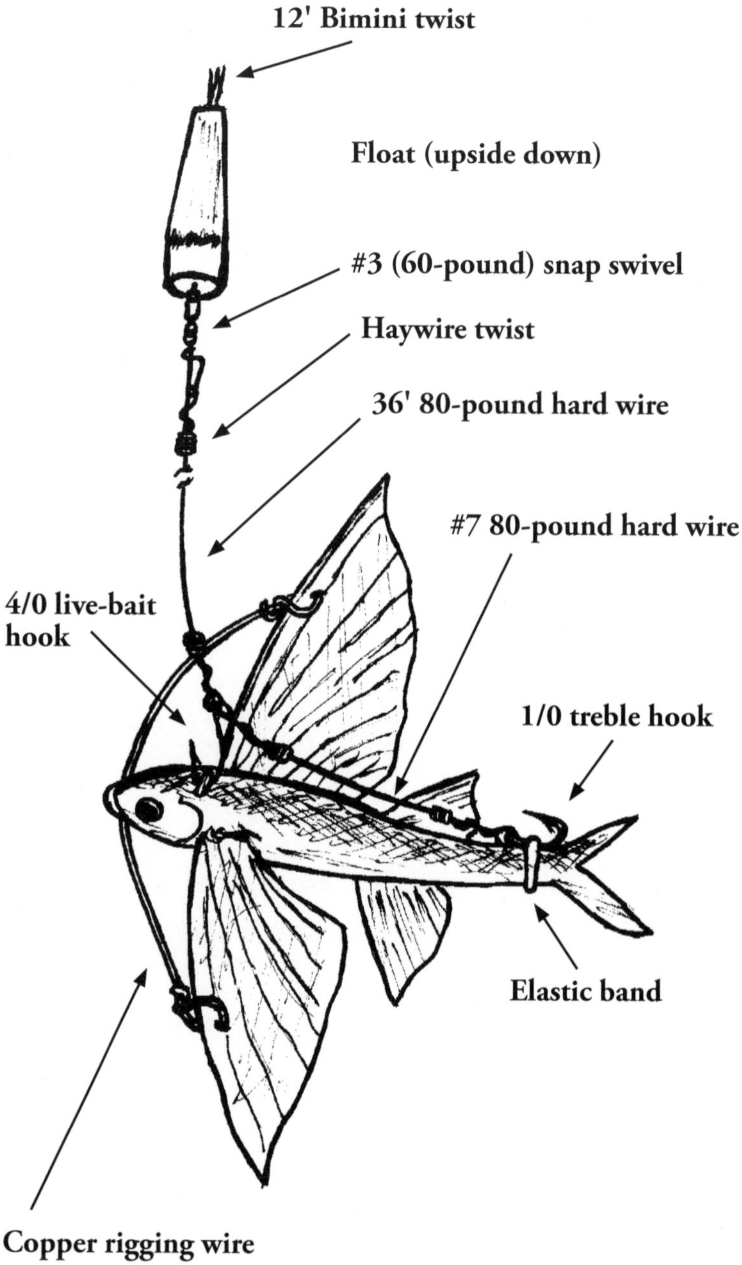
12' Bimini twist
Float (upside down)
#3 (60-pound) snap swivel
Haywire twist
36' 80-pound hard wire
#7 80-pound hard wire
4/0 live-bait hook
1/0 treble hook
Elastic band
Copper rigging wire

Dipsey Rig

(Shore, pier or trolling)

This rig is good for casting or trolling bait in shallow waters. The bait follows behind and off the bottom, the sinker bumps along the bottom as it is retrieved.

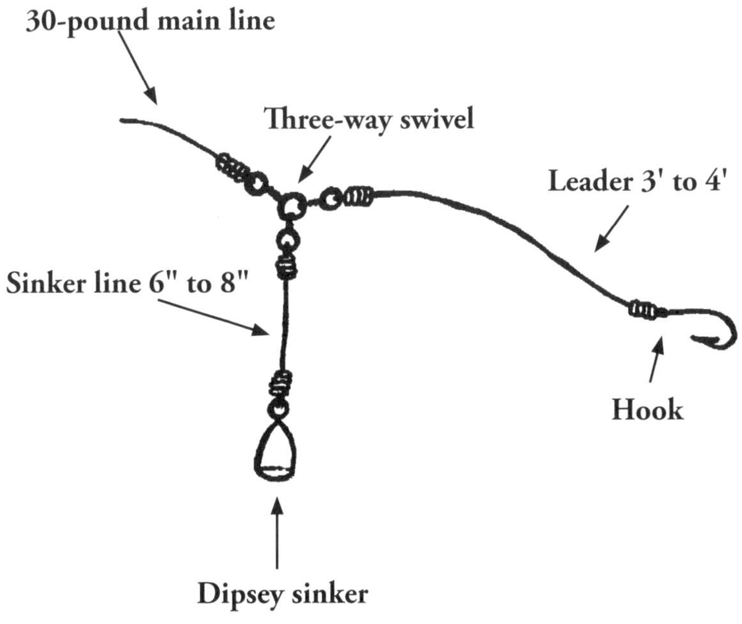

Note: The eye of the hook needs to be large enough to accept the double line of the dropper loop.

Double Pogy Rig

Rigging for kingfish

This rig is for big baits when fishing for kingfish.

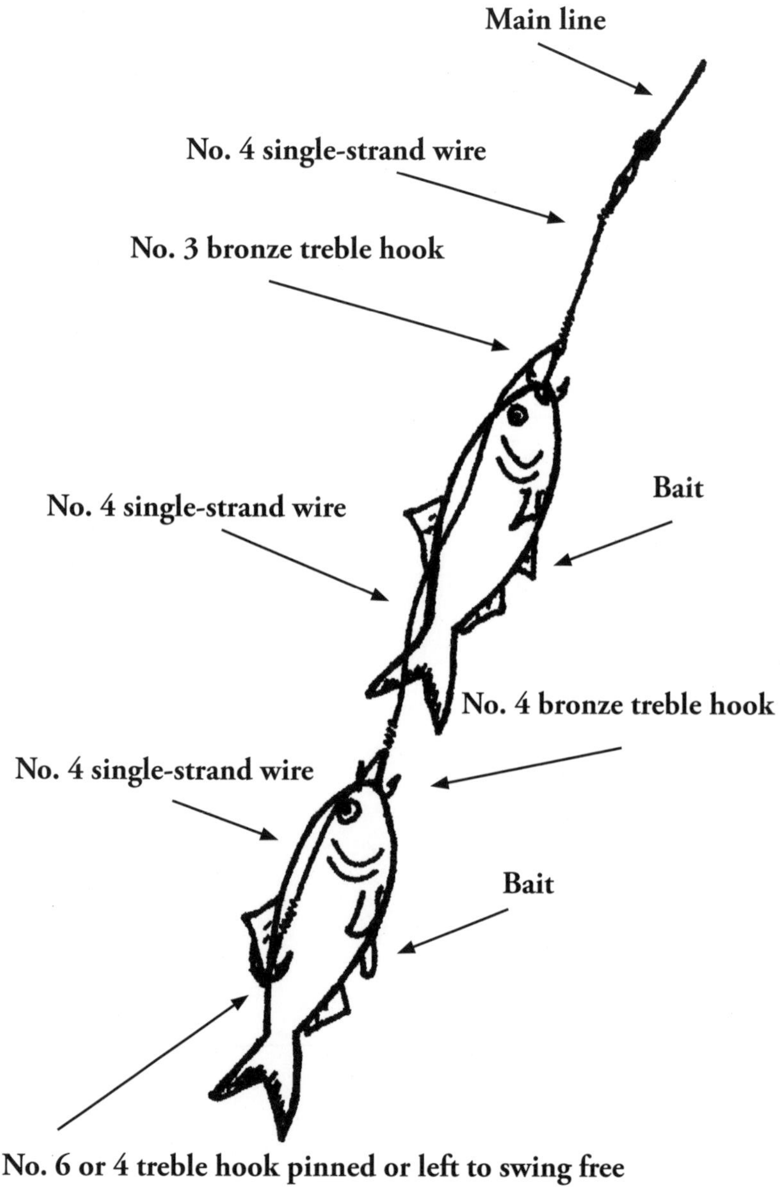

Dropper Loop Rig

An excellent rig when bottom fishing deep waters for grouper, red drum and the like. The Dropper Loop Rig is also known as the "guppy" rig. The rig is constructed by tying two Surgeon's Knots then attaching a sinker. The weight of the sinker is determined by the depth you're fishing and the strength of the current.

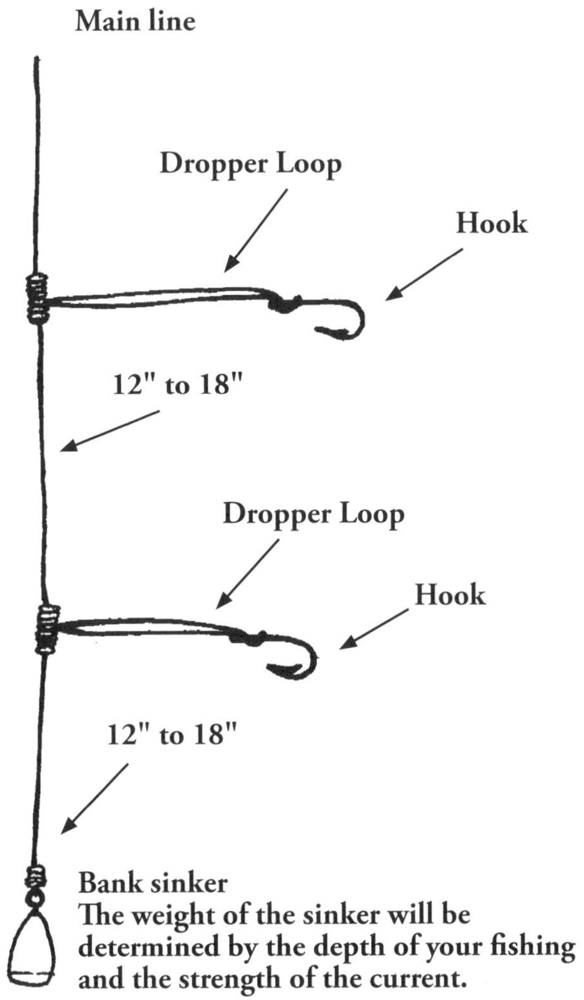

Drum Bait Rig

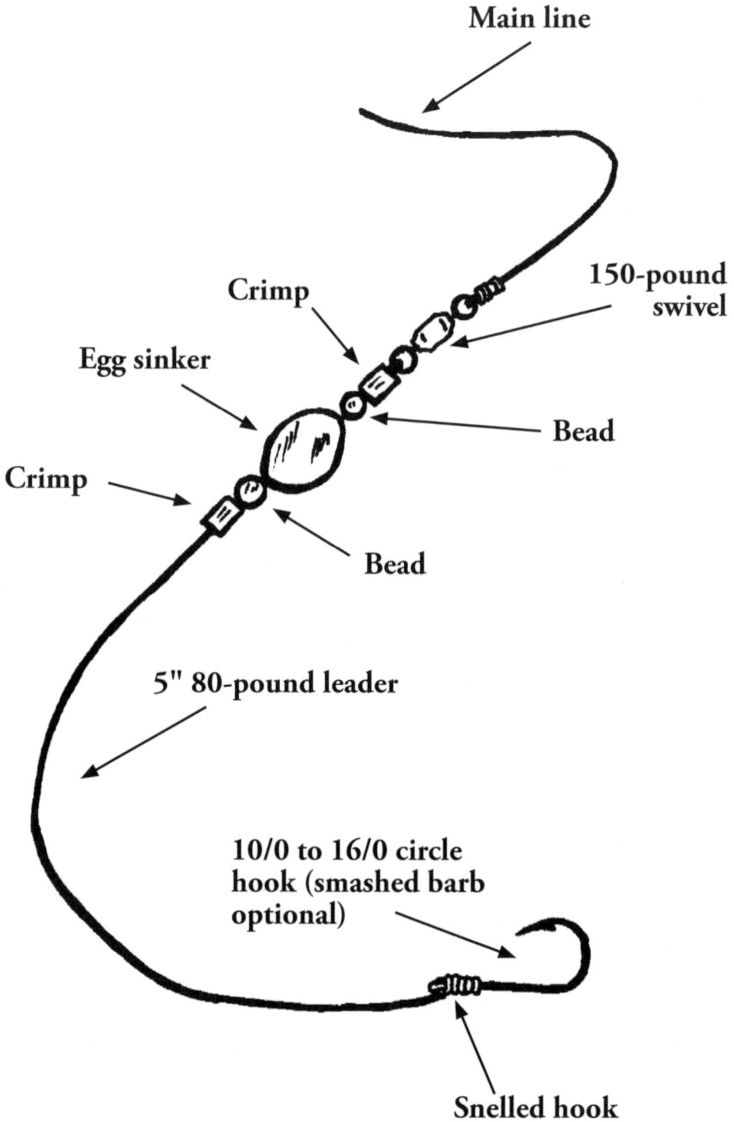
Main line
150-pound
swivel
Crimp
Egg sinker
Bead
Crimp
Bead
5" 80-pound leader
10/0 to 16/0 circle
hook (smashed barb
optional)
Snelled hook

Black Drum Rig

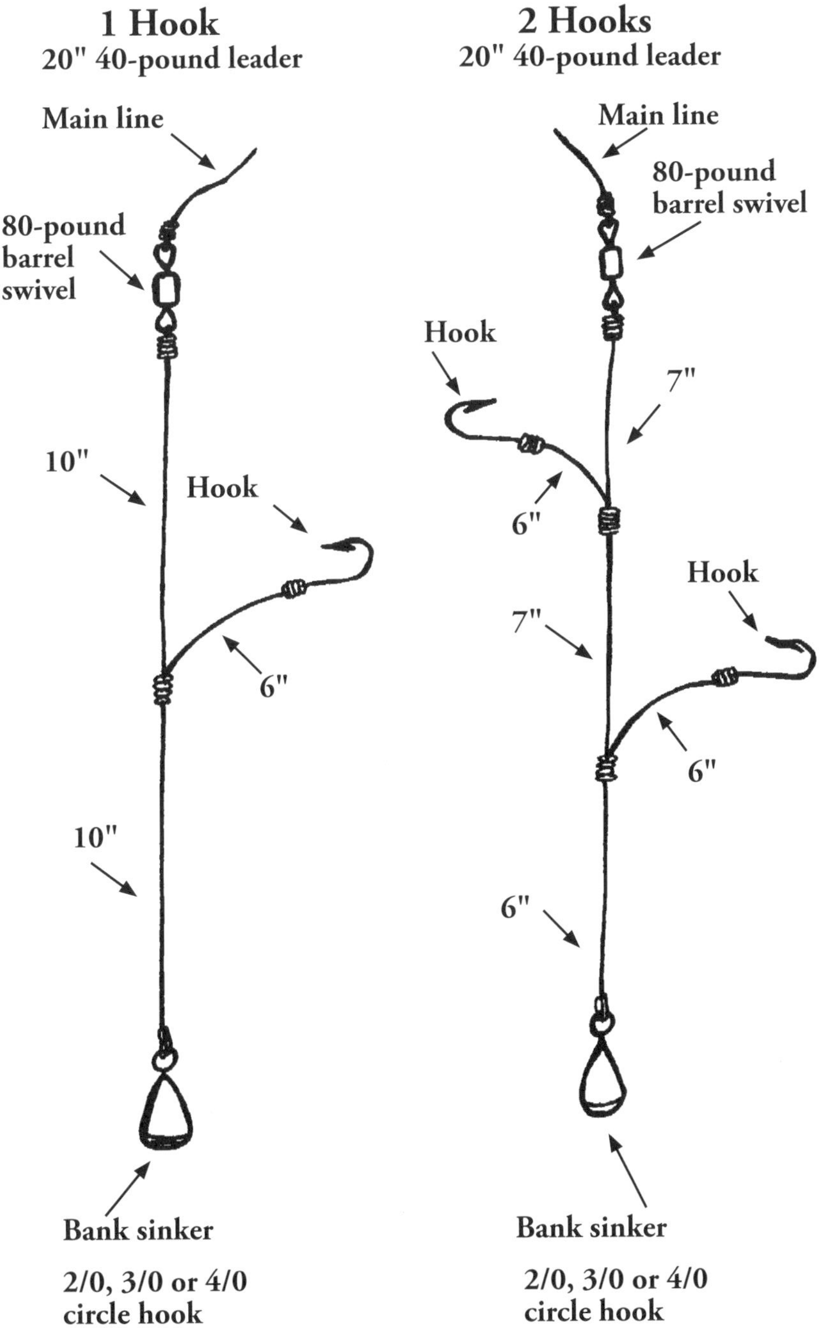
1 Hook
20" 40-pound leader
Main line
80-pound
barrel
swivel
10"
Hook
6"
10"
Bank sinker
2/0, 3/0 or 4/0
circle hook
2 Hooks
20" 40-pound leader
Main line
80-pound
barrel swivel
Hook
7"
6"
Hook
7"
6"
6"
Bank sinker
2/0, 3/0 or 4/0
circle hook

Drum Rig, Red

(For pier fishing)

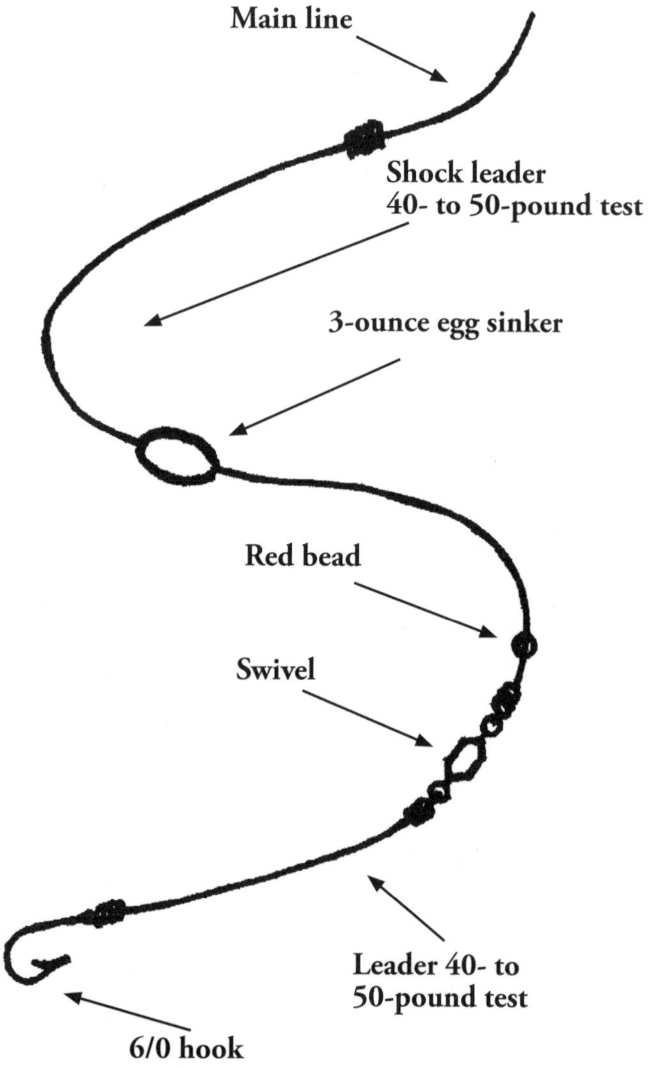

Note: This rig can be used with either cut or live bait hooked through the back. When using live bait wait a little longer before setting the hook.

Drum Rig, Red

(For surf fishing)

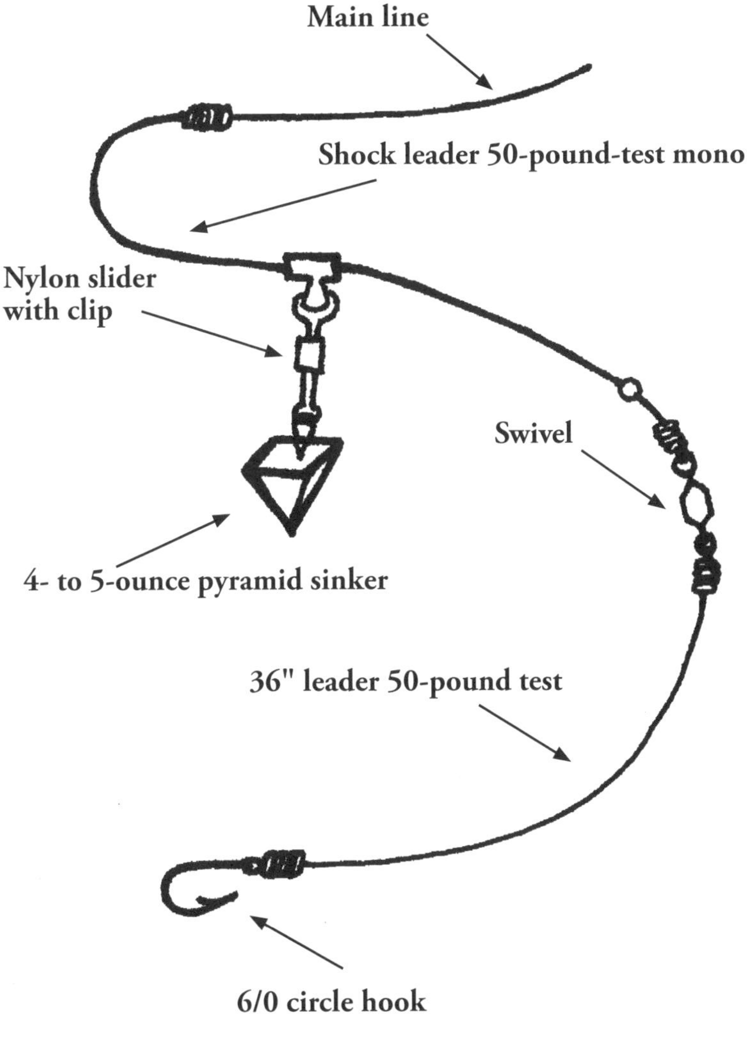

Note: When fishing for small sharks or blues replace the 50-pound mono leader with 45-pound-test wire leader.

Eel Trolling Rig

This rig is great for offshore big-game fish and an excellent rig for closer to shore striped bass, blues and snook.

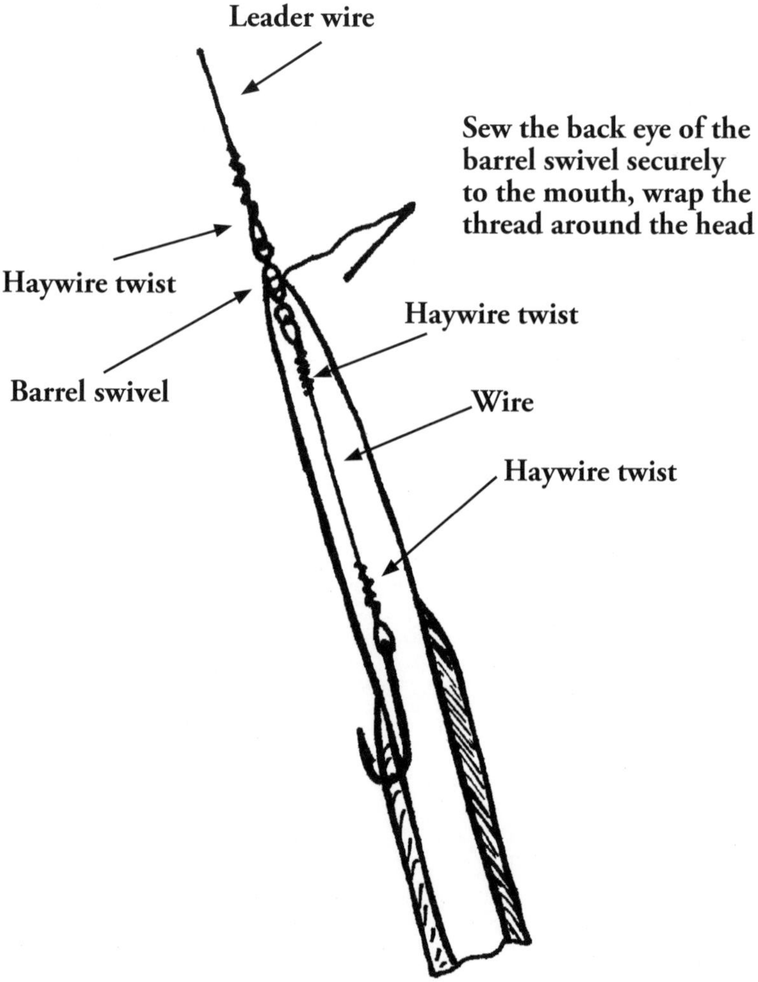

Note: Place the hook at the anal vent and measure the wire, then run the wire from the anal vent through the mouth. The Haywire Twist and barrel swivel should be half way in the mouth. Sew the back eye of the barrel swivel in position in the mouth.

Eelskin Rigging

Also known as the "plumber's special" because one of the major components is a rubber stopper with a lip. This bait is great for bluefish and striped bass.

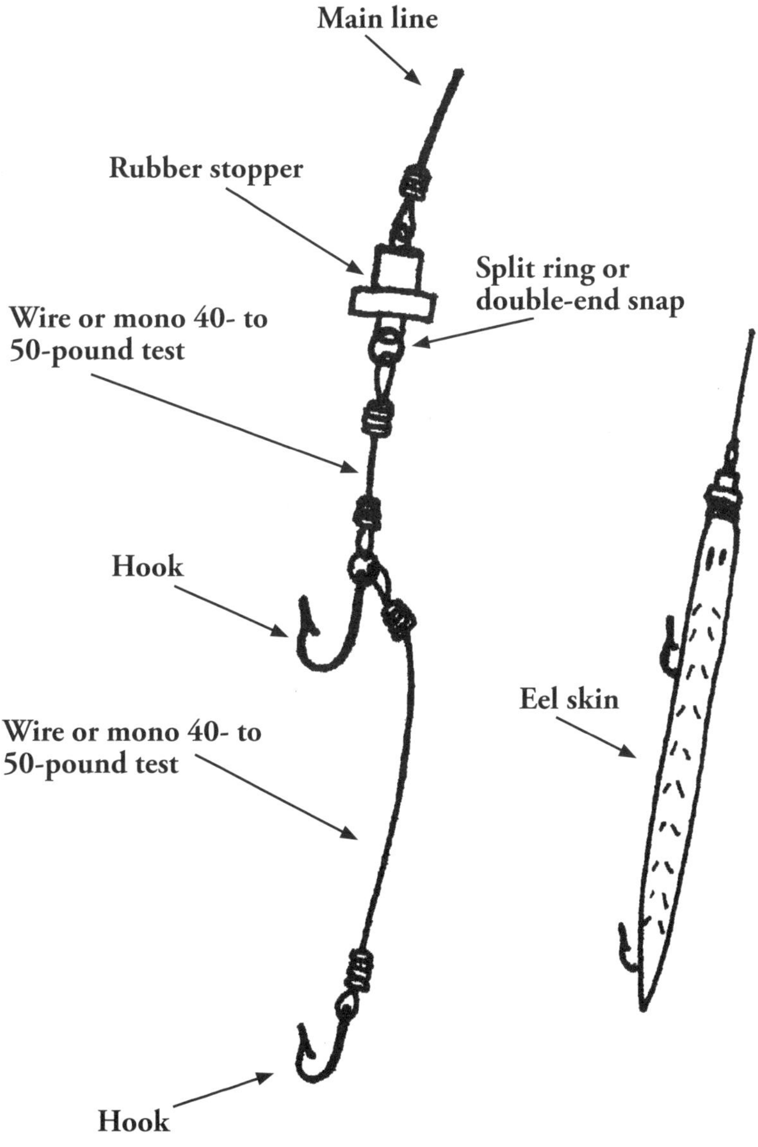

Feather-Strip Trolling Rig

This is one of the more popular trolling rigs, it's quick and easy to make.

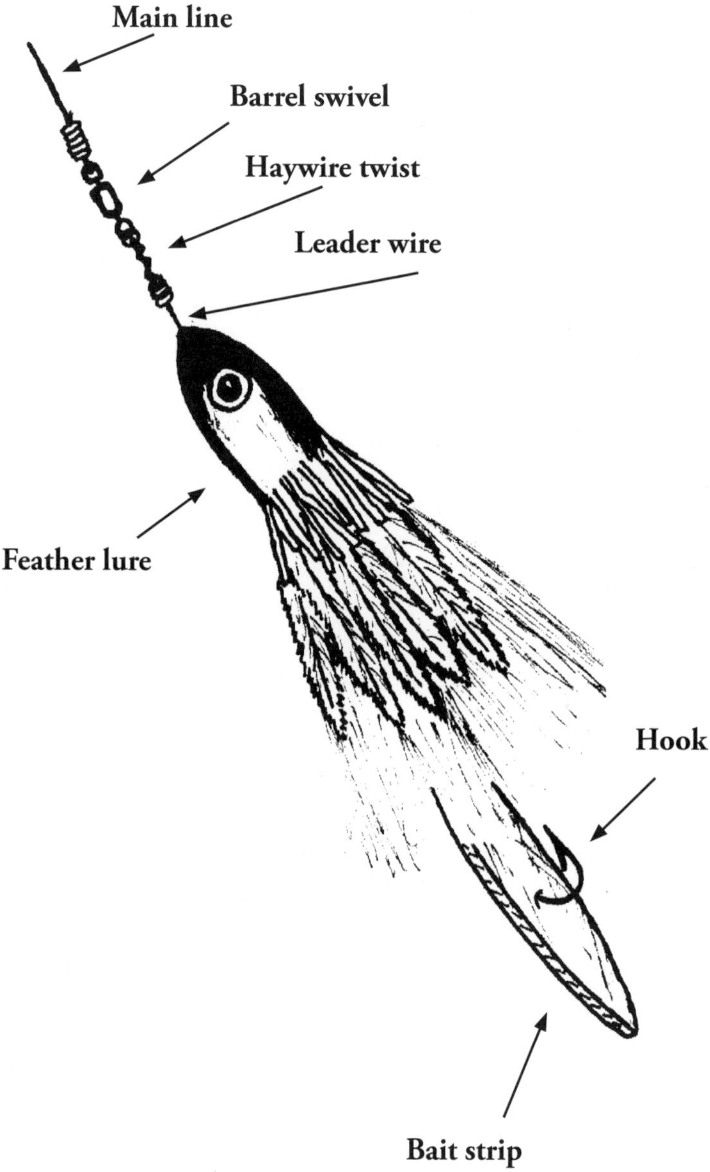

Feather-Strip Trolling Rig

(Continued)

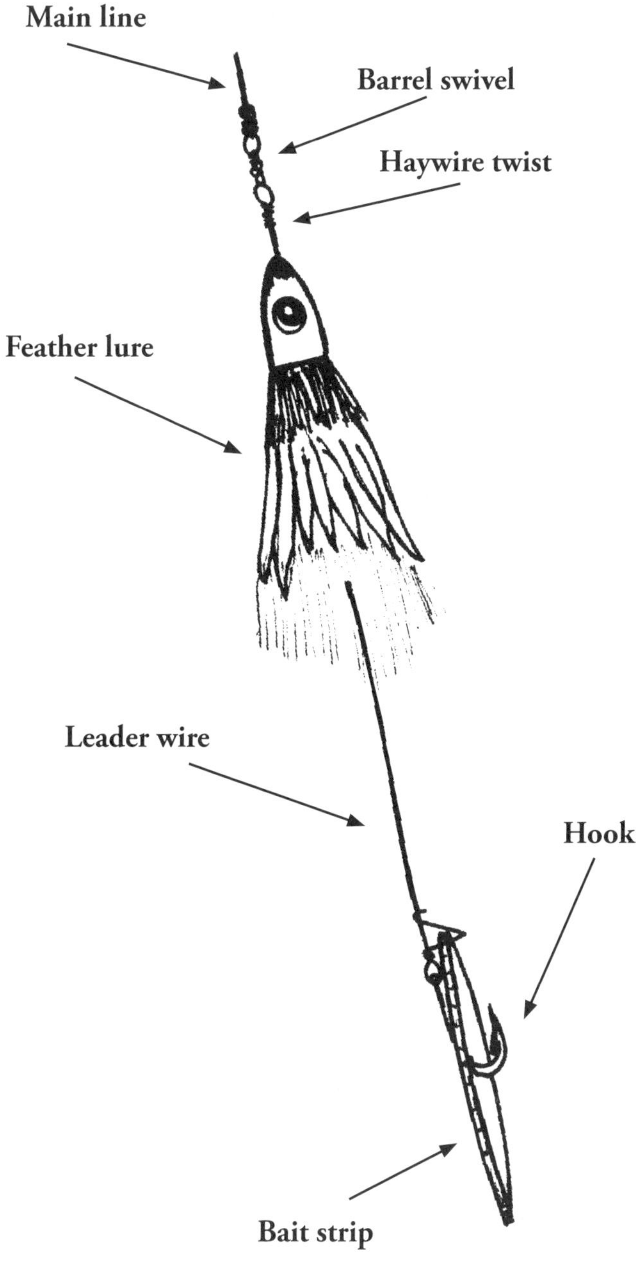

Fiddler Crab Rig

Fiddler crab is great bait for sheepshead, snapper, redfish, grouper and drum. When rigging the fiddler crab do not break off the claw.

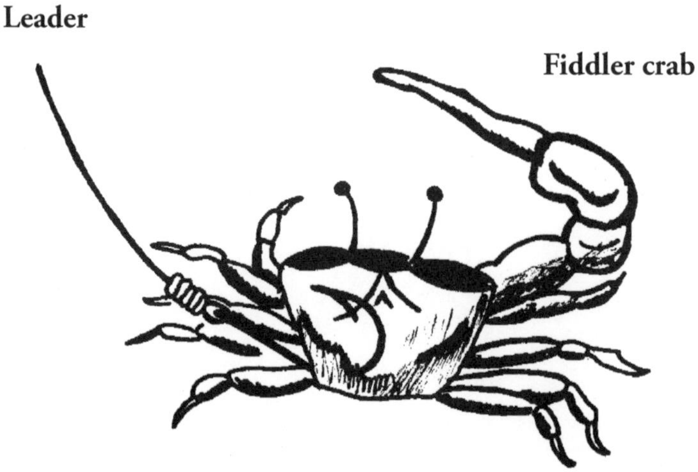

Live-bait hook. Place the hook in the base of any leg, and out anywhere under the shell.

Food for Thought

Fish love structure, fish near sunken wrecks, reefs (man-made or natural), oil rigs or other above-the-water structures.

Fish-Finder Rig

(Shore and pier fishing)

Ideal for sandy bottoms and a popular rig for use with seaworms, a chunk of baitfish, or clams. The cork keeps the bait off the bottom so it's somewhat protected from crabs.

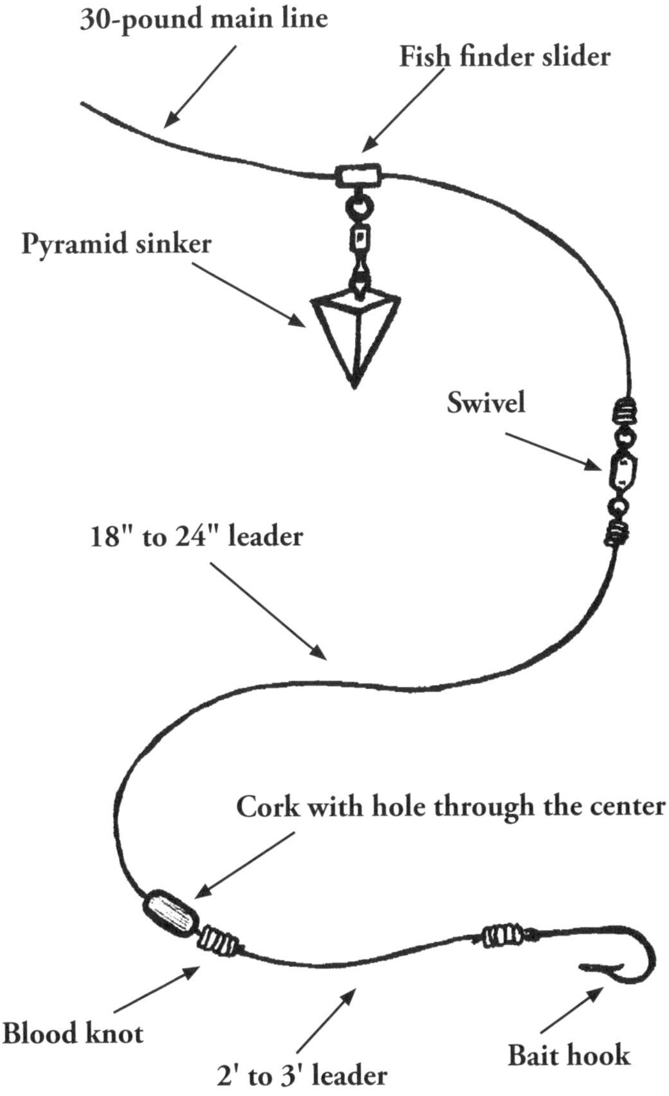

Float Rigs

Fixed Float Rig

Select the smallest float size that will support the bait being used. This rig is used to keep the bait off the bottom, away from crabs and sea lice.

Main line

Oval float fixed: Select the desired fishing depth between float and bait

Swivel: 40-pound

Live-bait hook

Popping Float Rig

The noise caused by popping floats vibrates through the water, drawing the attention of fish.

Main line

Popping cork

Swivel optional: 40-pound

Leader: 18 to 24 inches

Jig or live bait with live-bait hook

Floating Bead Trace Rig

The Floating Bead Trace System is ideal for floating the hook and bait off the bottom. The float slides back and forth from the stop to the bait when casting, making it easier to cast.

Main line

Options: Knot and bead, two-sided tape, small pinch weight

Popping cork

Swivel optional

Leader: 12 to 18 inches

Jig or live bait with live-bait hook

Float Rigs

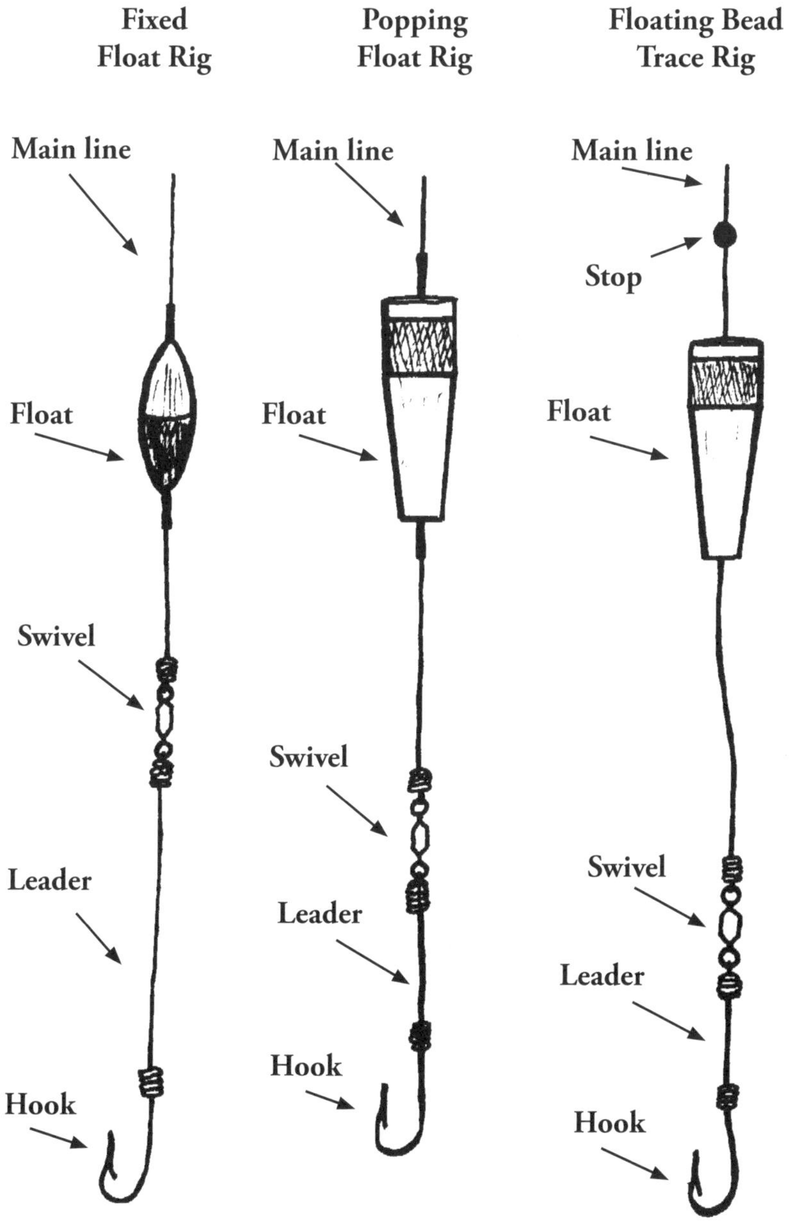
Fixed
Float Rig
Popping
Float Rig
Floating Bead
Trace Rig
Main line
Main line
Main line
Stop
Float
Float
Float
Swivel
Swivel
Swivel
Leader
Leader
Leader
Hook
Hook
Hook

Float Rigs

Working the Float

Take your float-fishing to the next level, try "popping the float." This technique is achieved by raising and lowering the rod tip; pausing between this rod action allows the jig or bait to flutter down and rest below the float. Continue this action through the entire retrieve, and then make your next cast. For additional action, move the rod tip from left to right as you raise and lower the tip. The noise caused by the popping action of the float will send vibrations through the water, drawing the attention of fish.

There are two options for attaching the float to make the popping action:

Option 1: Place the float in the conventional manner.

Option 2: Place the float up-side-down.

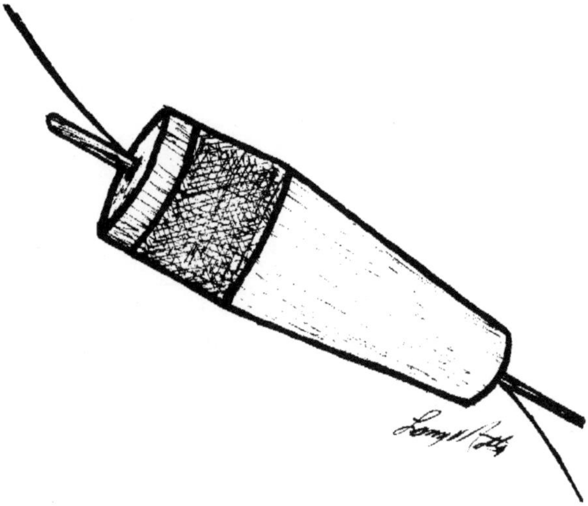

Float Rigs

Working the Float

Option 1: Float in the conventional manner with artificial bait

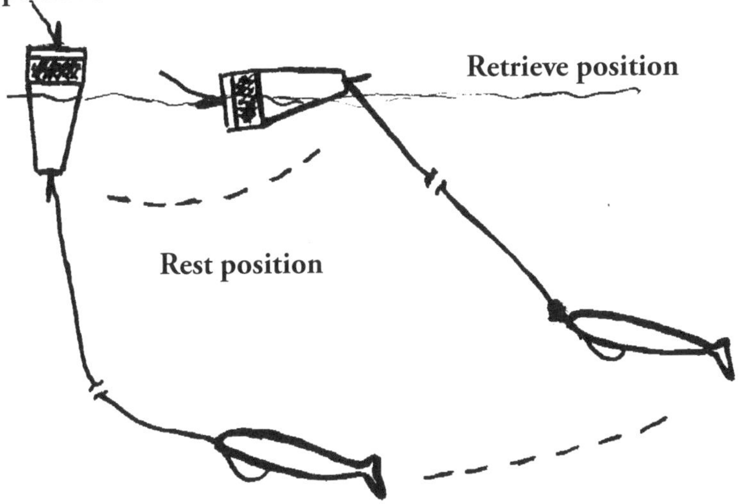

Option 2: Float in up-side-down position with live bait

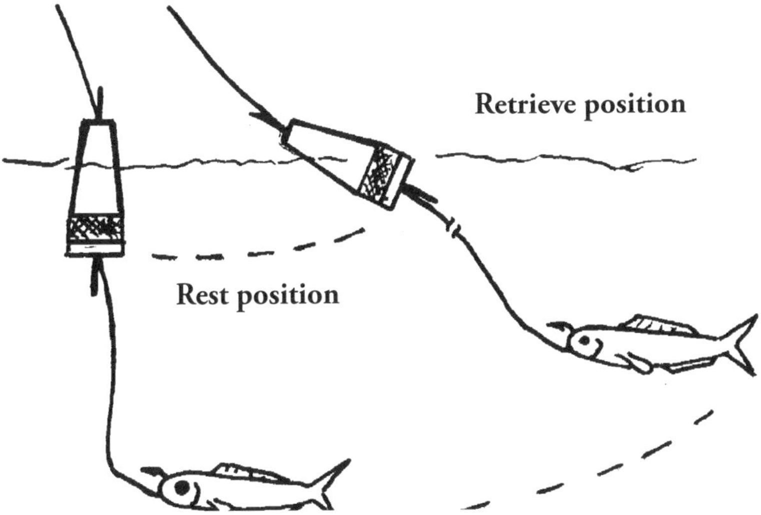

Flounder/Fluke Rig, Basic

This popular, simple rig is ideal for flounder or fluke and works great in all coastal areas. The rig can be fished with a plain bait hook or dress the hook with white or chartreuse bucktail.

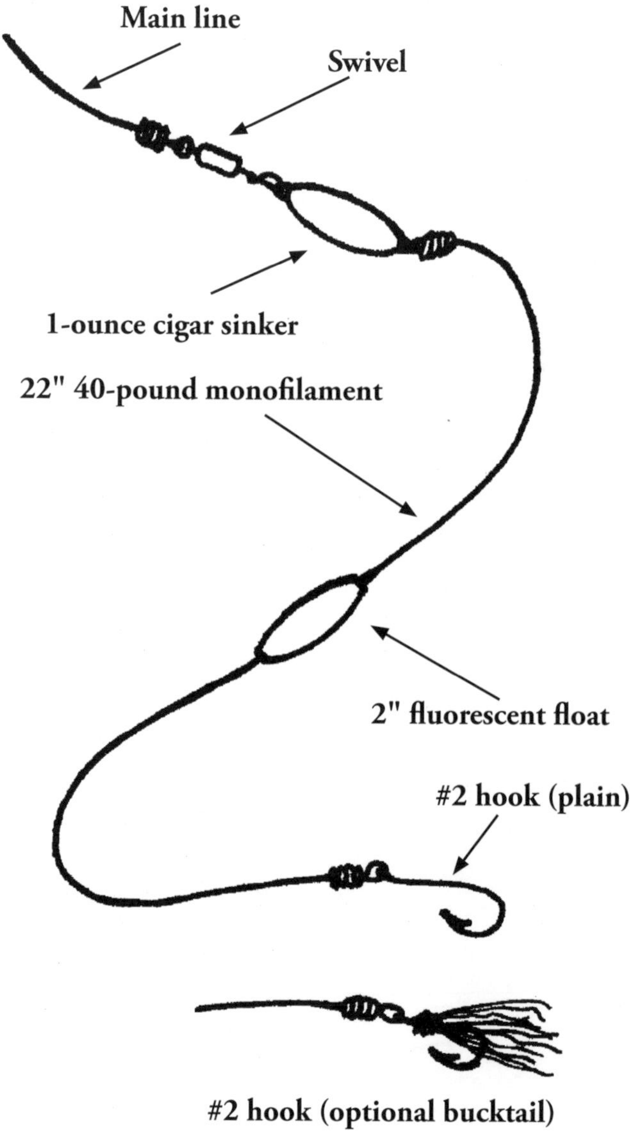

Flounder Bait Rig

Flounder are attracted to fresh, active live baitfish, such as minnows and shrimp. Other options are imitation baits, such as minnows, grubs and shrimp patterns or fly patterns.

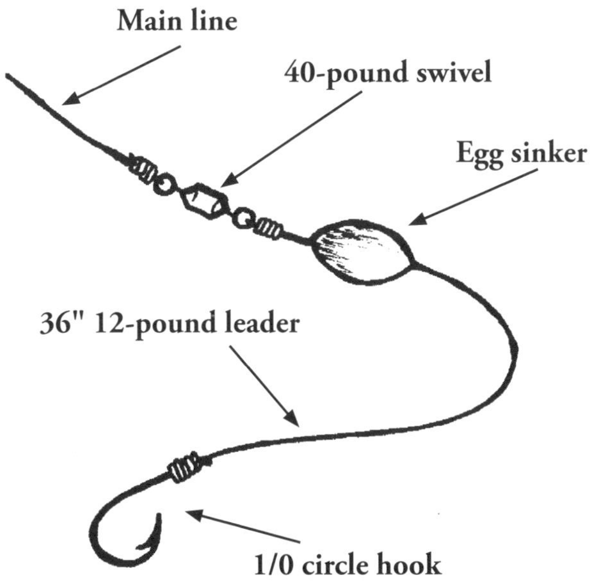

Flounder Chum Rig

Fill mini chum pot with rabbit food, crushed mussels or clams. The canister rides above the bank sinker disbursing morsels of food. Bounce the rig up and down occasionally to stir the food.

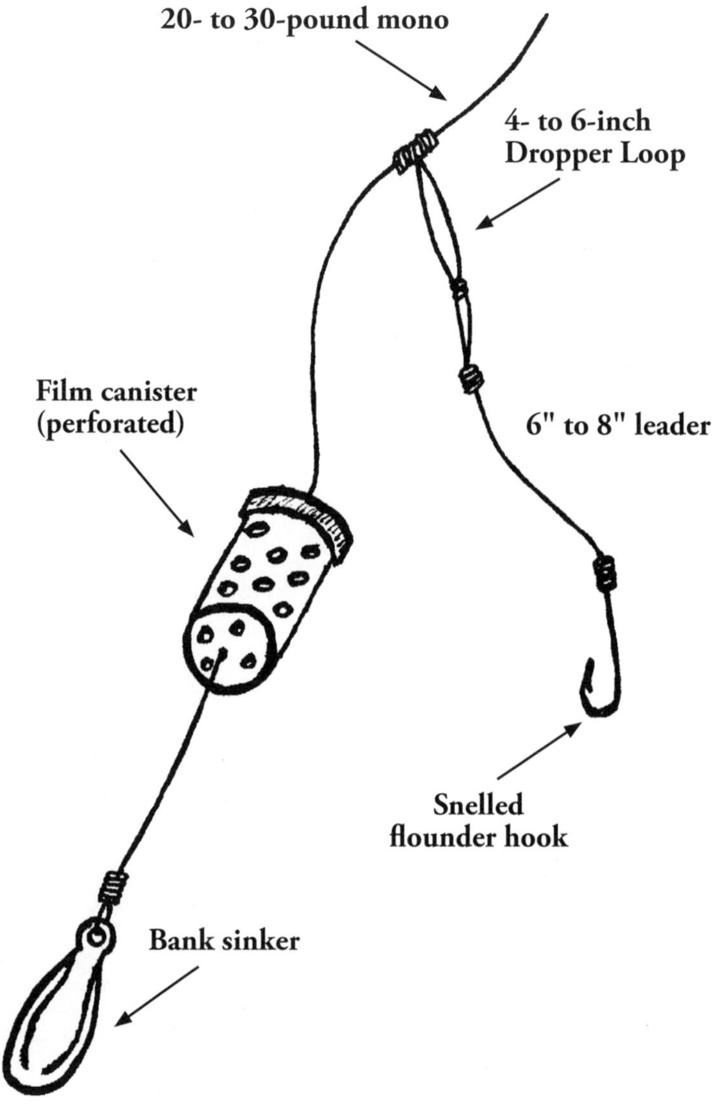

Fluke Drift Rig

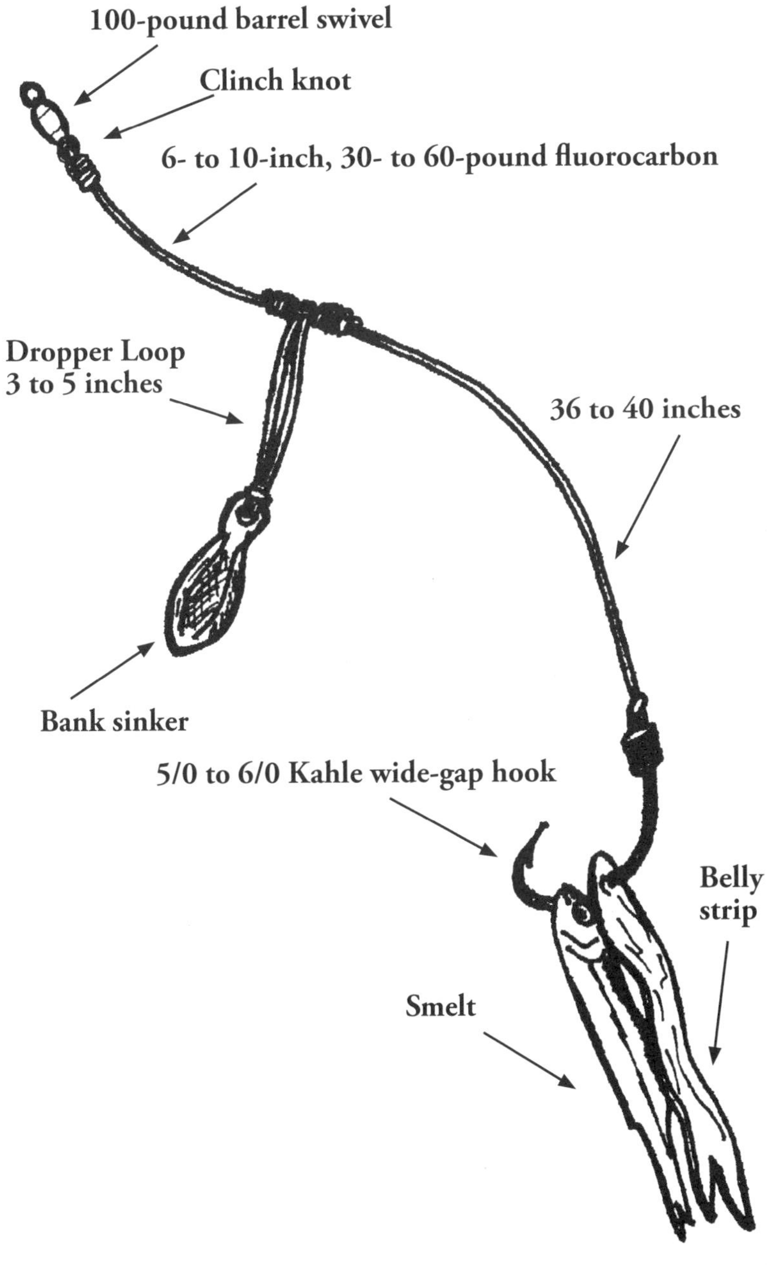
100-pound barrel swivel
Clinch knot
6- to 10-inch, 30- to 60-pound fluorocarbon
Dropper Loop
3 to 5 inches
36 to 40 inches
Bank sinker
5/0 to 6/0 Kahle wide-gap hook
Belly
strip
Smelt

Jig Rigged with Shrimp or Strip

These jig rigs can be fished off a pier, bridge or boat. Select the jig head weight that suits the depth you wish to fish and the water's current.

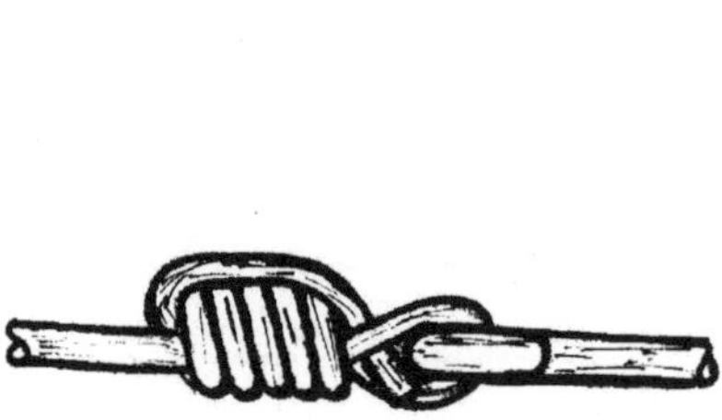

Mr. Clinch Knot

Kingfish, Spot Sea Trout and Whiting Bait Rig

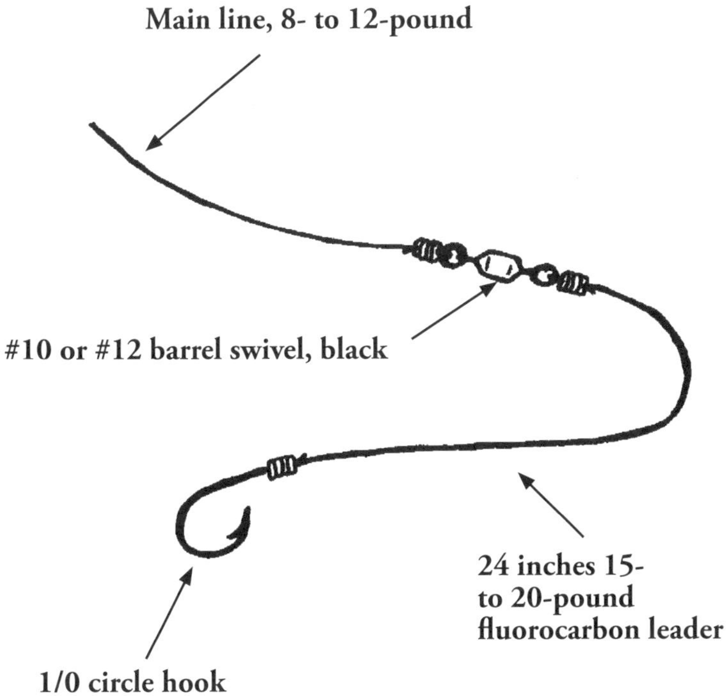

Note: When fishing for kings, always use low-visibility main line.

Kingfish Double-Hook Rig

Push the hook through the anal vent, then push it forward and out of the mouth. To camouflage the hook's position, point it upward and flush against the body and tail.

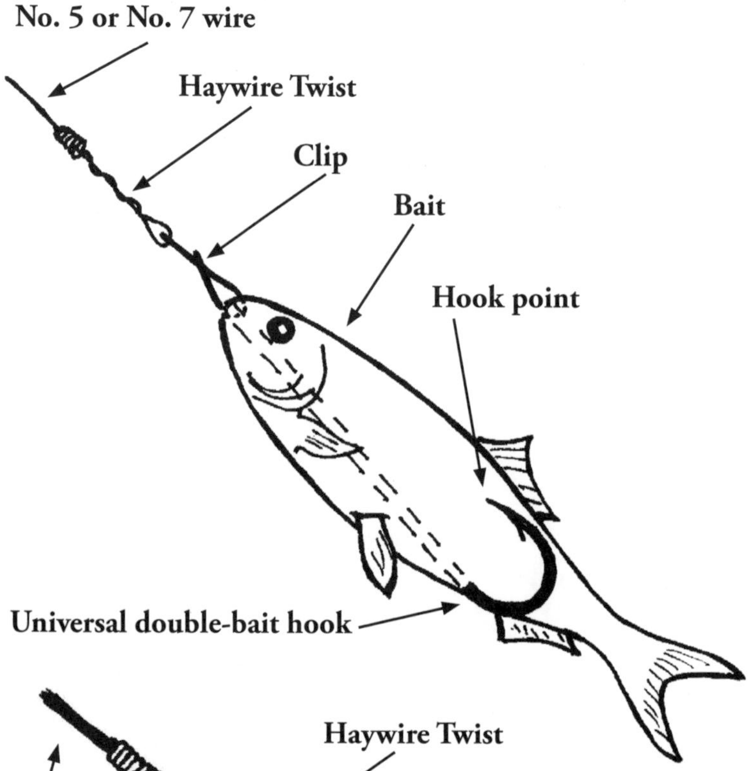

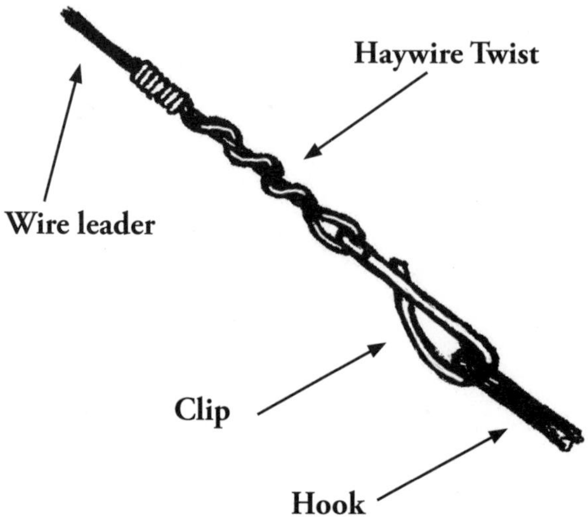

Kingfish Stinger Rig

This is a basic starter rig. Select the hook, wire and swivel sizes that suit your fishing style and the size of the kings you're stalking.

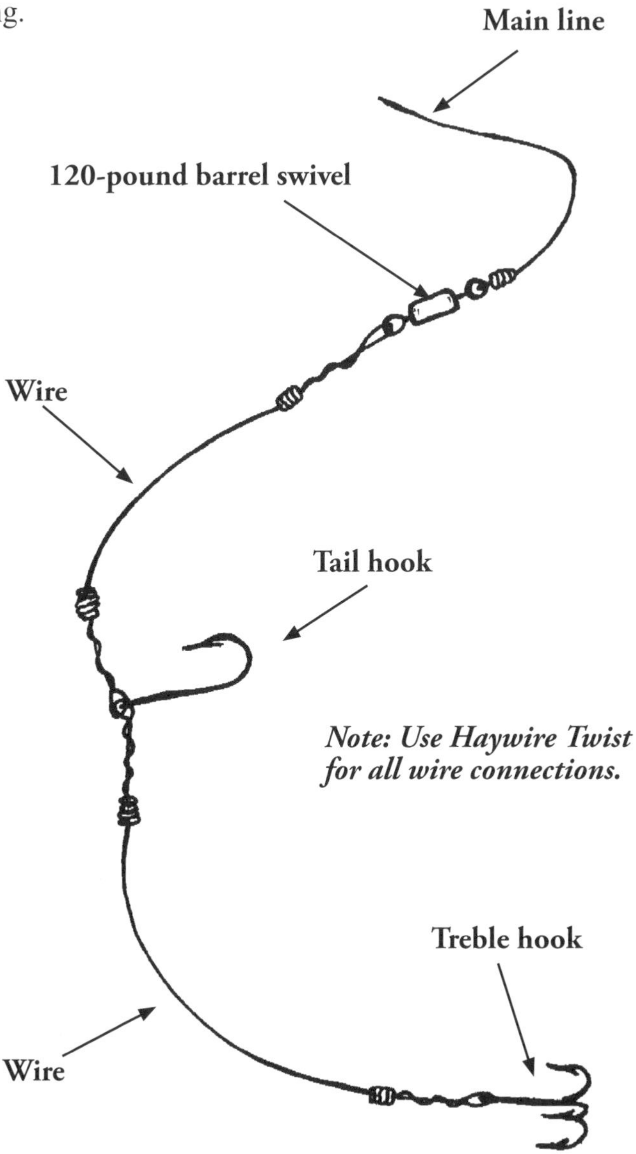

Kingfish are called "smokers" because of their speed and power.

Live Bait Rig No. 1, Catch-All

This rig is used when fishing small baits, such as pilchards, sardines, threadfin herring or the like; drop down to a smaller circle hook or live-bait hook when looking for your desired species. If the smaller baits have a hard time staying down, place a 1/4-ounce split shot several feet up the leader.

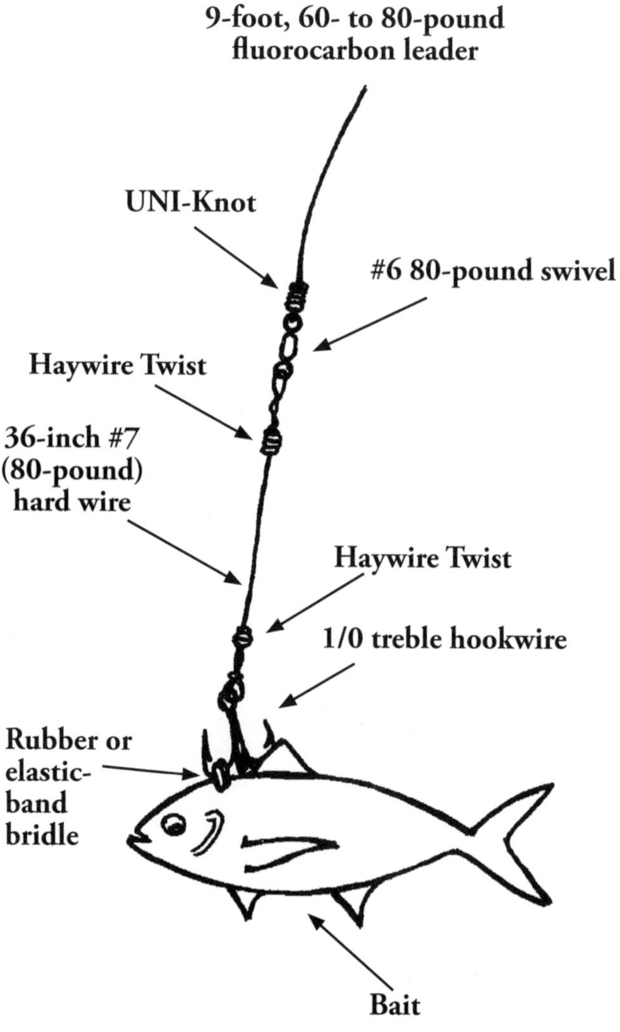

Live Bait Rig No. 2

This rig is ideal when fishing for kingfish, wahoo and other fish that strike short. The cork is attached up-side-down to make a popping noise, attracting attention, as the bait is retrieved.

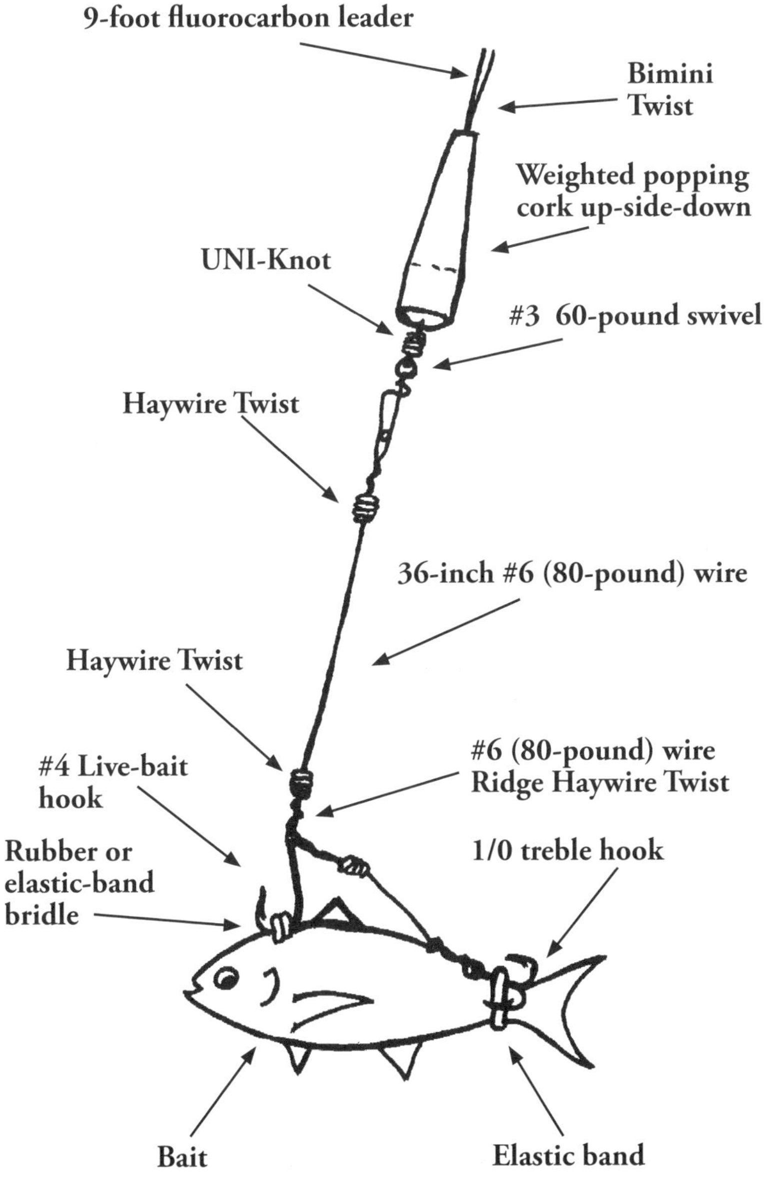

Live Bait Rig No. 3

Circle-Hook Rig

This rig is used with large baits such as blue runners, goggle eyes, Speedos or the like. Smaller baits drop down to a smaller circle hook or live bait hook. If the smaller baits have a hard time staying down, place a ¼-ounce split shot several feet up the leader.

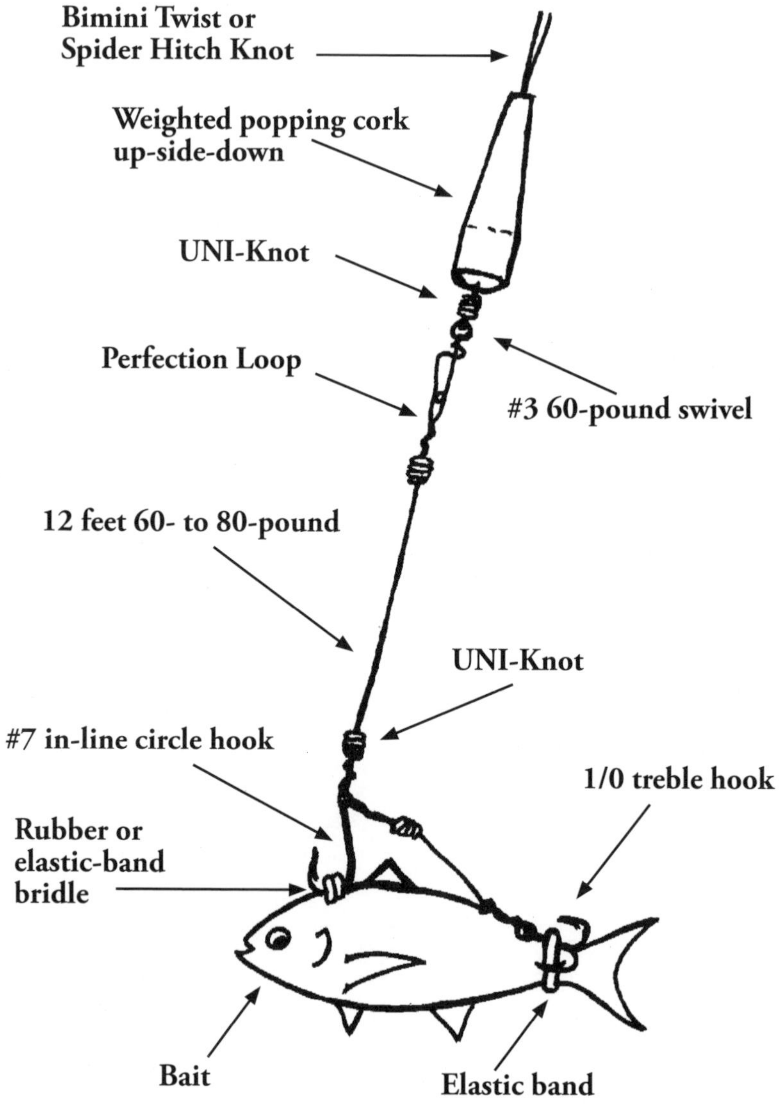

Marine Worms

Worms (sandworms, bloodworms, clamworms, nightcrawlers, angleworms, etc.) one of the most popular and effective all-around baits.

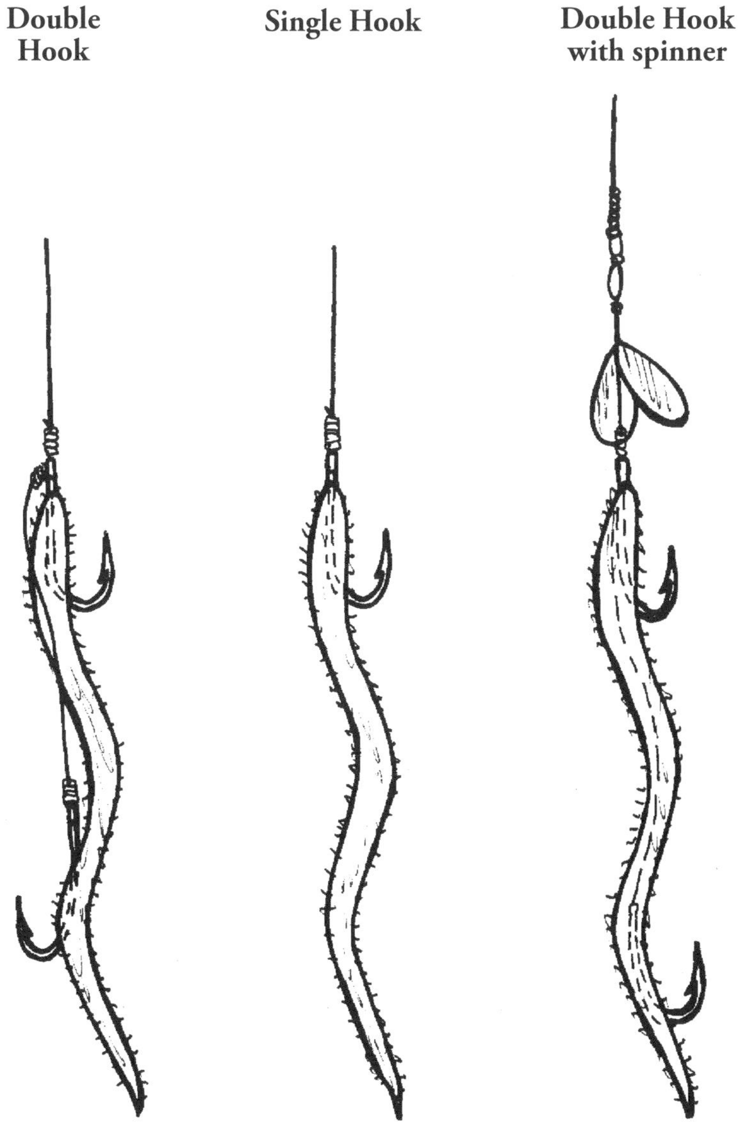

Marlin Rig with Mackerel

This rigging is good when trolling for large gamefish such as marlin.

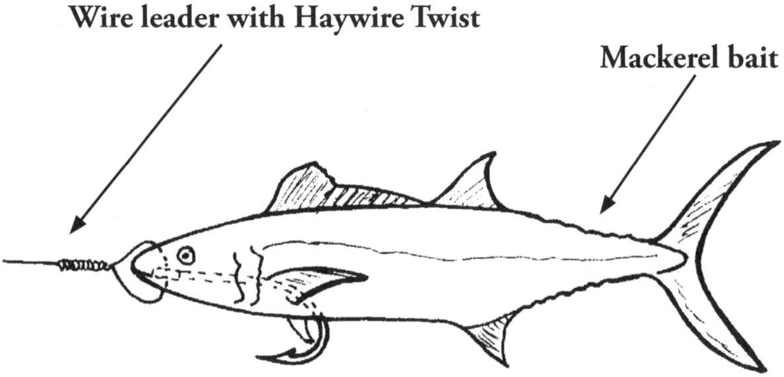

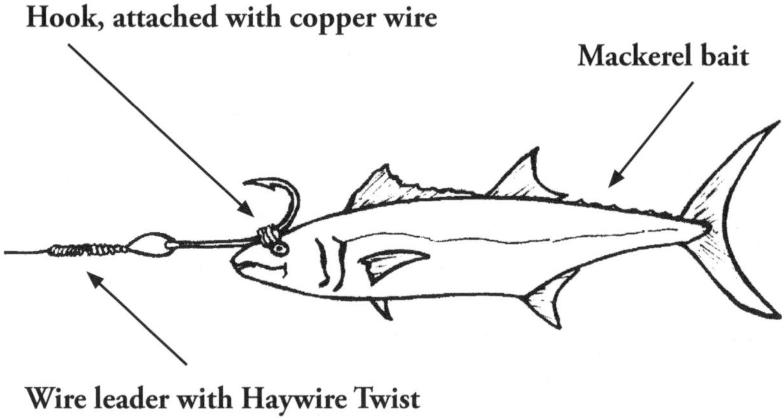

Mullet Head Rig

Large mullet are used for marlin and tuna fishing and are also great for trolling deep for amberjack and large grouper. These rigs require flexible mullet; instead of de-boning, flex the bait back and forth breaking the backbone in several places.

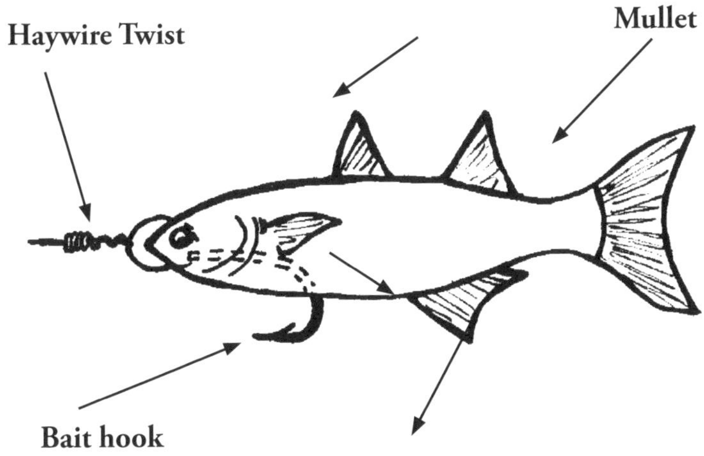

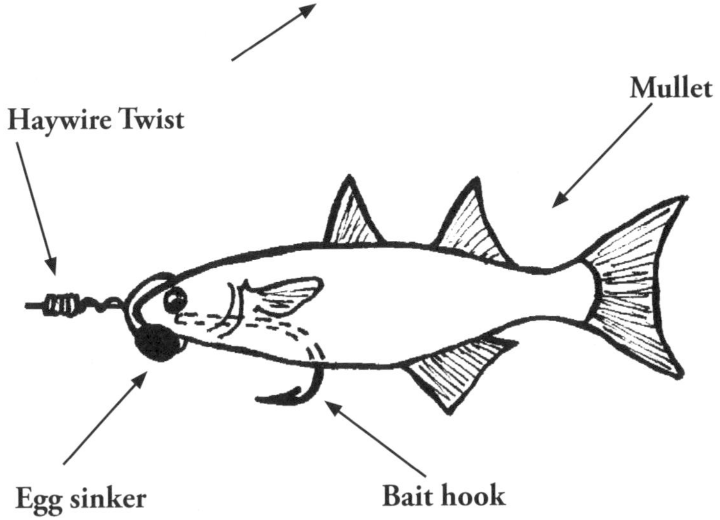

Mullet Rig
(Continued)

Match hook and mullet head size to your quarry.

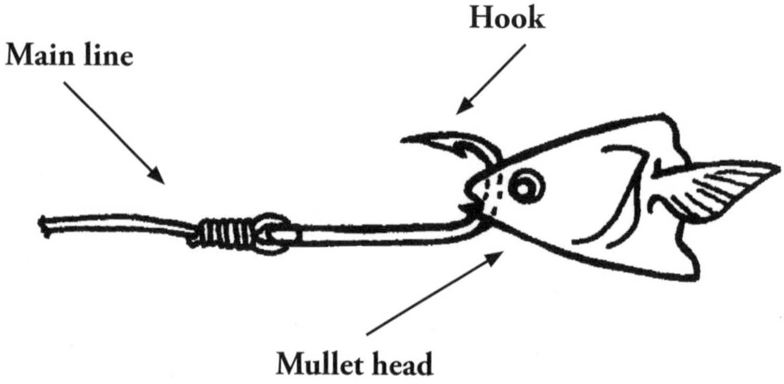

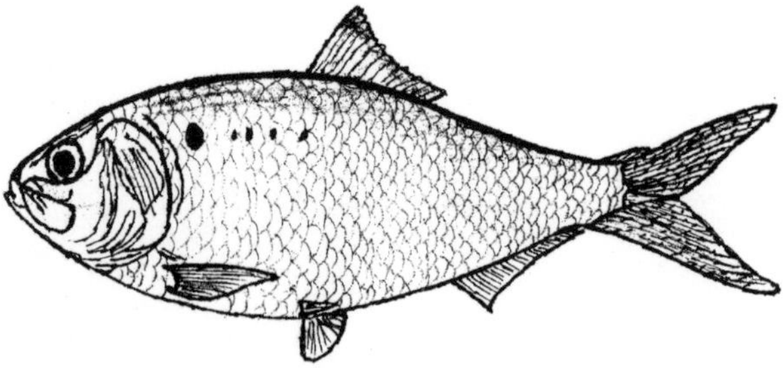

Offshore Trolling

When trolling, these double-hook rigs can be customized to fit your fishing needs with the lures or bait targeting your desired species.

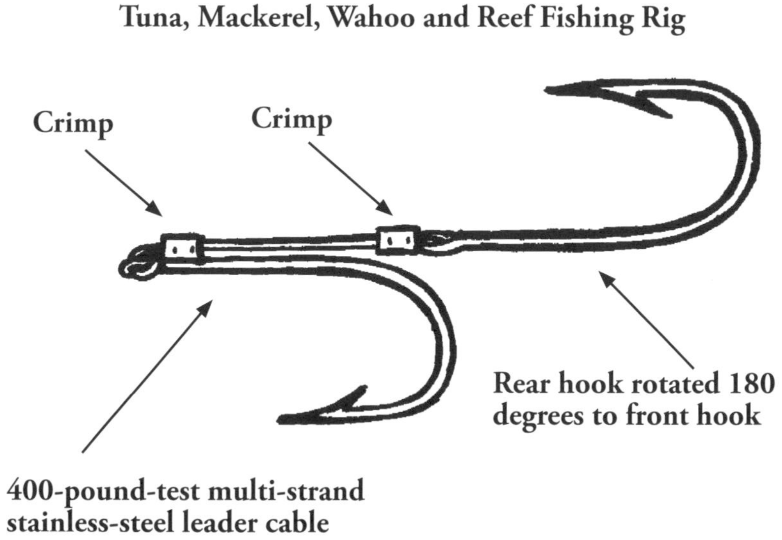

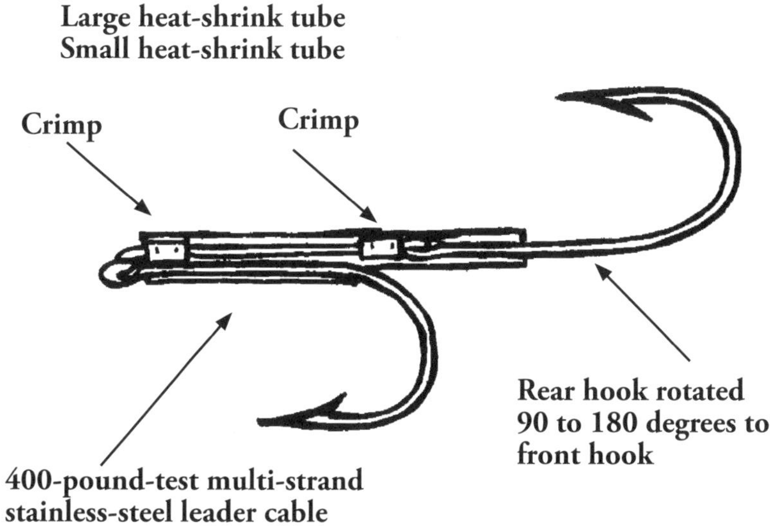

Permit Bait Rig

A permit's favorite food is crab. It's important to present the bait so the current drifts and carries it to the fish. Hook the crab from the bottom up. Once the hook is through the shell move it around to create a larger hole so the crab can move around.

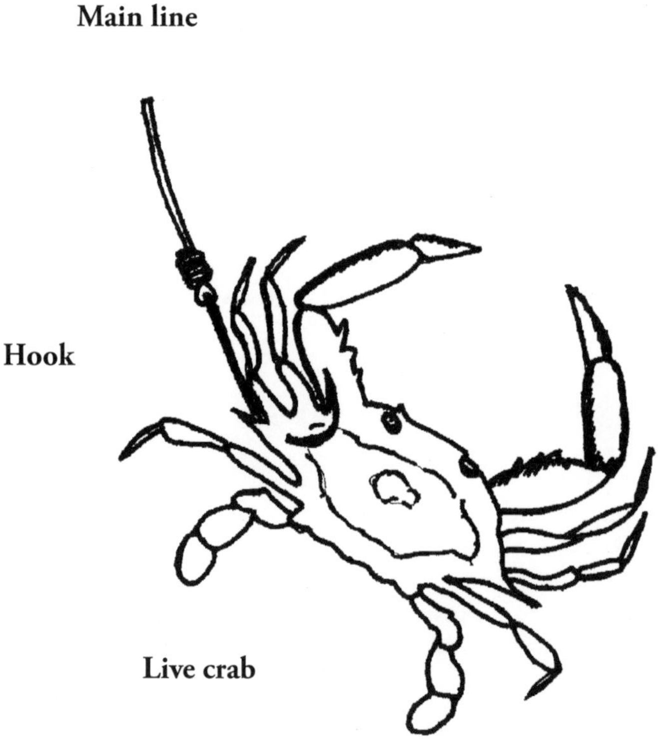

Food for Thought

When stalking permit it's extremely important to be as stealthy as possible at all times. The shallower the water the spookier the fish will become so approach and fish with caution.

Pier Rig for Live Bait

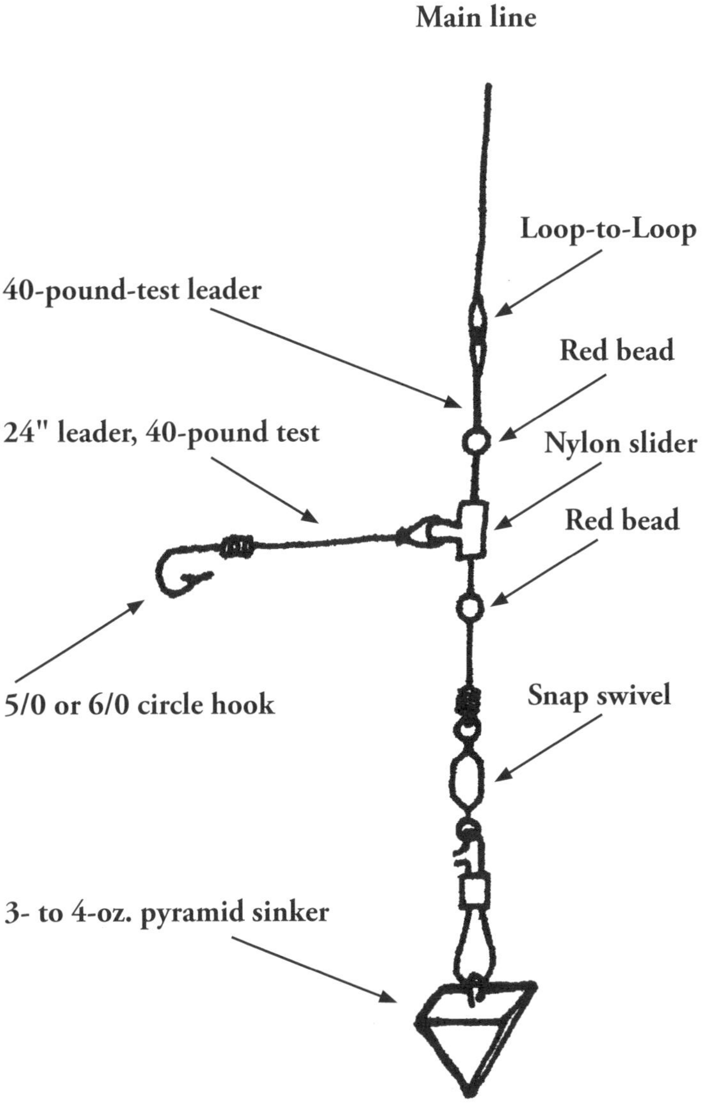

Hook the live bait (spot or pin fish) at the rear of the dorsal fin. This allows the bait to swim freely around the leader.

Pollock Jigging Rig

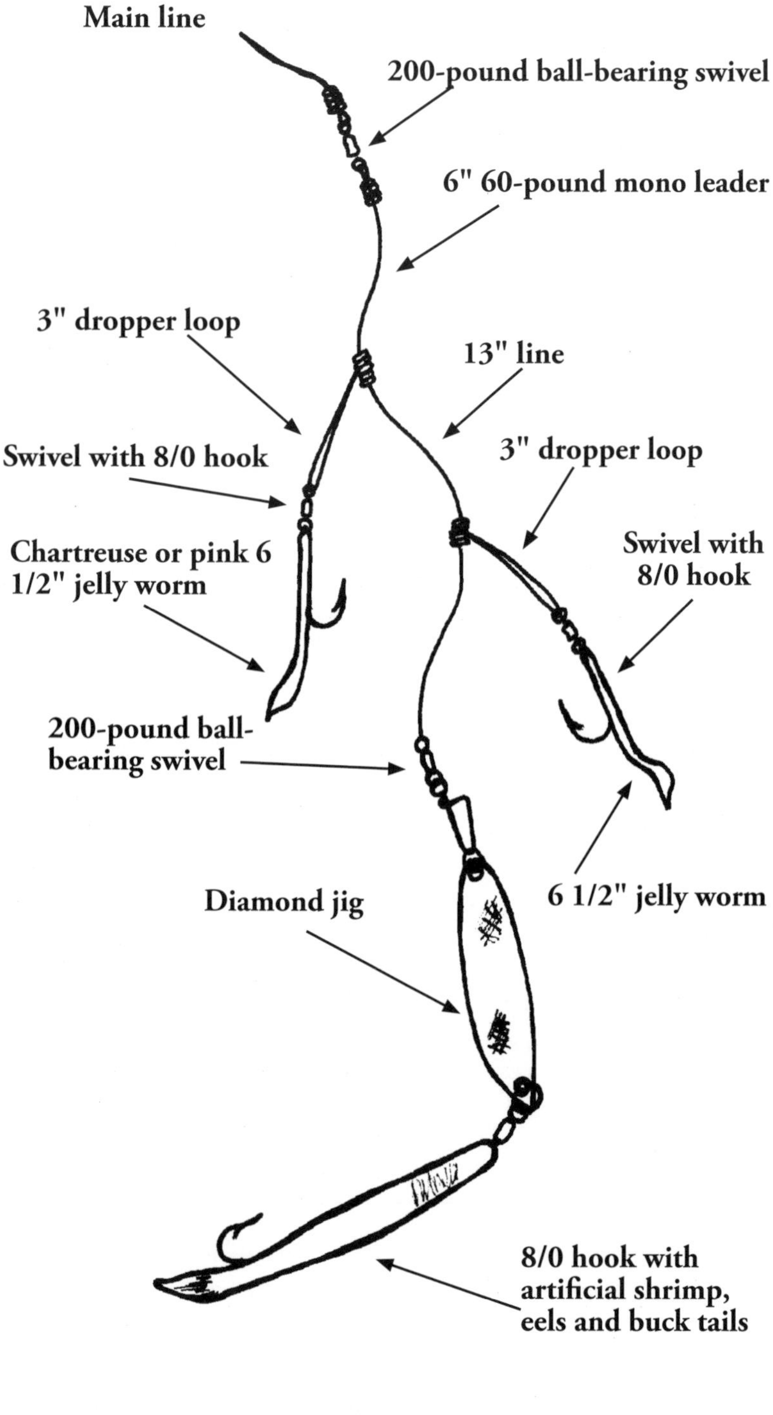
Main line
200-pound ball-bearing swivel
6" 60-pound mono leader
3" dropper loop
13" line
Swivel with 8/0 hook
3" dropper loop
Chartreuse or pink 6 1/2" jelly worm
Swivel with 8/0 hook
200-pound ball-bearing swivel
Diamond jig
6 1/2" jelly worm
8/0 hook with artificial shrimp, eels and buck tails

Popping Cork Rig

With its loud popping and splashing sound on the surface, the Popping Cork Rig is a valuable fish-attracting device that is extremely effective at triggering strikes. This device works well with surface plugs or baits under the surface.

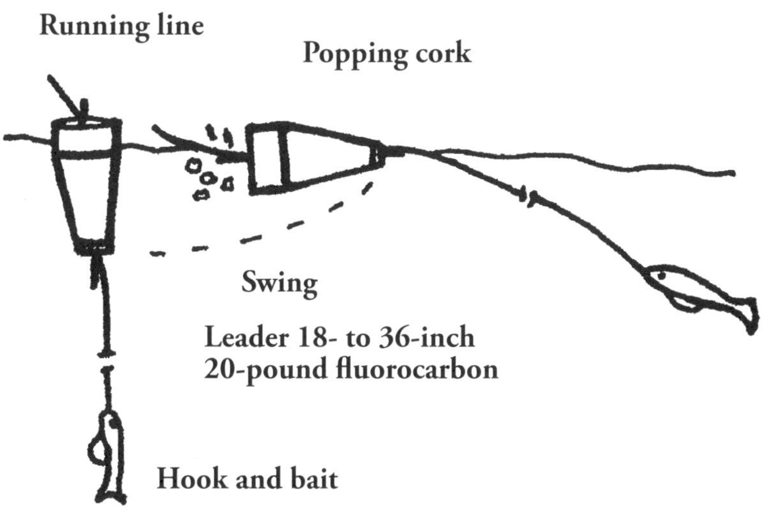

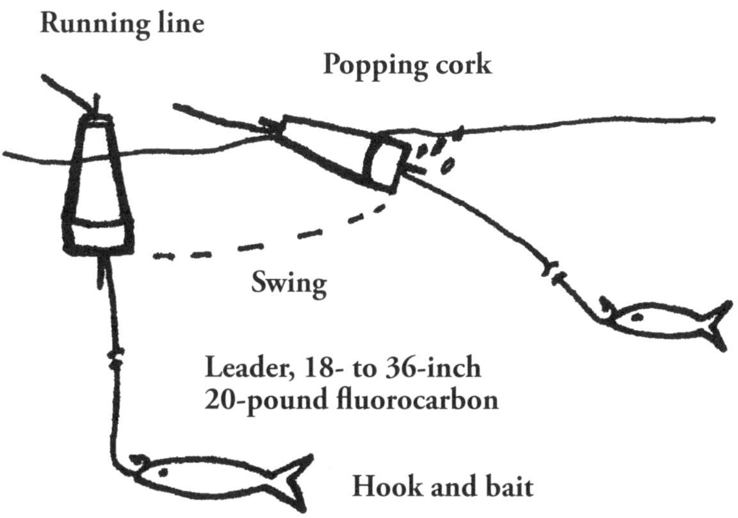

Redfish Bait Rig

This is a good all-round basic bait rig for redfish that can be modified to water, wind and bottom conditions. The bait can be crab, shrimp or other redfish. Adjust the line size to your preference, but remember that redfish can be leader shy.

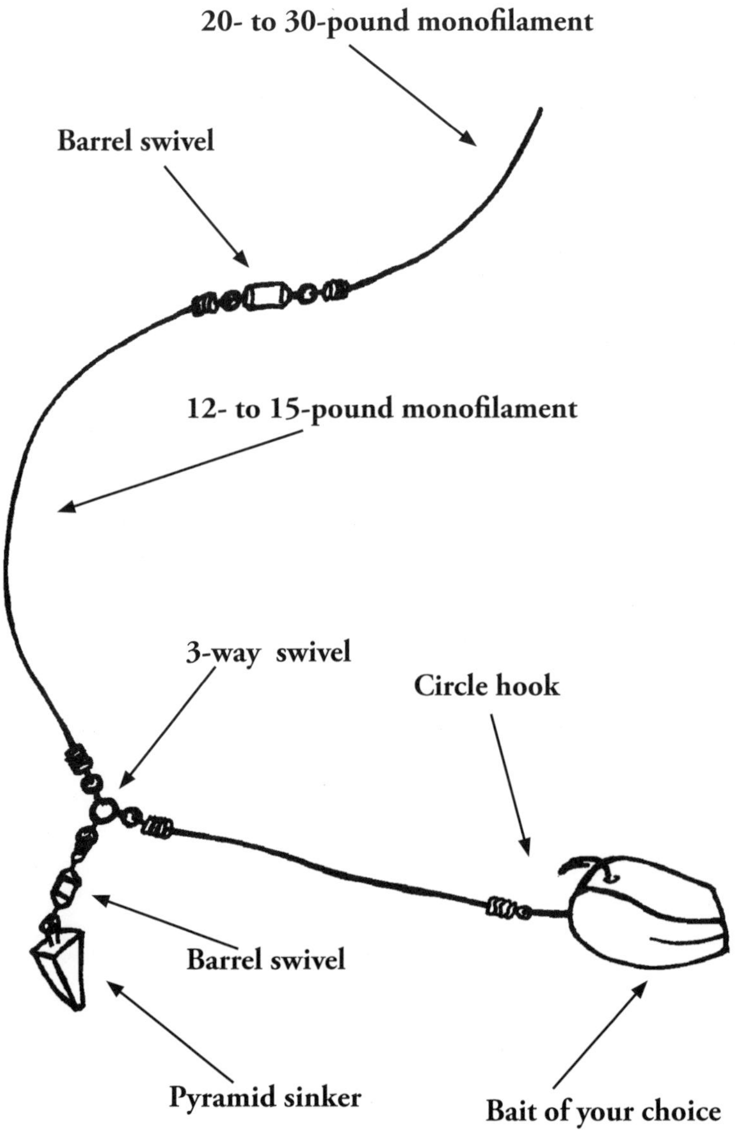

Red Gill Rigging

Run the leader through the hole in the nose of the red gill then through body cavity and pull out through the anal vent. Attach leader to hook eye then pull the leader and bring the hook back into the body. Use an egg or bullet weight on the main line above the leader if weight is needed.

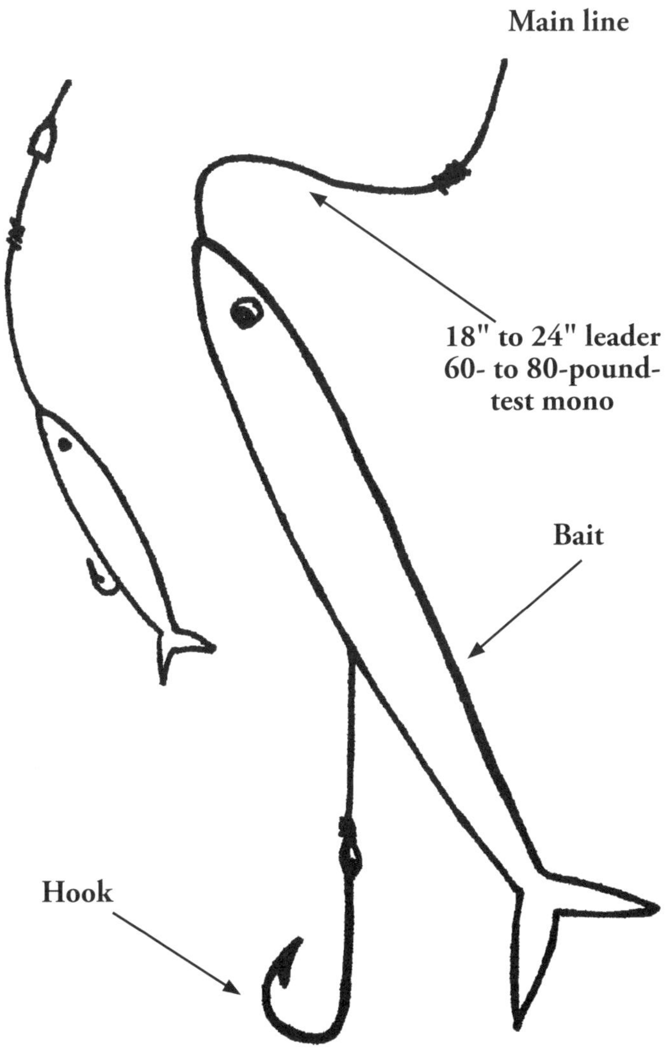

Ribbonfish Rig

(rigging for kingfish)

A dependable trolling or fixed rig for kingfish.

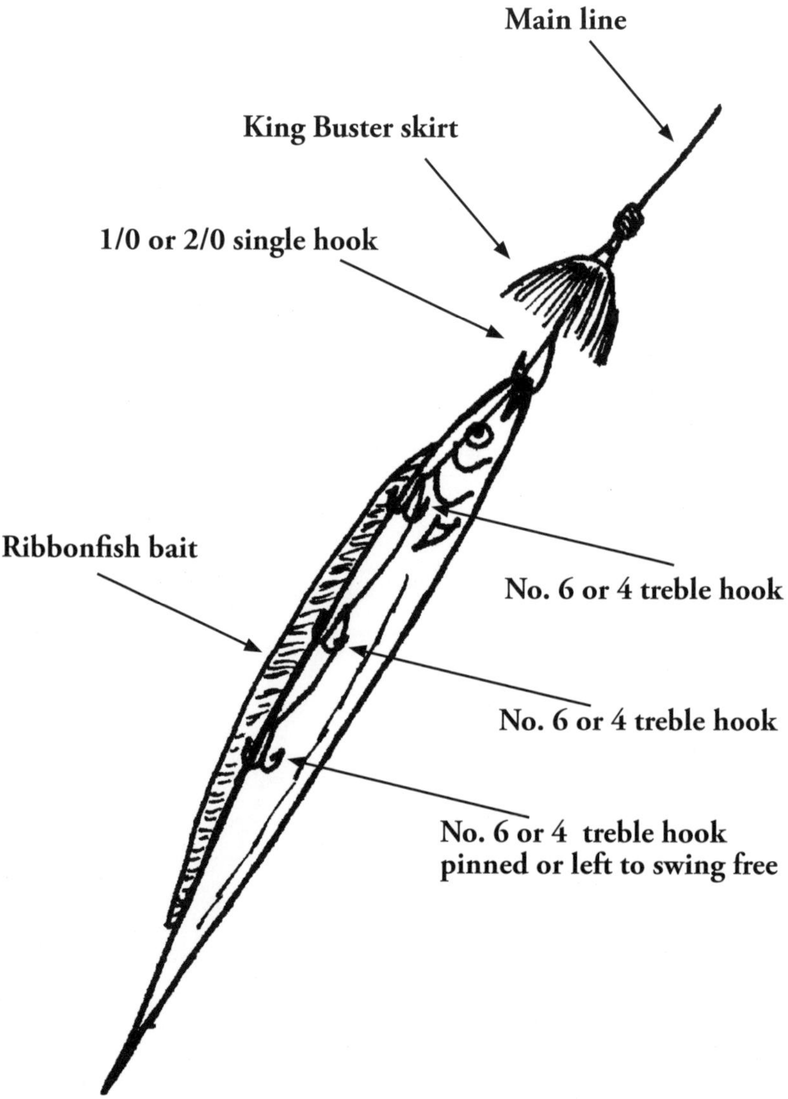

Note: No. 3 Bronze wire is used between all treble hooks and single hook.

Rig for Reds No. 1

This rig works best when you're anchored, and is also known as the fish-finder rig. Use an egg that's just heavy enough to keep the bait on the bottom in one spot.

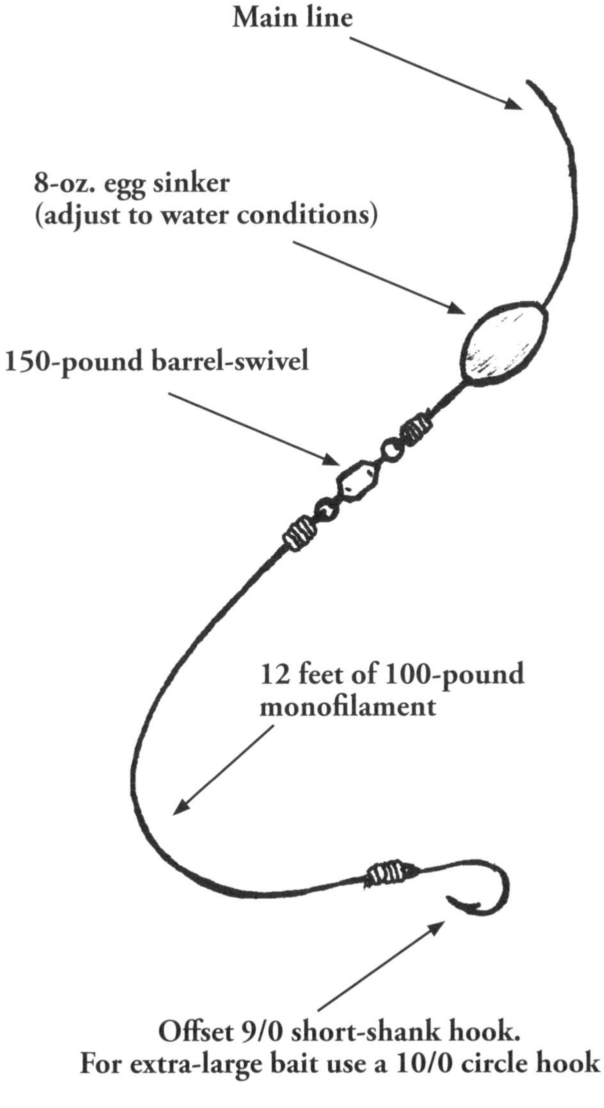

Rig for Reds No. 2

This rig works well when drift fishing in deep water and/or in heavy current. It's also called a chicken rig. The heavy sinkers will get the bait down quickly and hold bottom.

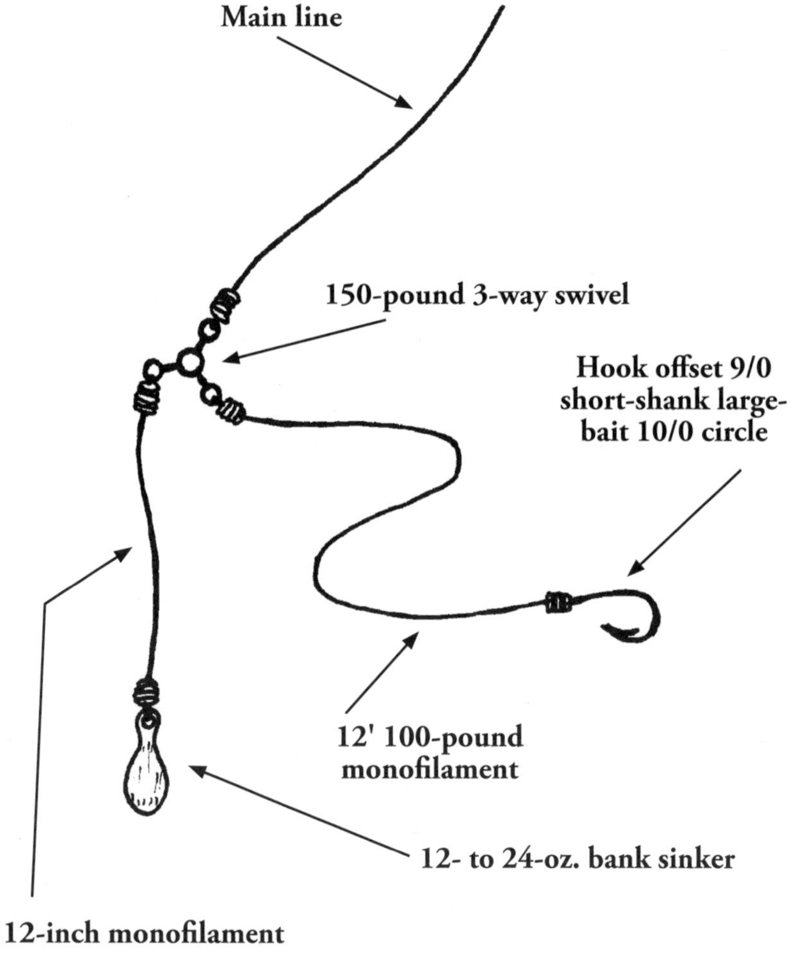

Rigging Trolling Baits

This is the standard simple and fast construction of a ballyhoo (Balao) offshore bait for trolling.

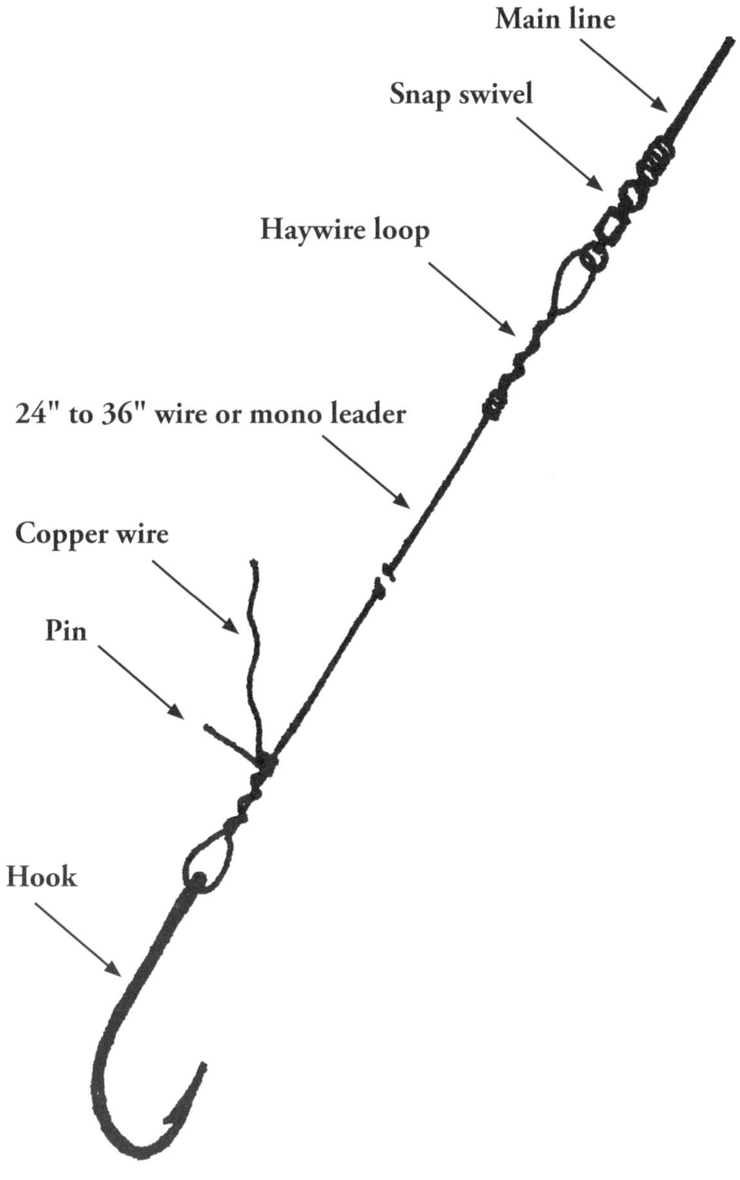

Rigging Trolling Baits
(Continued)

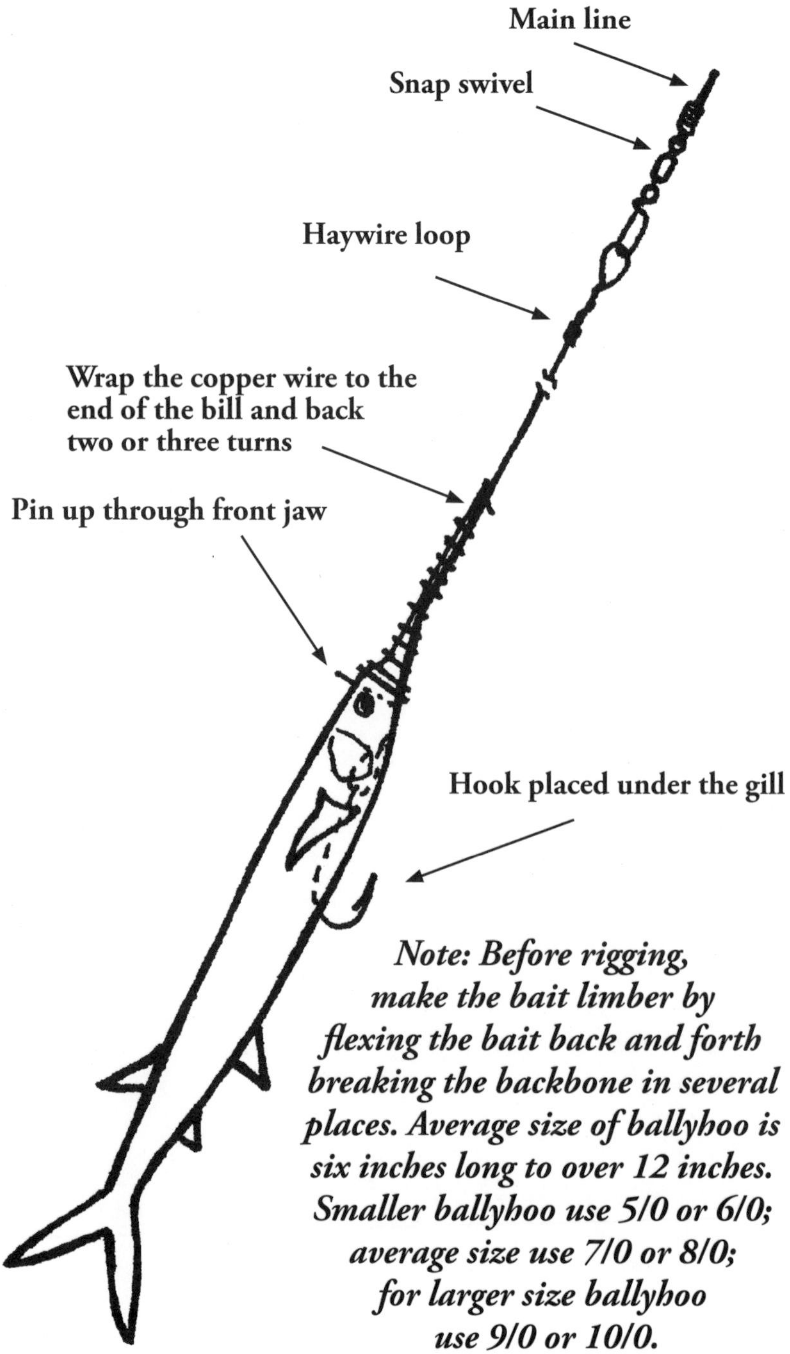

Note: Before rigging, make the bait limber by flexing the bait back and forth breaking the backbone in several places. Average size of ballyhoo is six inches long to over 12 inches. Smaller ballyhoo use 5/0 or 6/0; average size use 7/0 or 8/0; for larger size ballyhoo use 9/0 or 10/0.

Rock Fishing Rig

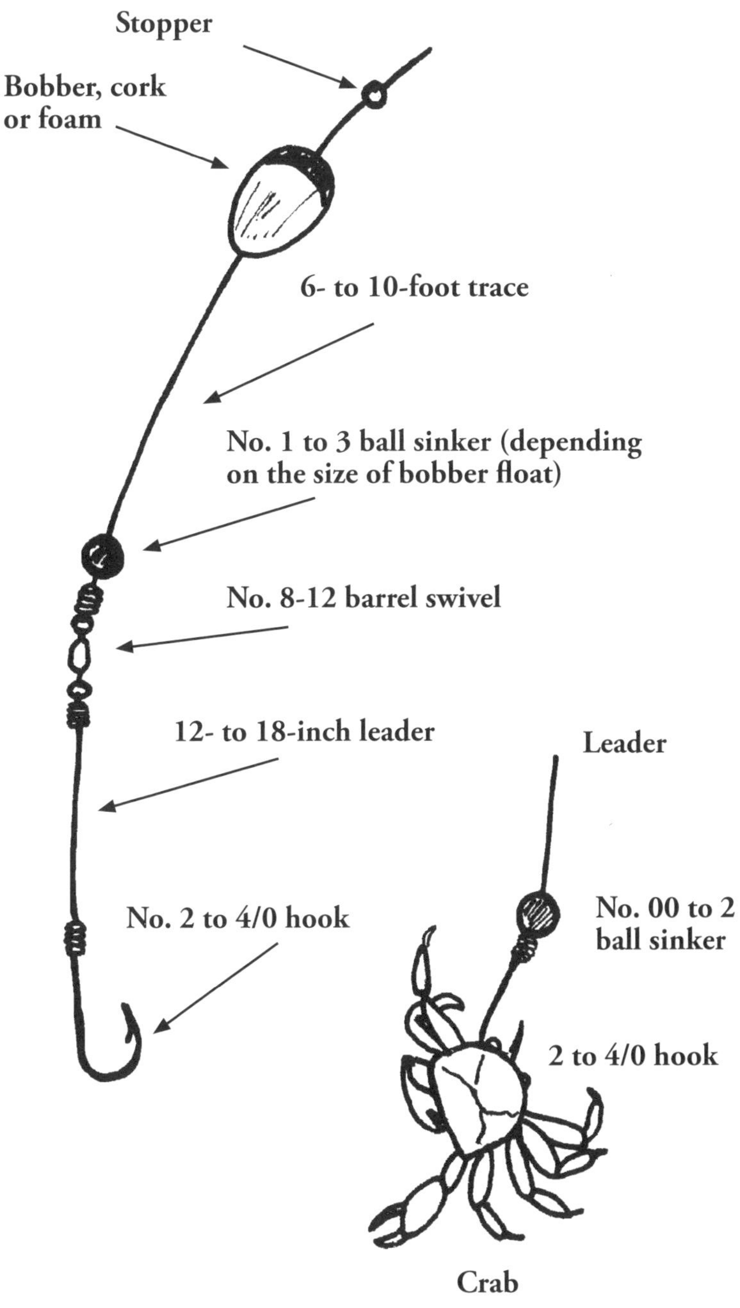
Stopper
Bobber, cork or foam
6- to 10-foot trace
No. 1 to 3 ball sinker (depending on the size of bobber float)
No. 8-12 barrel swivel
12- to 18-inch leader
No. 2 to 4/0 hook
Leader
No. 00 to 2 ball sinker
2 to 4/0 hook
Crab

Rock Fishing Pulley Rig

This rig is ideal when fishing over submerged structures, large rocks and the like.

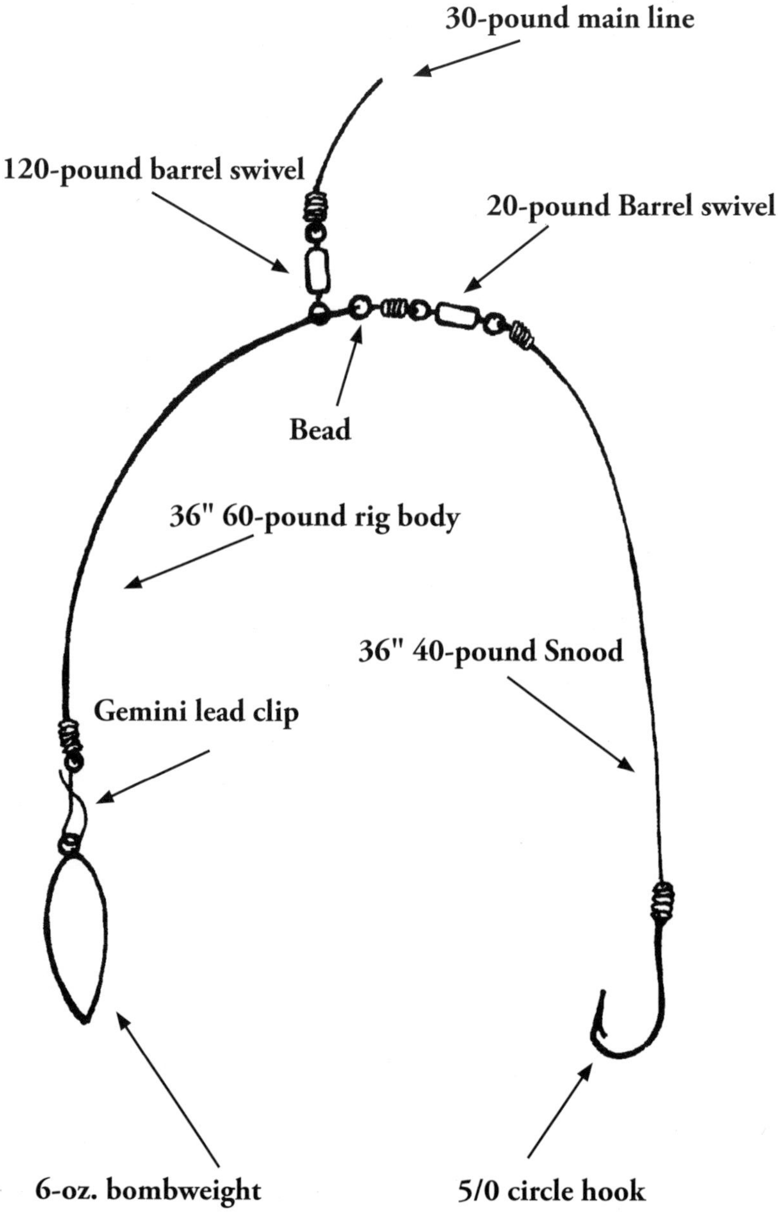

Ron Schatman's Wire-Line Rig

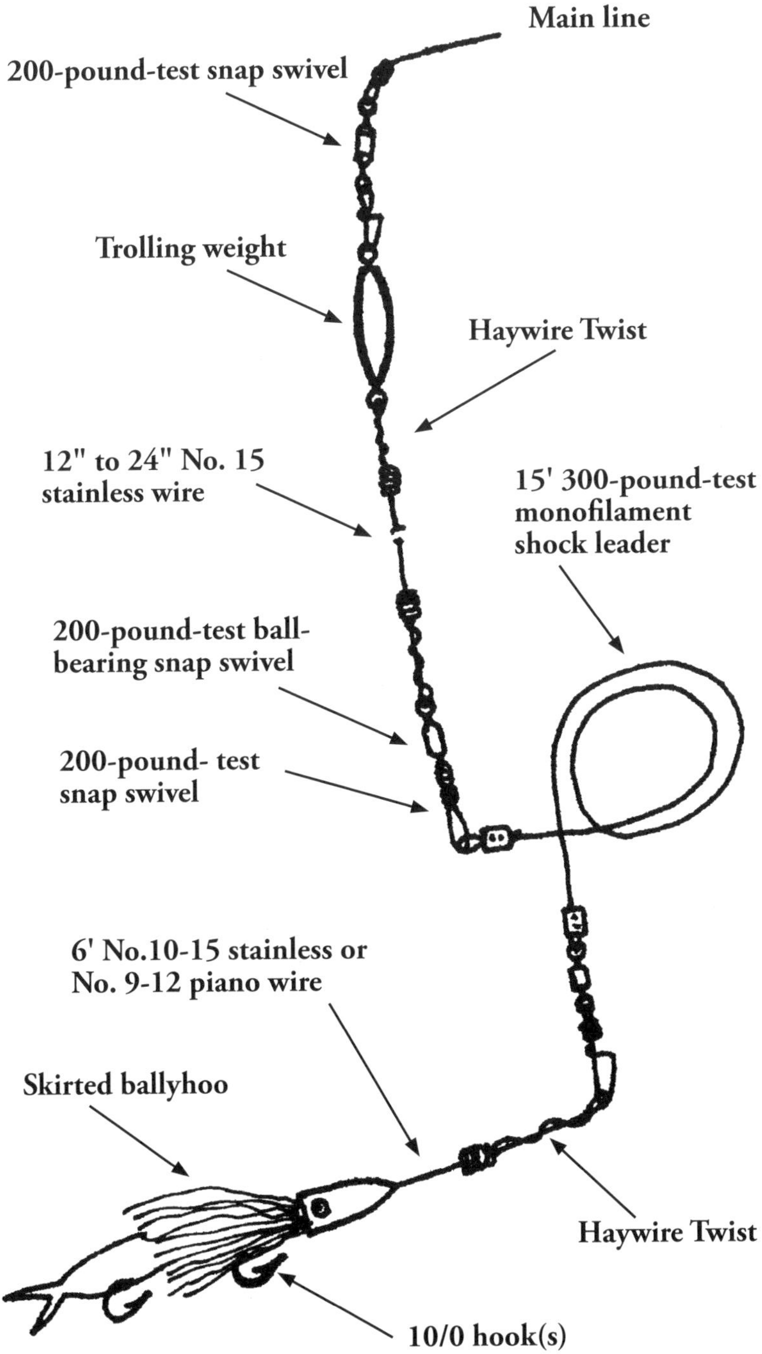
Main line
200-pound-test snap swivel
Trolling weight
Haywire Twist
12" to 24" No. 15 stainless wire
15' 300-pound-test monofilament shock leader
200-pound-test ball-bearing snap swivel
200-pound- test snap swivel
6' No.10-15 stainless or No. 9-12 piano wire
Skirted ballyhoo
Haywire Twist
10/0 hook(s)

Sabiki Bait-Catching Rig

The Sabiki bait-catching rig is used for catching schooling baitfish, such as herring and small jacks. This rig can be made or purchased with five to six small hooks or lures. The rig is made with a series of Blood Knots with one tag end attaching to the hook and the other trimmed off.

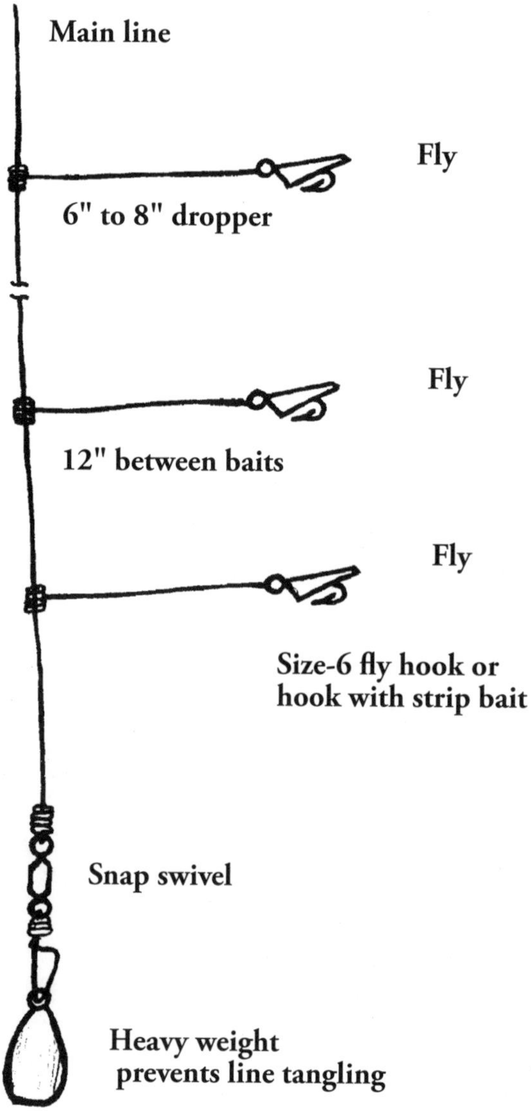

Salmon Flasher Trolling Rig

This is a standard salmon flash trolling rig used for trolling fly or strip bait. The rig can be used with a downrigger or simply use a short stiff trolling rod, heavy-duty reel and heavy weight. Attach a UNI-Line release to break away your main line on a strike.

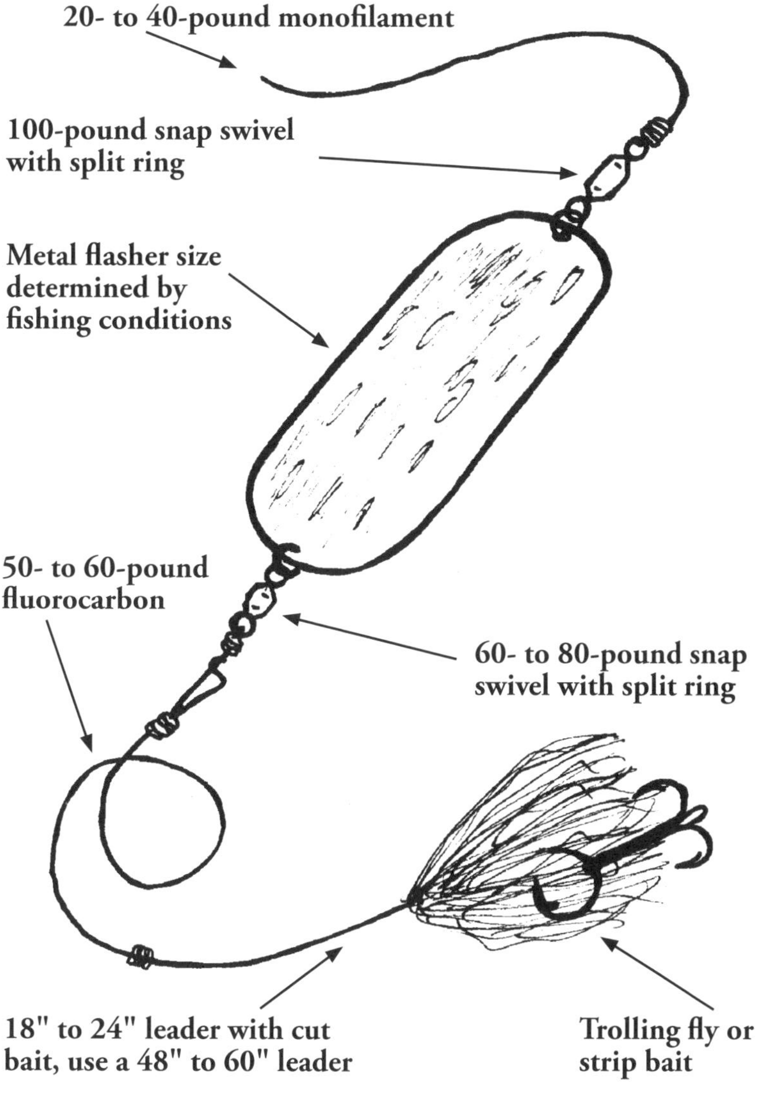

Sand Flea Rig

Sand fleas are mostly fished in the surf, off ocean-pier and from the beach for pompano and other surf fish. Sand fleas are best hooked from the bottom to top.

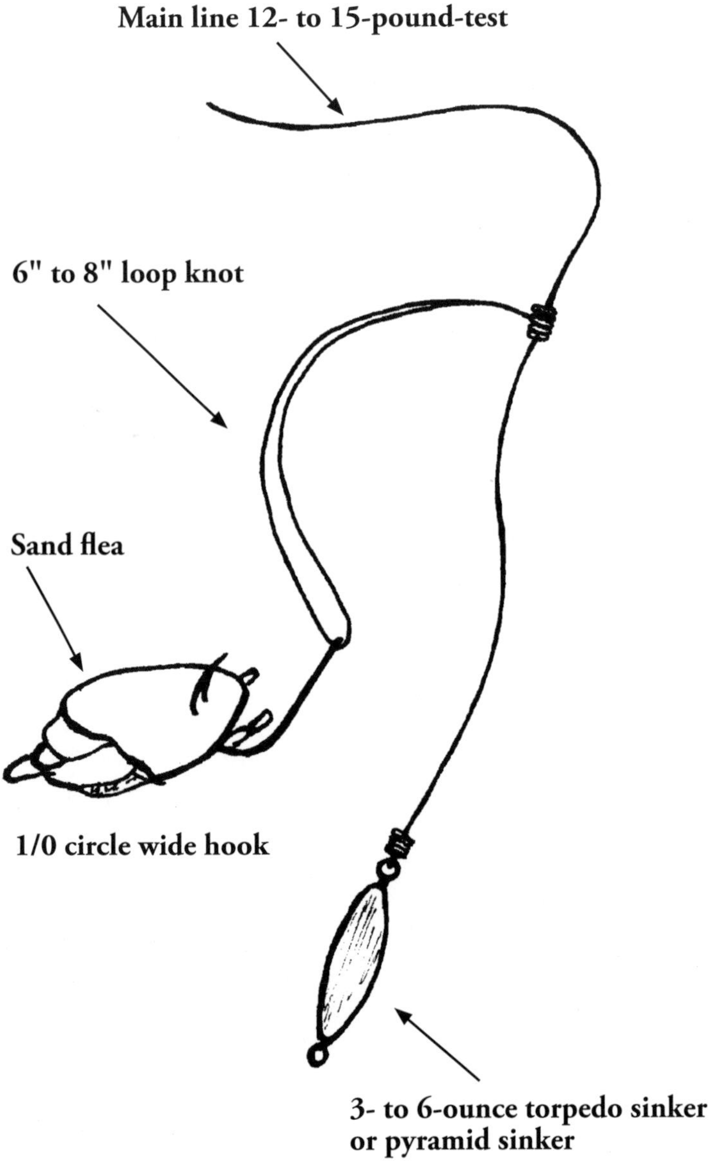

Shark Bait Leader Rig

Medium Sized Sharks

This leader should be a minimum of 50% longer than the size shark you expect to catch.

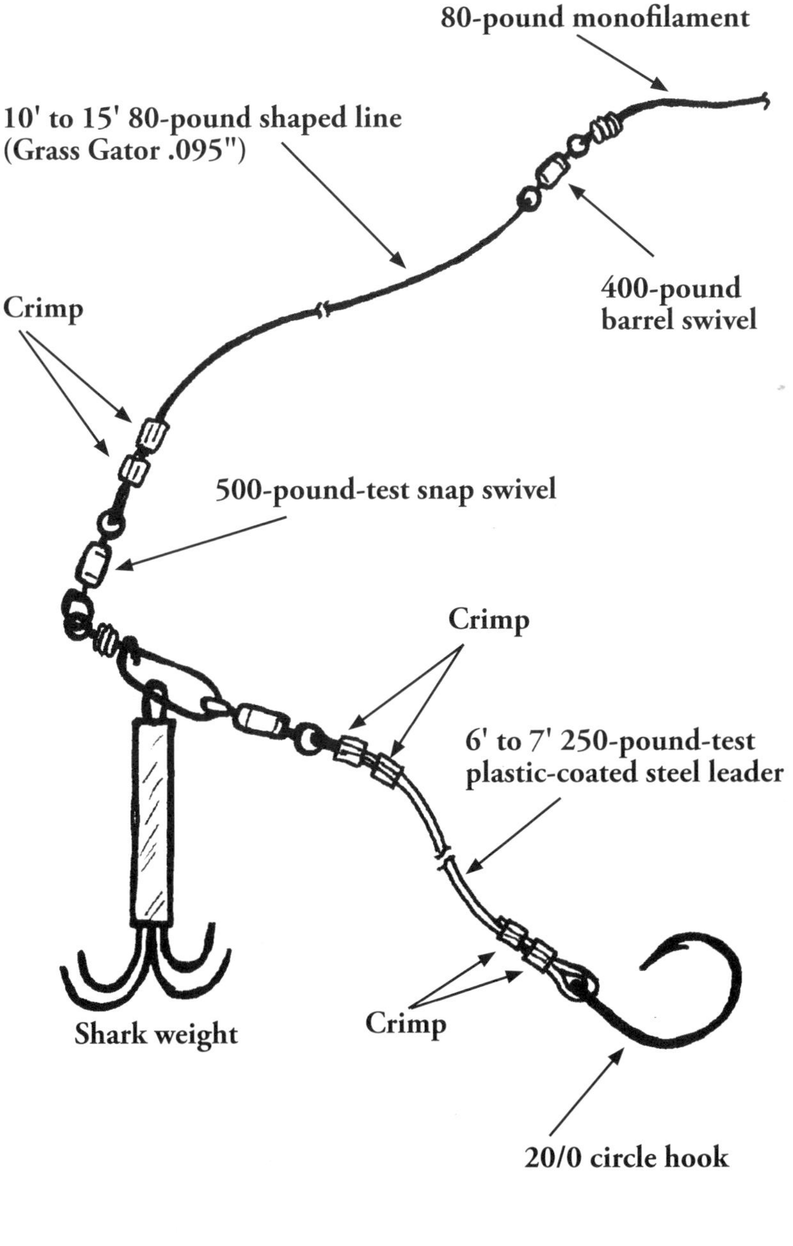

Shark Rig, Large Sharks

This 9-foot 480-pound-test stainless-steel cable rig is for the serious shark fisherman. The solid wire will slip between the shark's teeth and he is unable to bite this part of the leader.

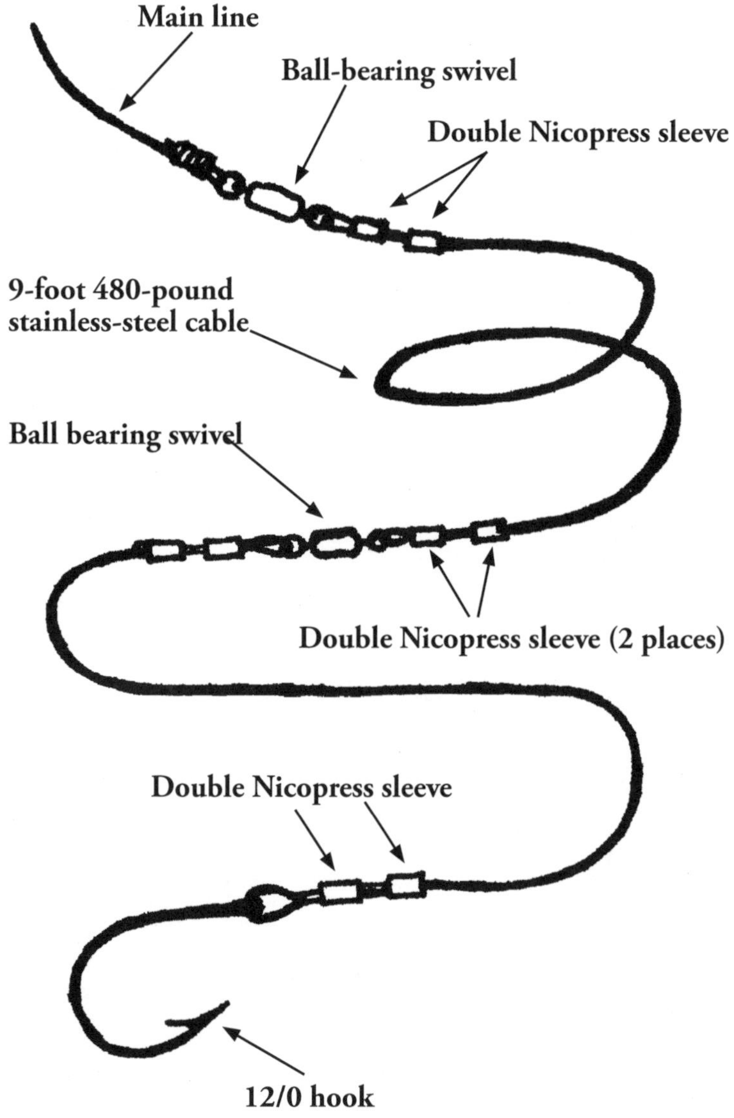

Sheepshead Rig No. 1

This is a standard "fish finding" rig and one of the most common used for locating desired species, in this case Sheepshead.

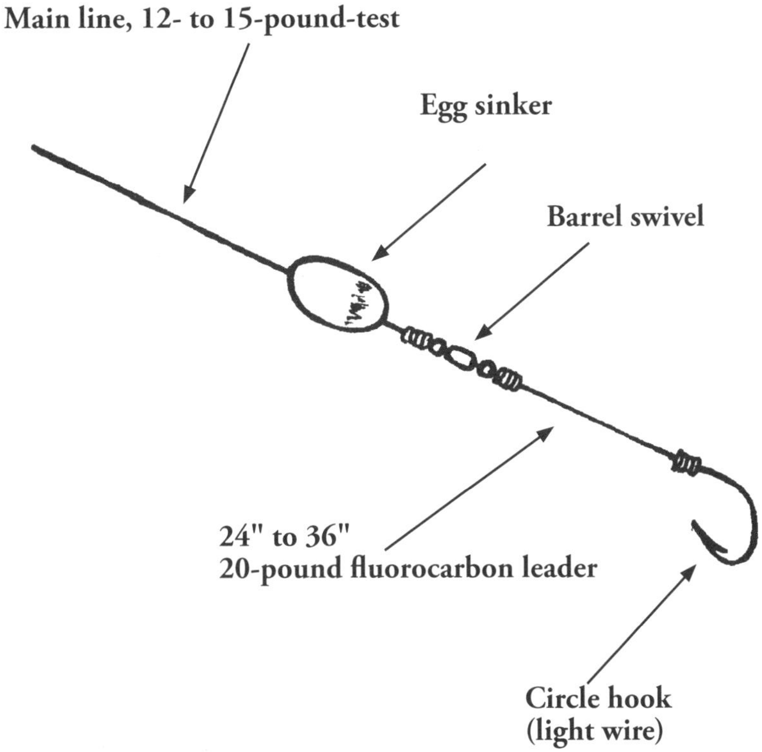

Food for Thought
Fish love clams, so when fishing is slow, fish near clam beds.

Sheepshead Rig No. 2

When fishing strong current or off piers, docks, jetties and bridges, the dropper loop rig works well. Use only enough weight to hold the rig in position.

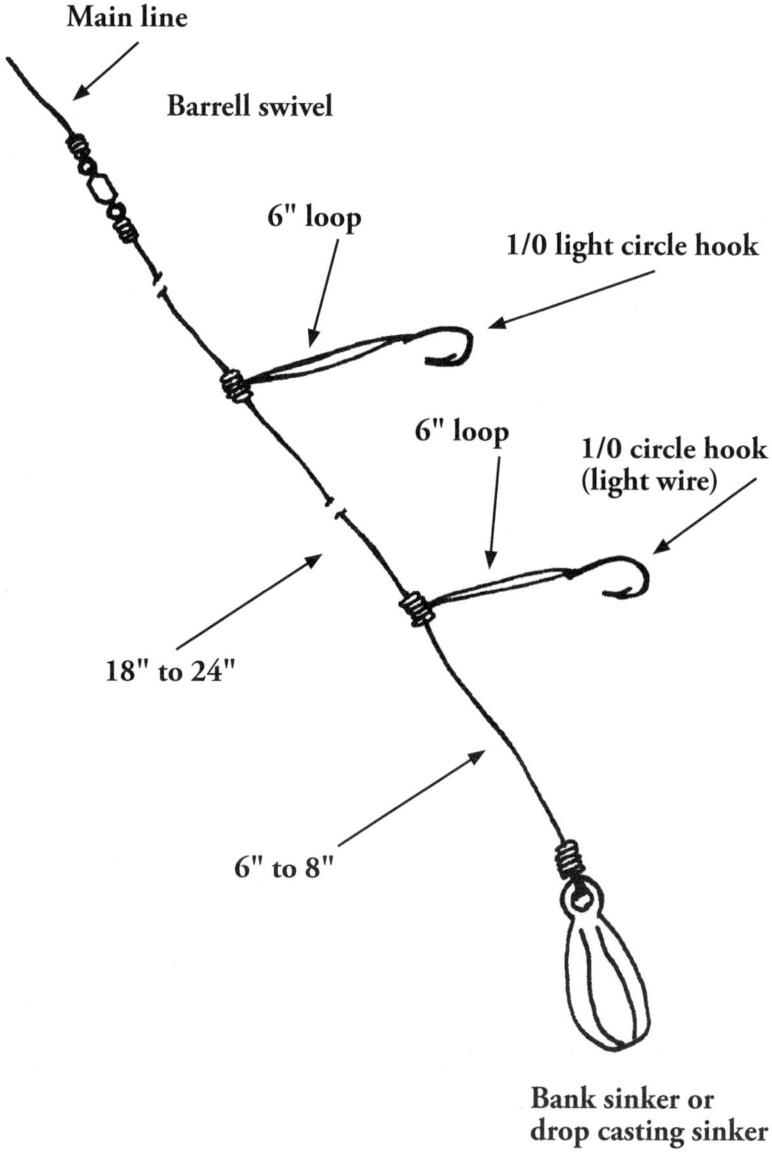

Sheepshead Rig No. 3

A 1/8- to 1/4-ounce jig head, weight depends on the size of shrimp, sinks slowly and less likely to snag. Use a Perfection Loop that allows the jig to wobble and wiggle giving your bait an additional fish attraction. This rig works best with freshly peeled shrimp.

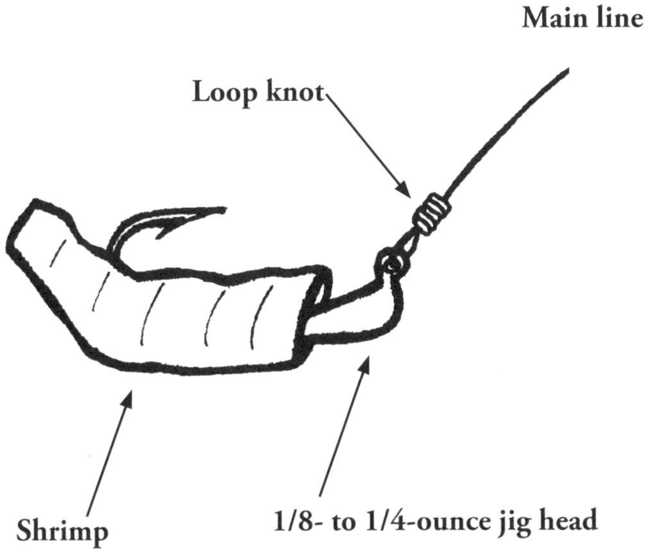

Shiner Tail Strips Rig

Use this rig with small fish such as pinfish cut bait for drift fishing and bottom fishing. This fish and rig is widely used when fishing for sea trout.

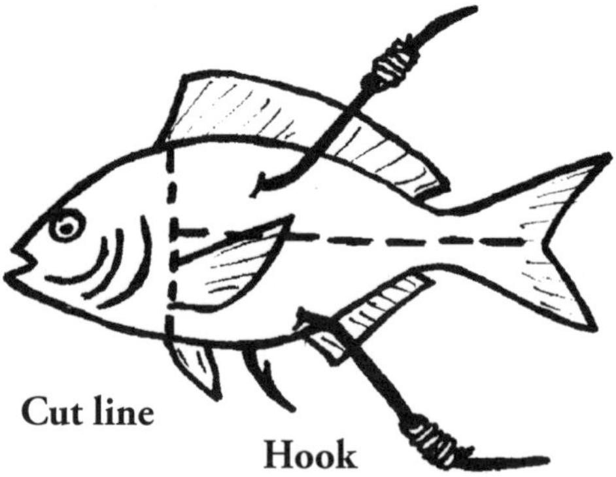

Bottom Fishing

Position the hook near the center of the bait.

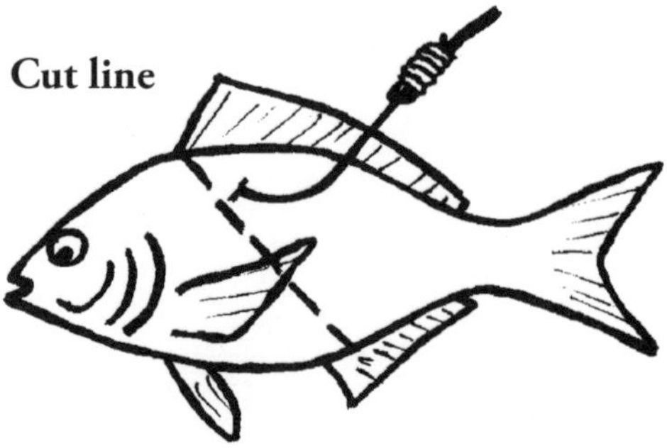

Drift fishing

Position the hook near the head end of the bait.

Shock-Absorber Rig

This rig is effective when fishing for small to medium size powerful-hitting fish. The absorber gives the rig a little give on the strike and strong fighters.

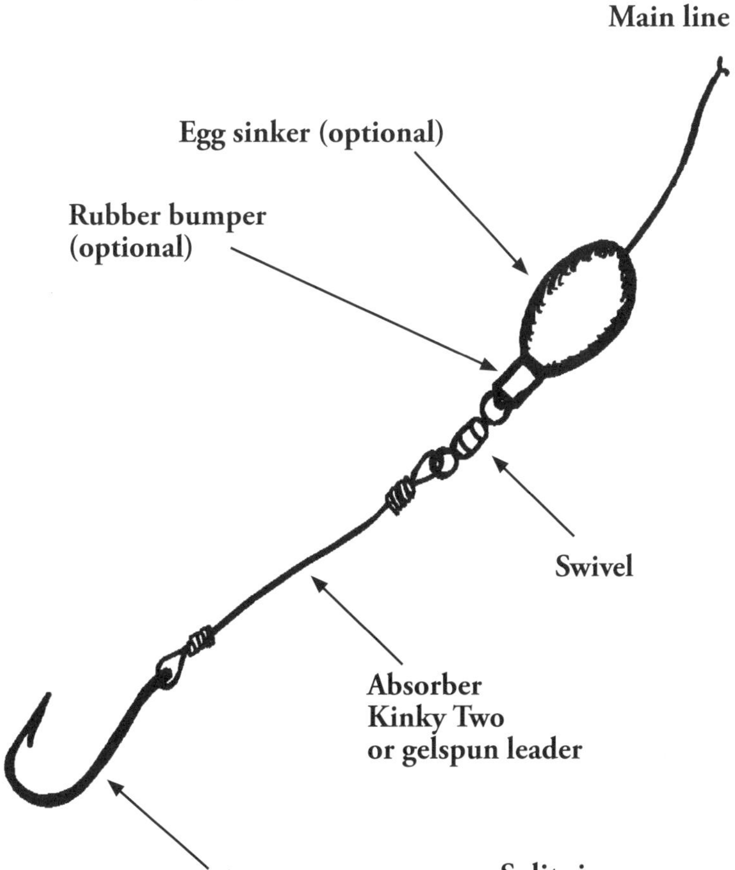

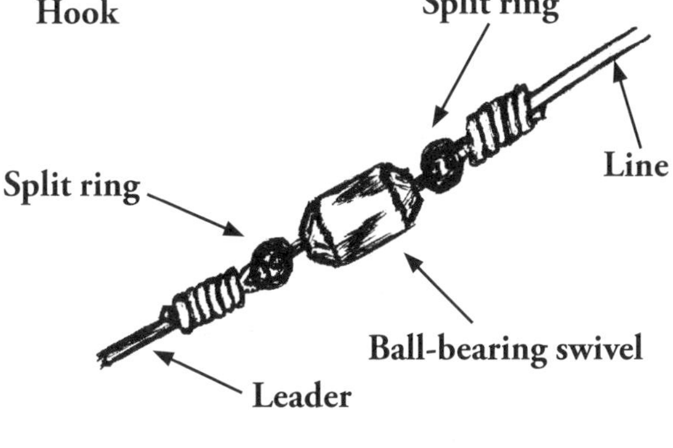

Shore/Surf-Fishing Rig

A simple all-around rig should not let you down in your favorite shore or surf-fishing spot. The sinker should be changed to perform best with bottom conditions.

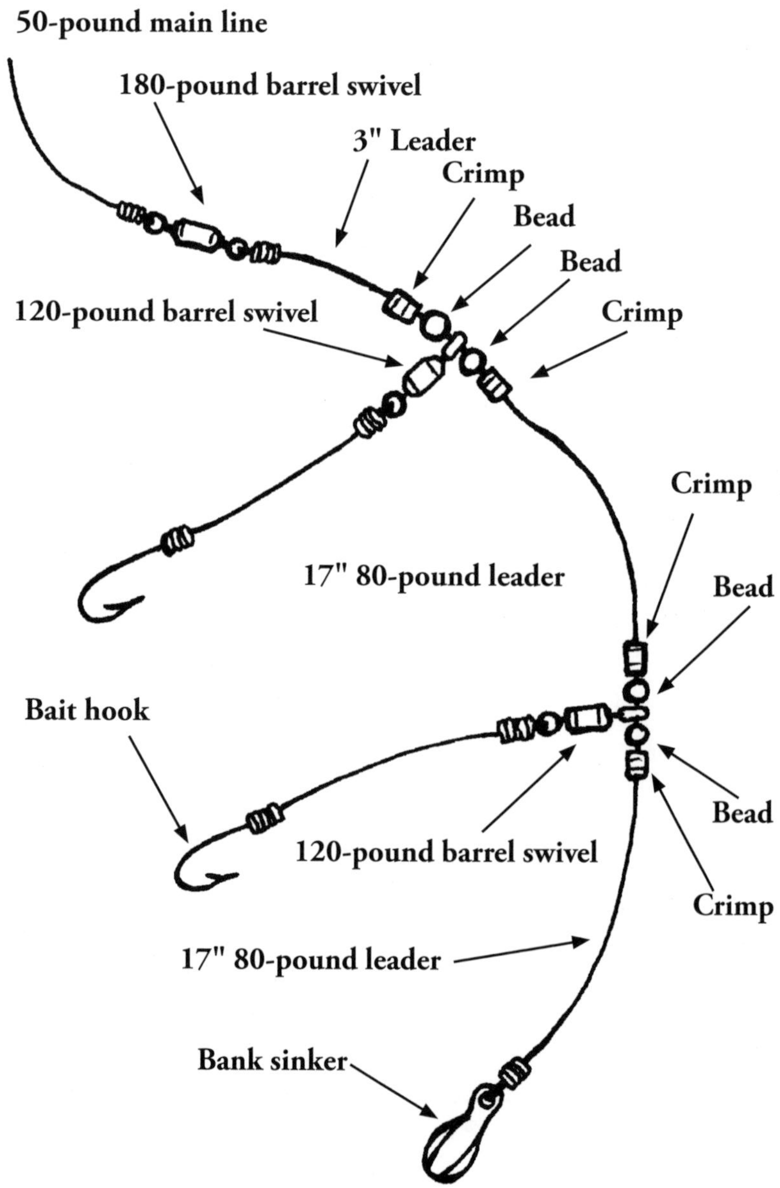

Shrimp Rig, Weedless

This is a live shrimp weedless rig for fishing in thick grass, weedy bottoms and shallow water. This rig is also affective rigged as a "Texas Rig."

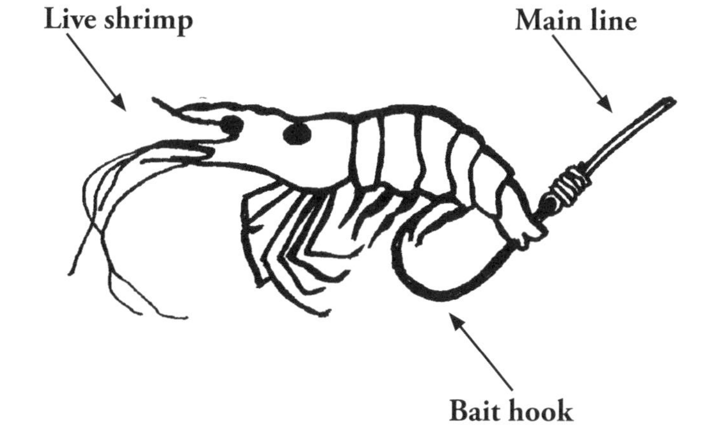

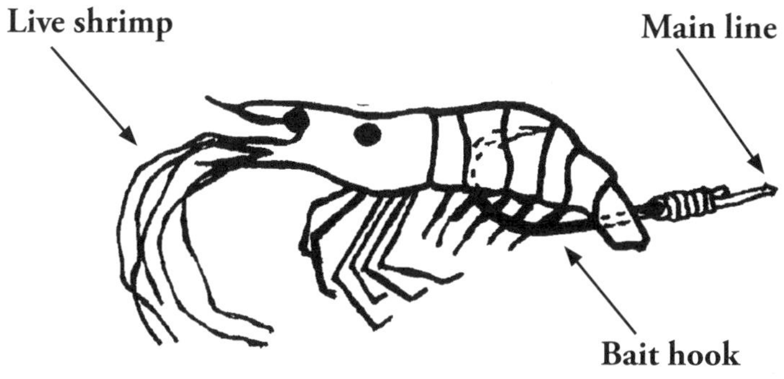

Sliding Bait Rig

This rig works well with either live or dead bait. It allows you to adjust to any size bait. The rig can be made with braided wire or monofilament.

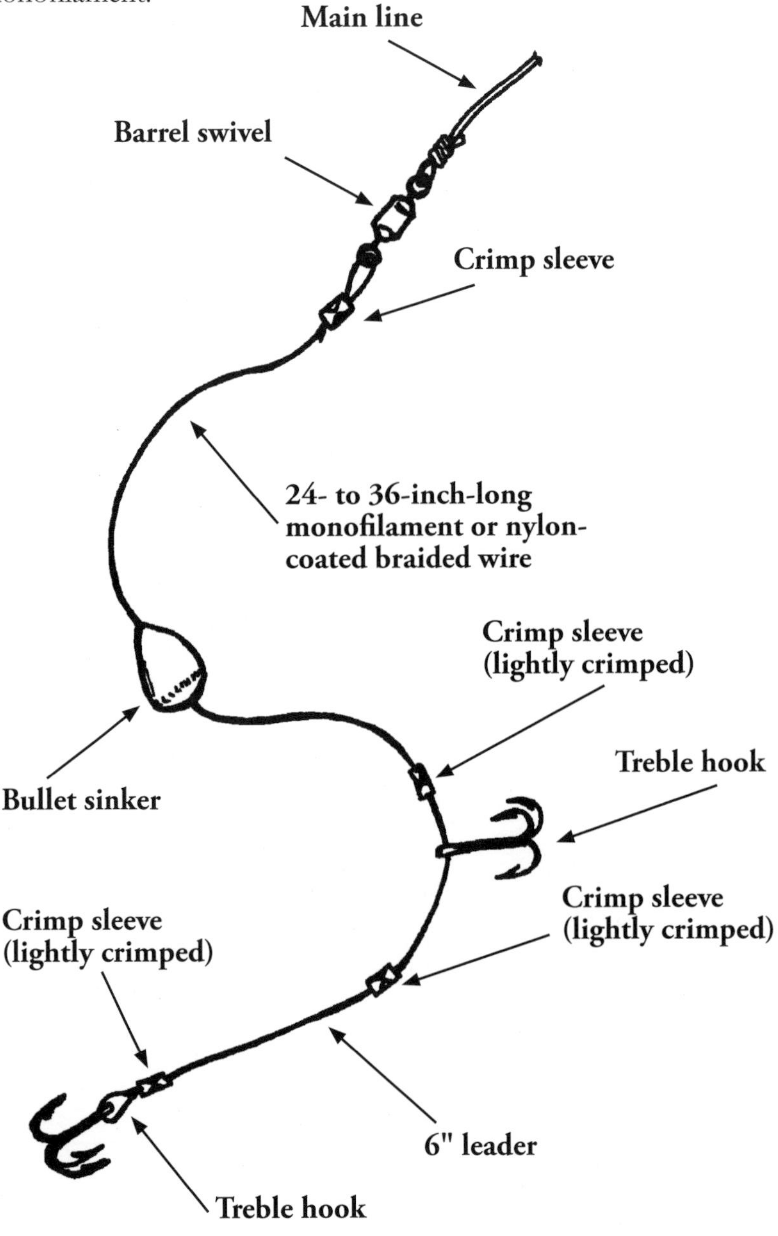

Snapper Rig with Octopus

(also used for kingfish and mulloway)

Floating Rig

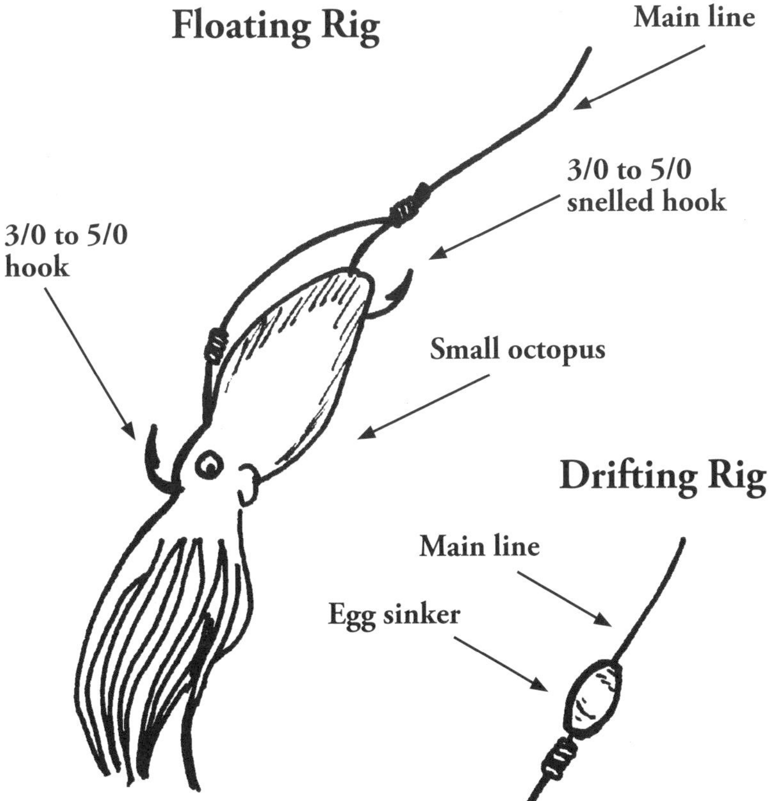

Drifting Rig

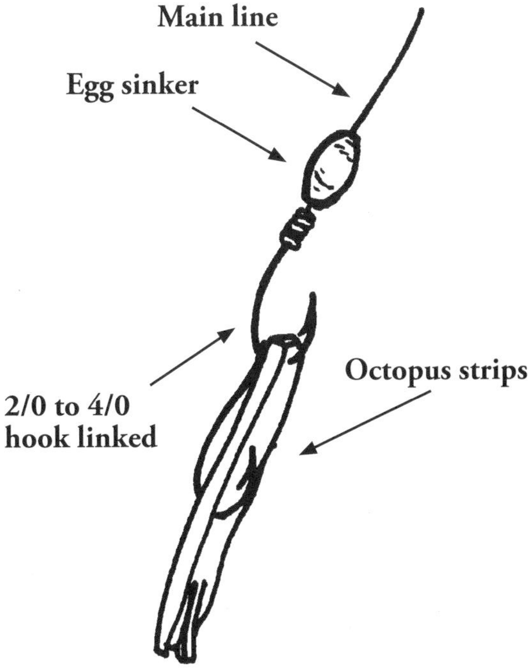

Stinger Rig

For short-striking fish, excellent with either live or dead natural baits. The rig can be made with wire or monofilament and a variety size of hooks.

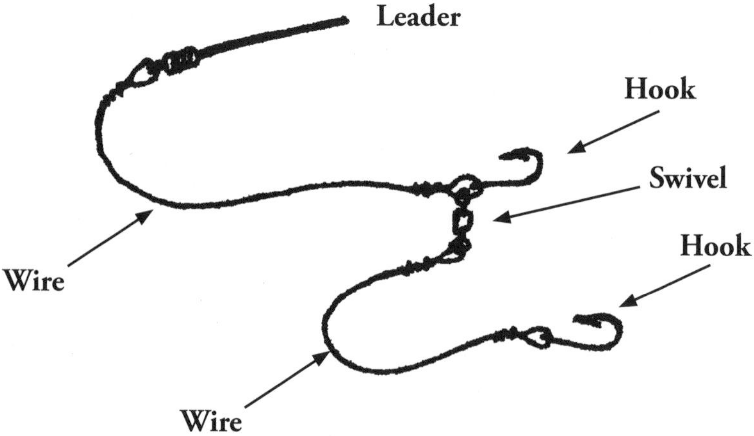

Stinger for bait

Stinger for cut bait

Stinger for worms and eels

Strip-Bait Rigs

Hook a rough-cut piece of bait and hook it to one end of the bait.

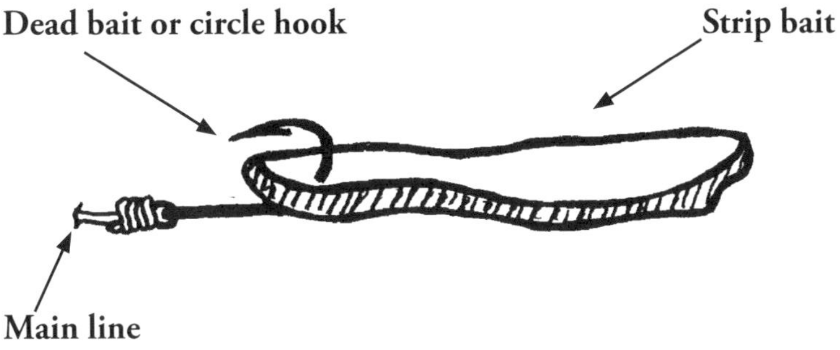

For Drifting Fishing

This rig is good when drifting for speckled trout.

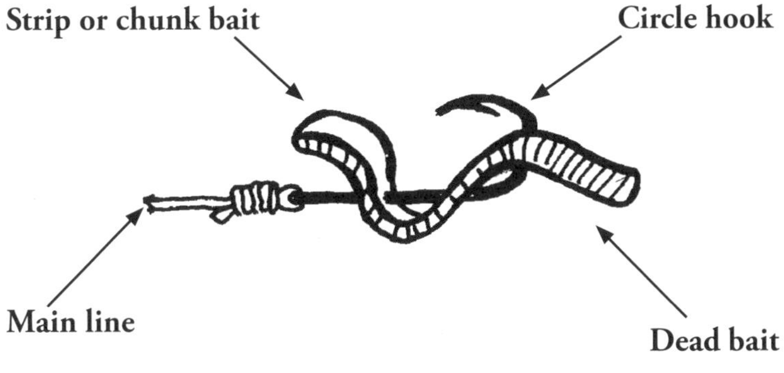

For Bottom Fishing

Striped Bass Rig

36" 50-pound Leader

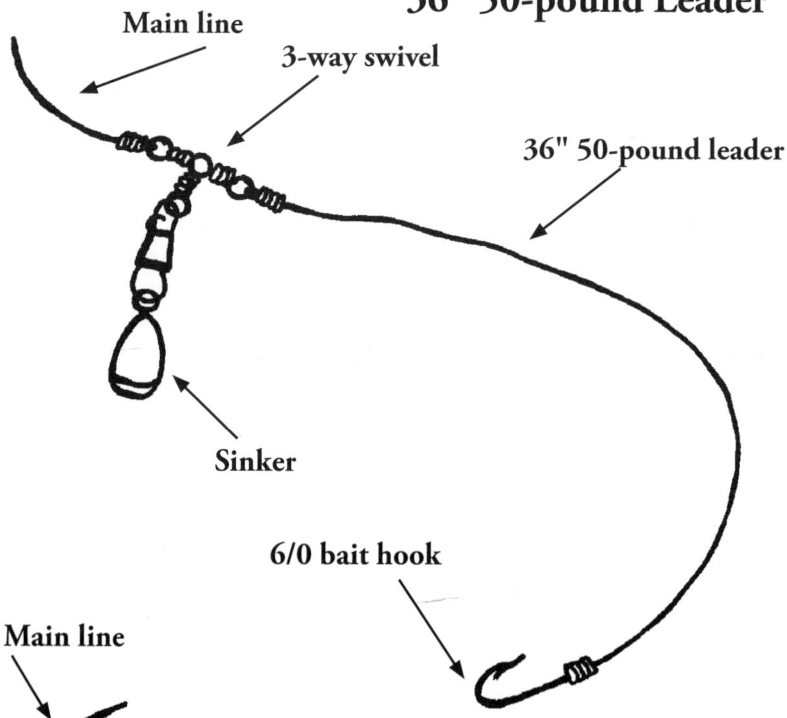

60" 50-pound Leader Dead Drift

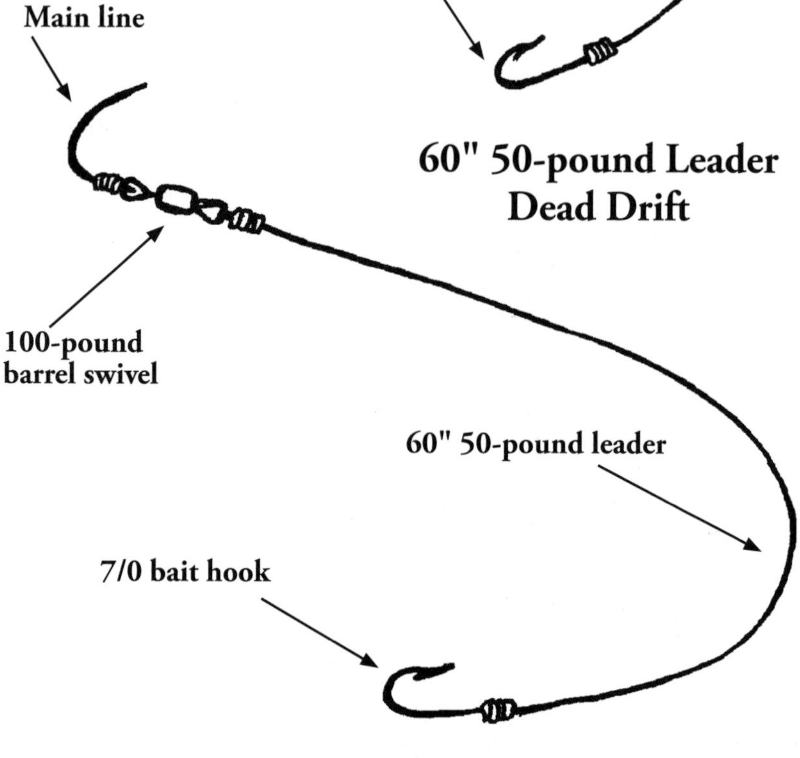

Striped Bass Rig

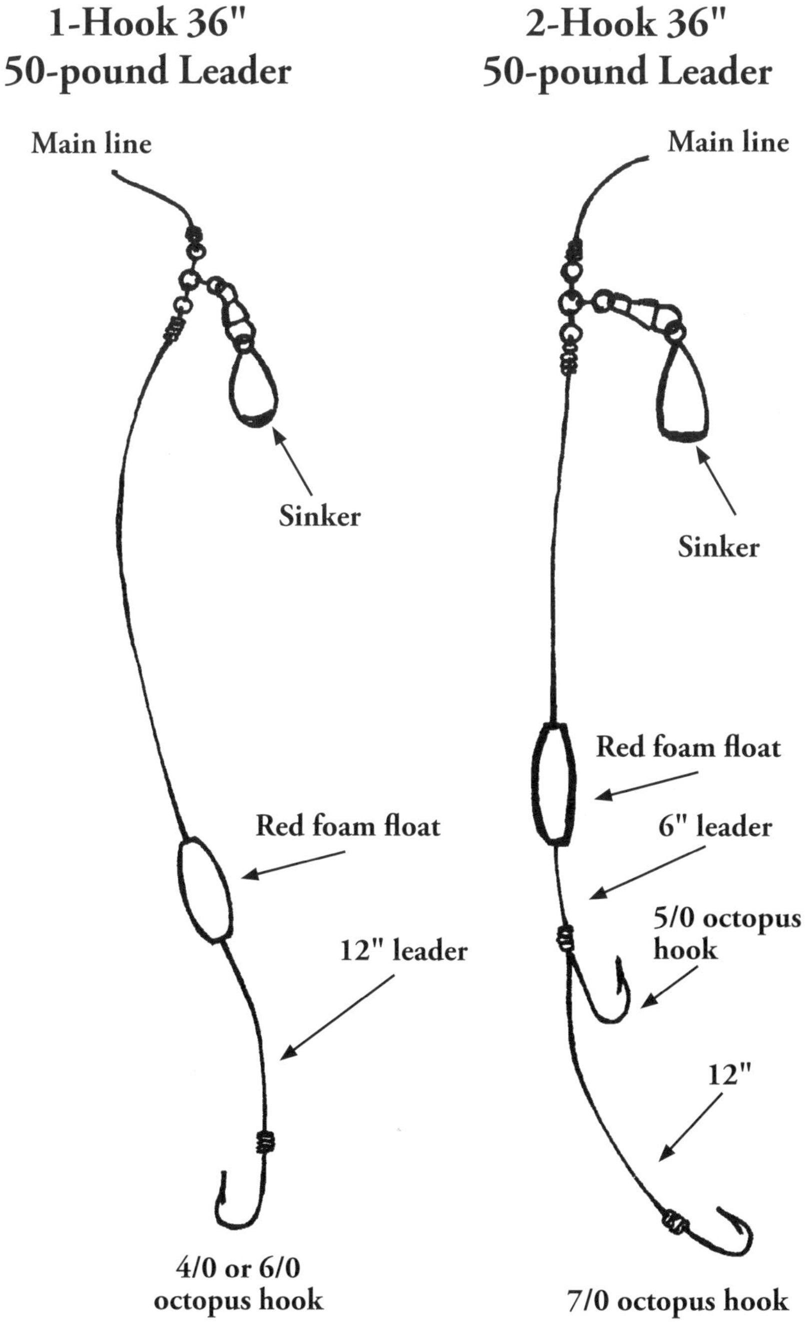
1-Hook 36"
50-pound Leader
Main line
Sinker
Red foam float
12" leader
4/0 or 6/0
octopus hook
2-Hook 36"
50-pound Leader
Main line
Sinker
Red foam float
6" leader
5/0 octopus
hook
12"
7/0 octopus hook

Striped Bass Rig

2-Hook 39" 50-pound Leader

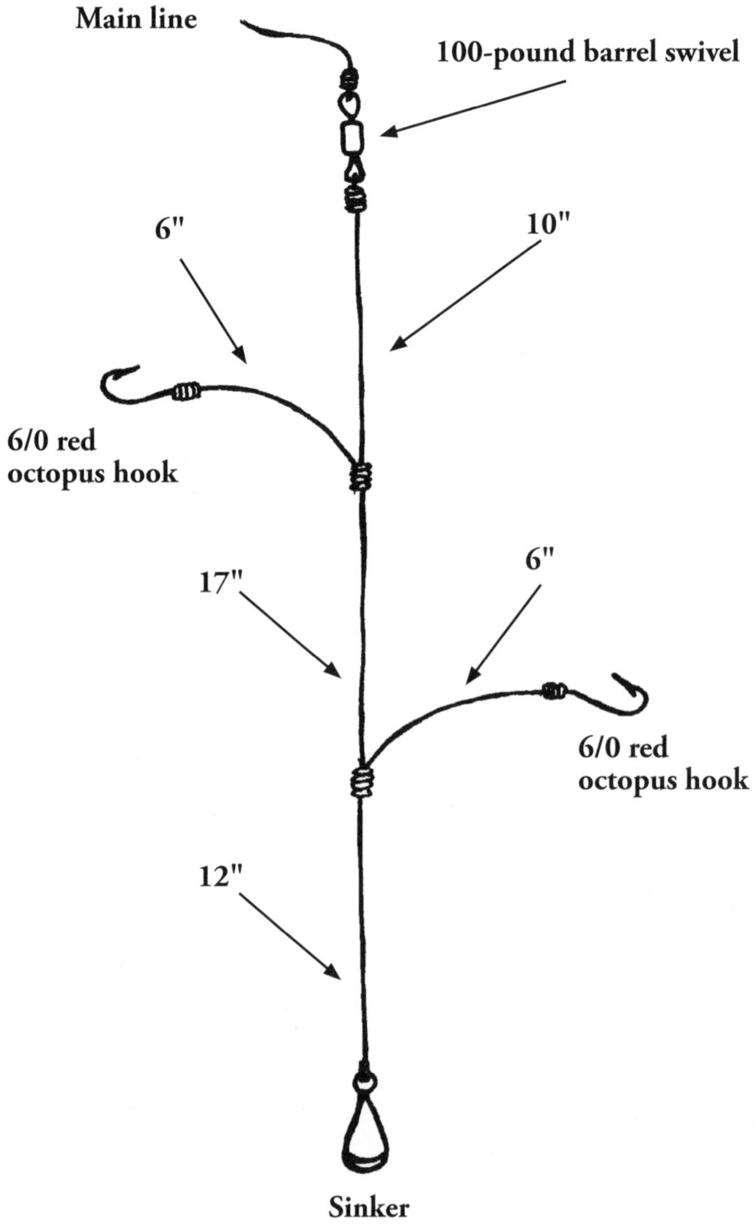

Surf Rig, Basic

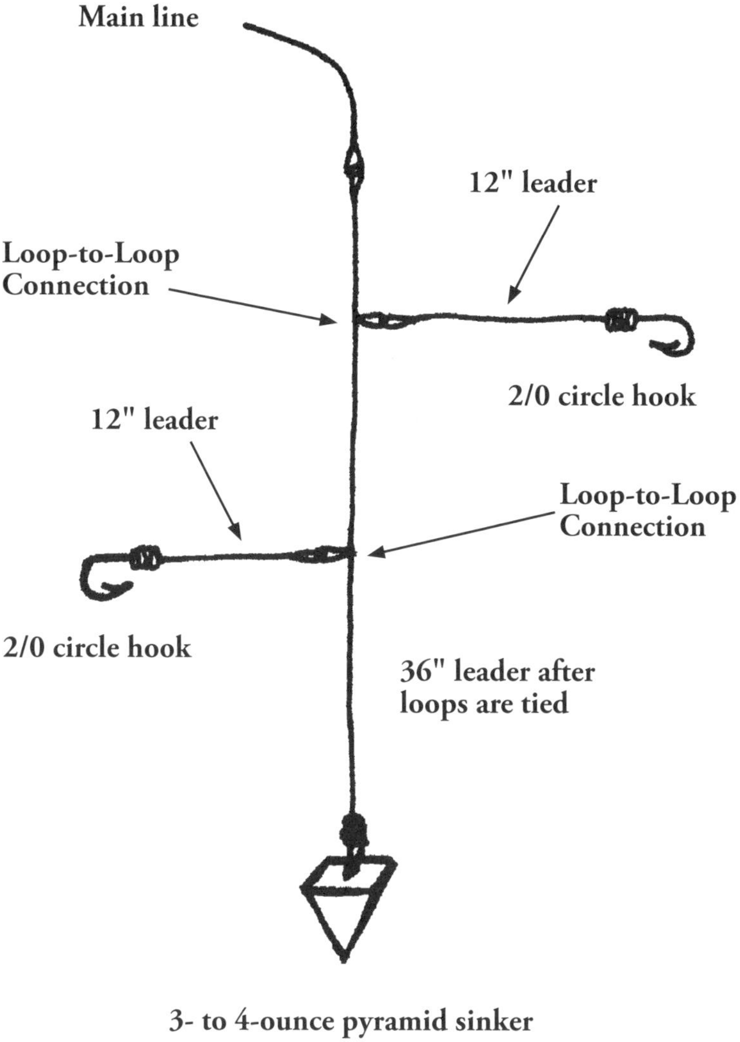
Main line
12" leader
Loop-to-Loop
Connection
2/0 circle hook
12" leader
Loop-to-Loop
Connection
2/0 circle hook
36" leader after
loops are tied
3- to 4-ounce pyramid sinker

Surf Rig for Long Distances

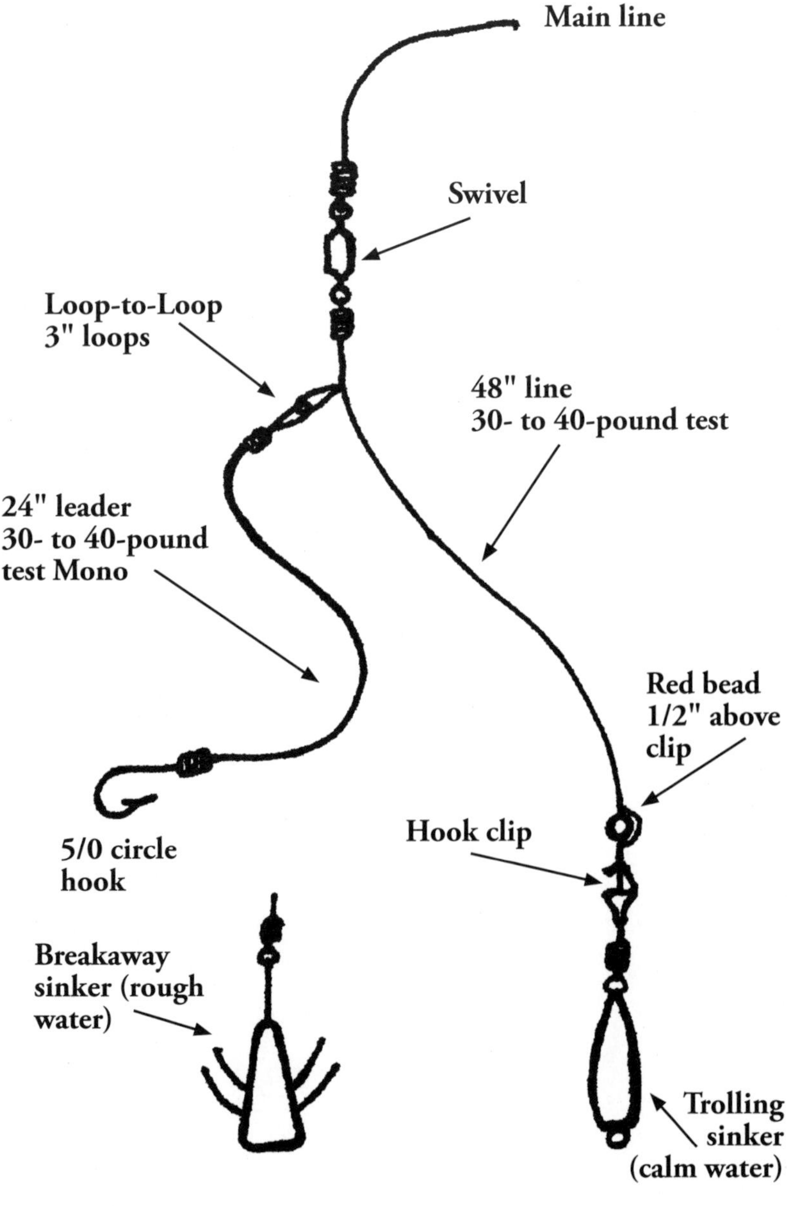

Adjust the 24" leader to clip so hook releases easily when the rig hits the water.

Tandem Bucktail Rig

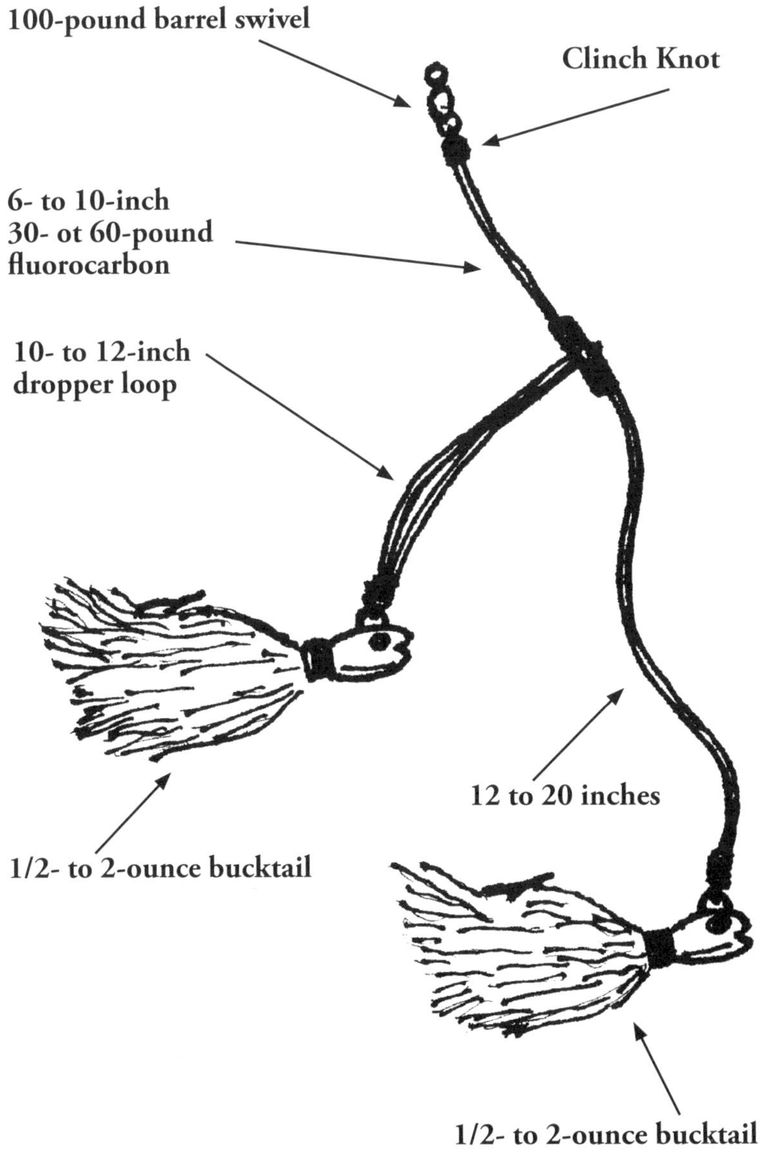

Tarpon Bait Rig

Tarpon feed on crabs and a variety of fish, including sardines, anchovies, mullet and pinfish. These baits are ideal for drifting or still-fishing. Shallow runners jerked, paused, then jerked often works. Jig it in deep water and passes works nicely too.

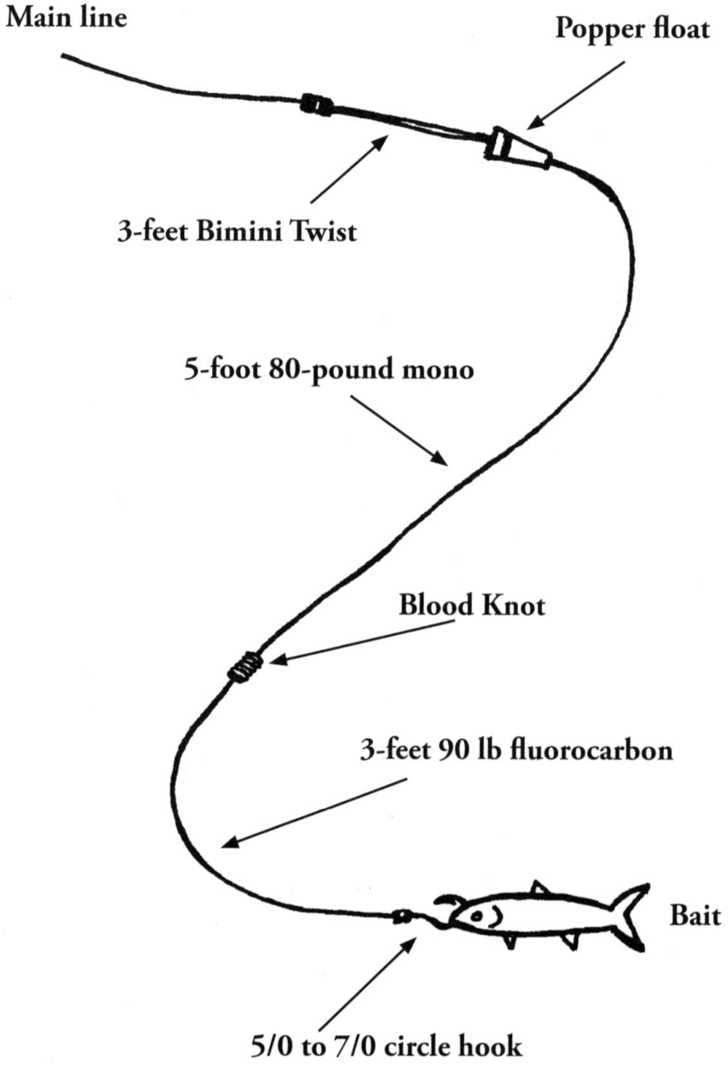

Teaser Rig

(shore and pier fishing)

A main key to success with this rig is slow, consistent movement. Keep this rig simple, the teaser should be small and light.

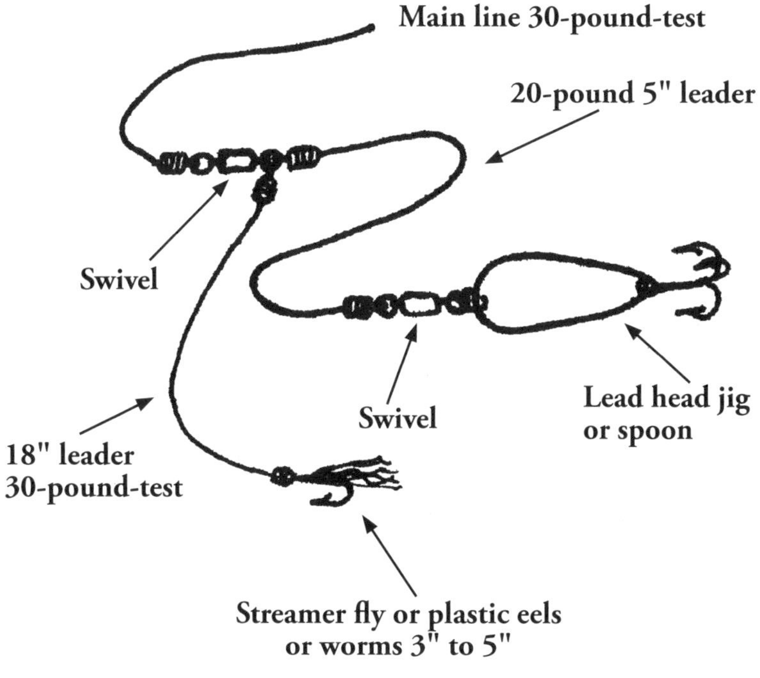

Tile Fish Rigs

2-Hook 39" 80-pound Leader

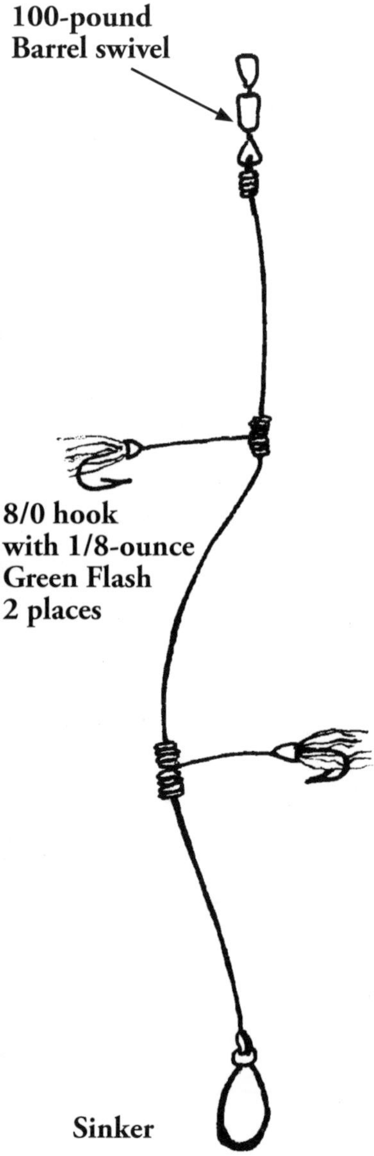

3-Hook 45" 80-pound Leader

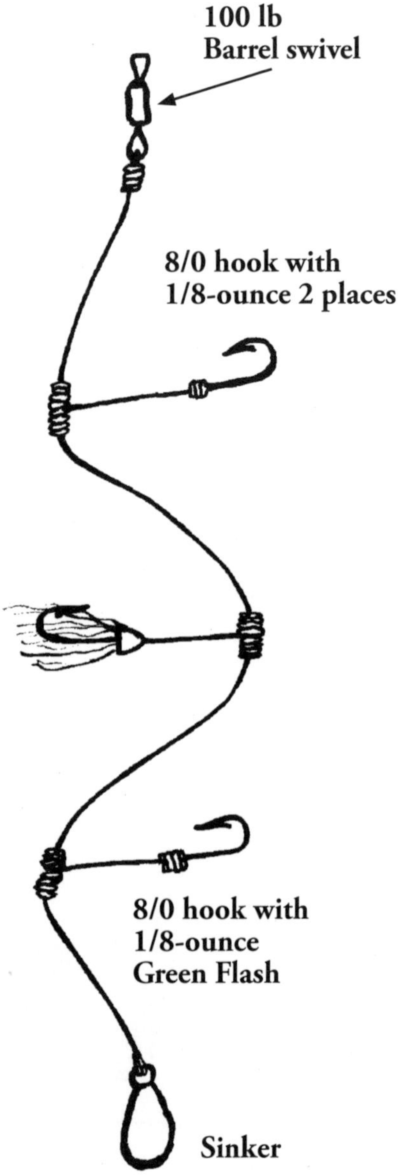

Tooth-Fish Rig

These two rigs are good when fishing salt or fresh water for tooth fish such as bluefish, mackerel, walleye and pike to name a few.

Single-Strand Wire Leader

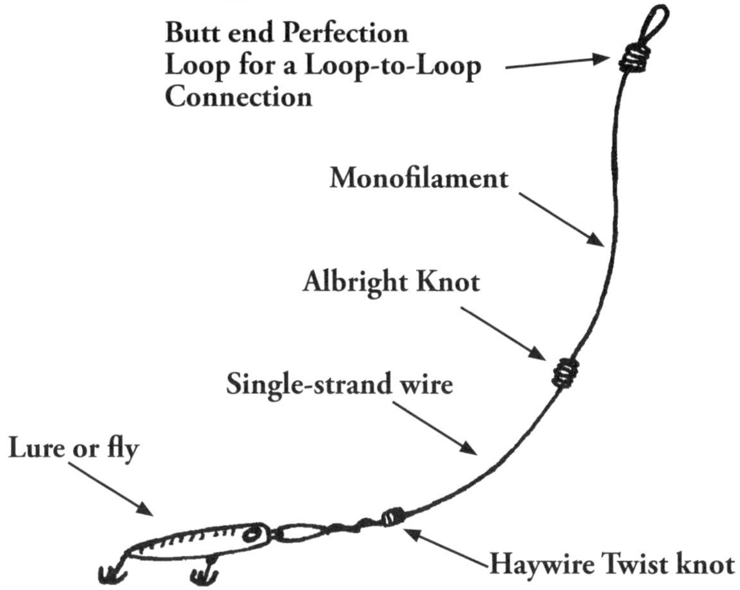

Monofilament Shock Tippet

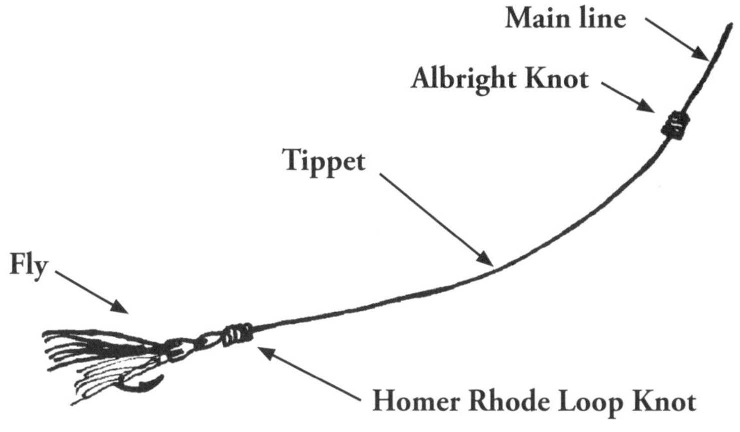

Trolling Rig and Sinkers

General trolling sinkers weigh several ounces for medium or heavy fishing tackle. Select weight, wire and hook according to your fishing preferances.

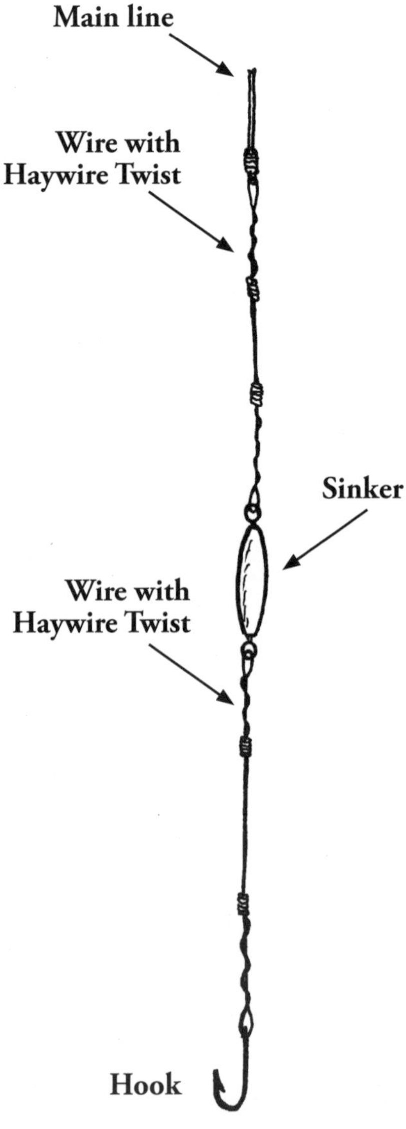

Cigar sinker

Spin sinker
(banana weight)

Keel sinker

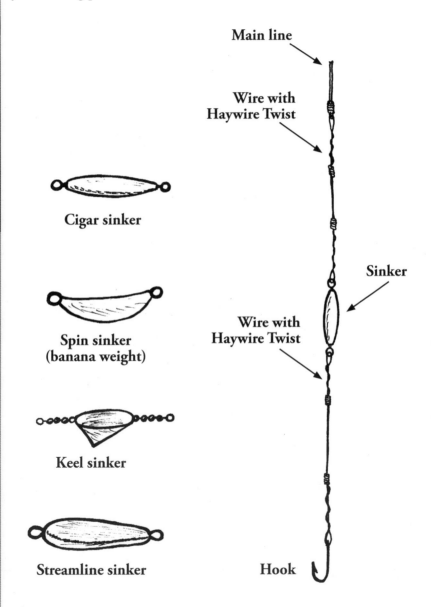

Streamline sinker

Tuna Dead-Drift Rig

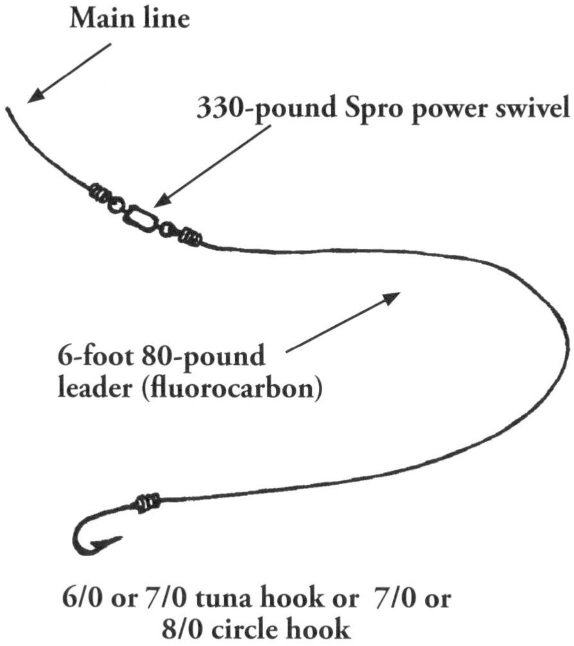

Whiting Bait Rig
32" Leader

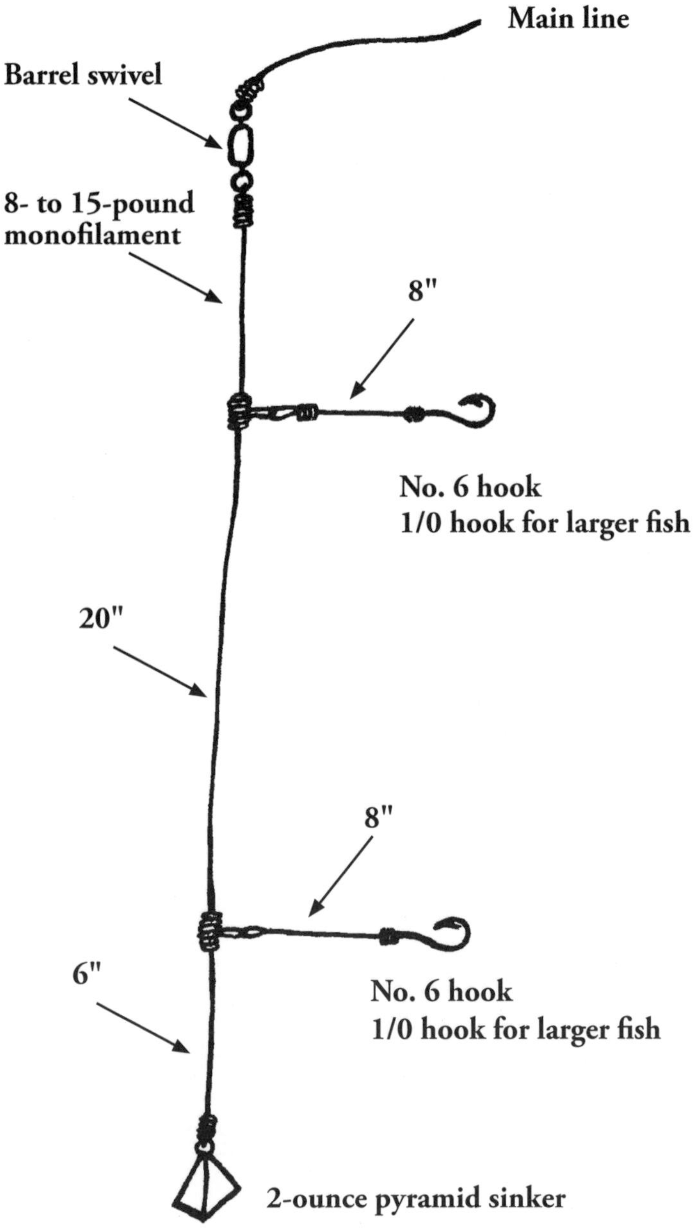

Whiting Bait Rig
48" Leader

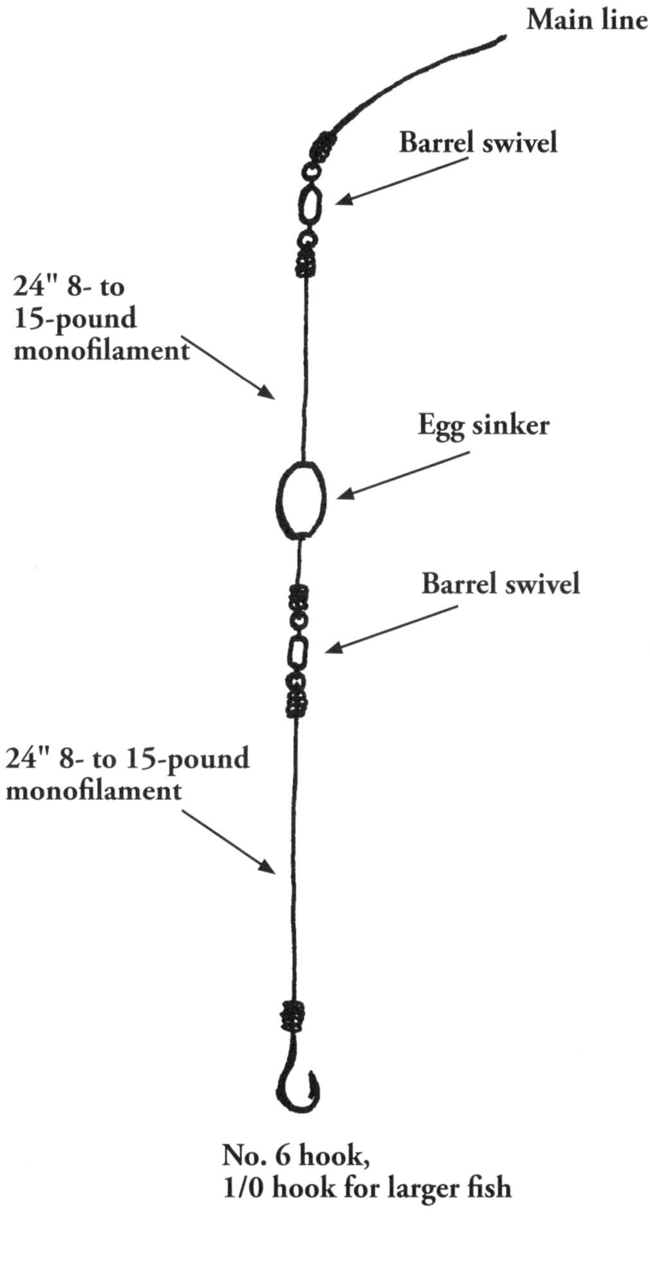

Yellowfin Tuna Rig

Since yellow fin tuna are leader shy this leader may prove invaluable in tough situations. A 12-foot length of cable is attached to a tuna hook on one end and a welded rig on the other. Cable and hook size to be determined by the size fish in the area. The cable is wrapped into a tight coil and attached to the hook shank with a strong rubber band. Then add bait of choice.

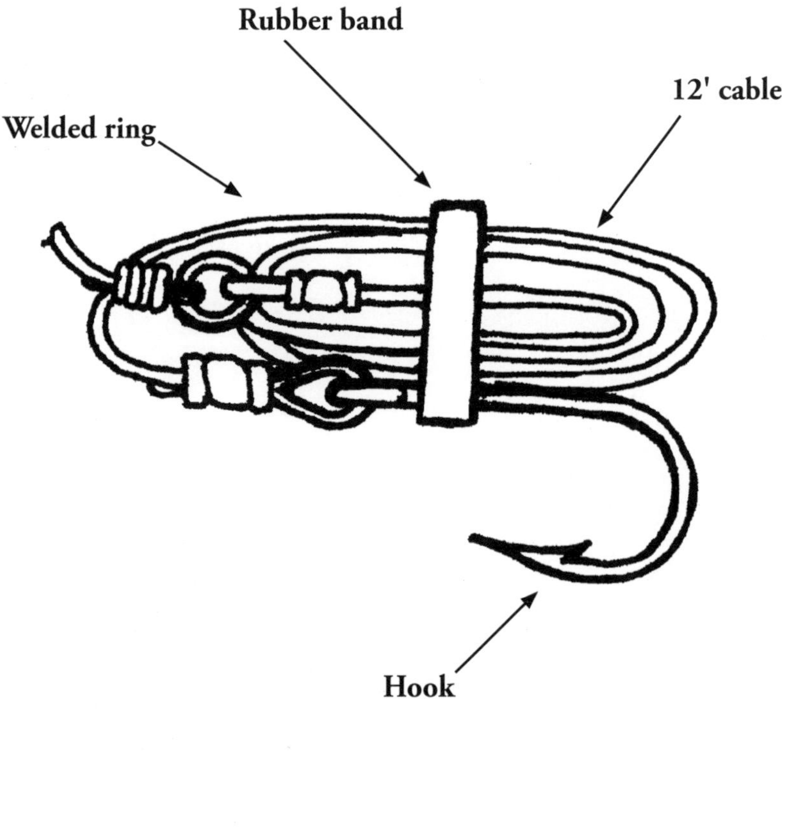

Yellowfin Tuna and Dolphin Rig

These two rigs are designed to be fished just under the surface for feeding yellowfin and dolphin.

#1

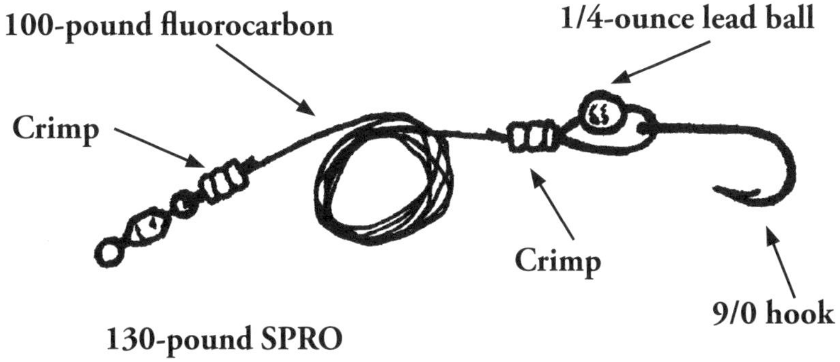

Note: Bait with medium size ballyhoo.

#2

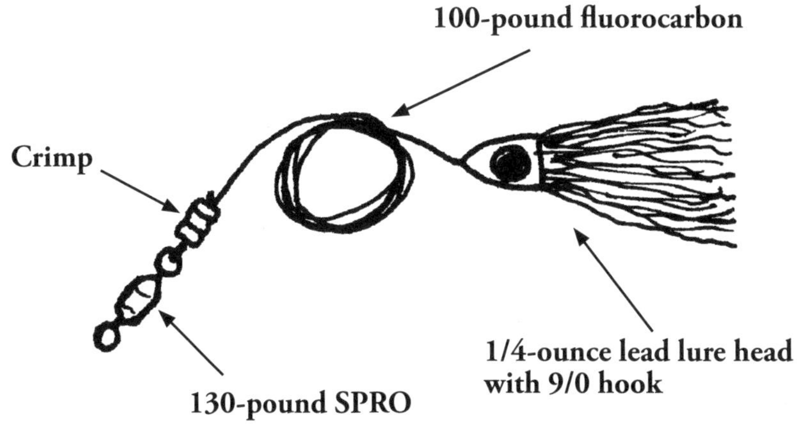

Chapter 4
Fly-Fishing Leaders and Rigs

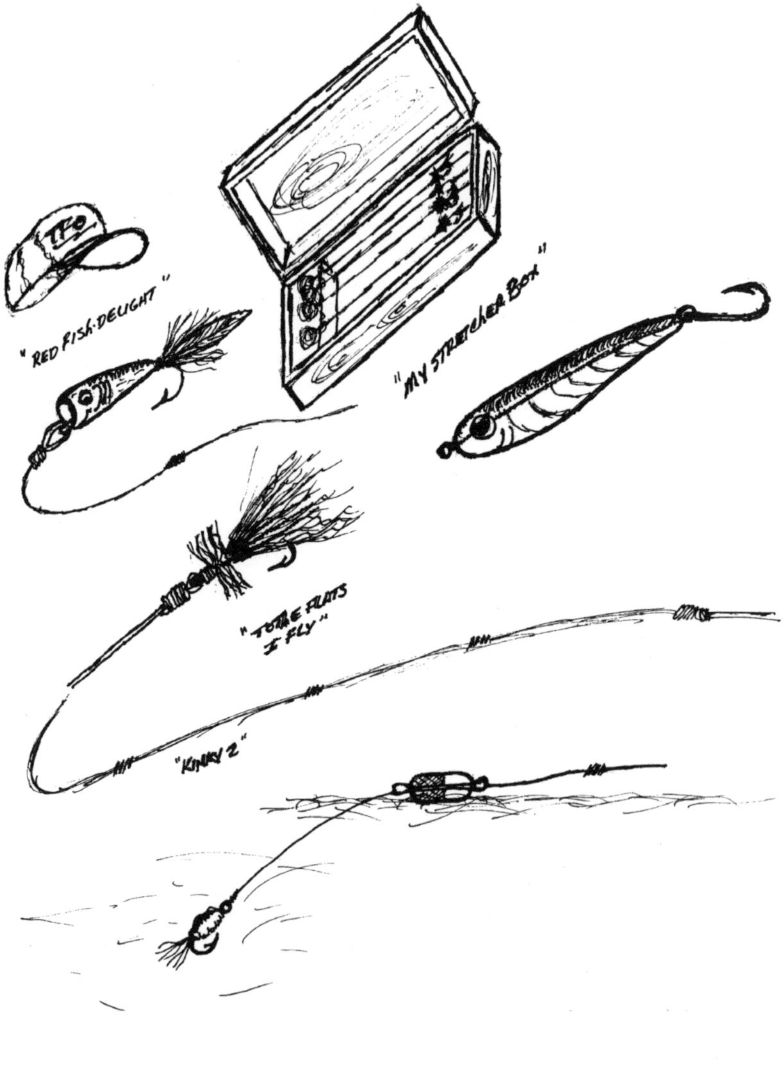

Straightening Shock Tippet

1. Heat a pan of water on the stove. **DO NOT BOIL.** Boiling damages the monofilament.

2. Put the monofilament in the heated water and allow to soak for one to two minutes. This will help "un-kink" the monofilament. Caution: Use tongs to remove the monofilament.

3. Pull each end of the pre-cut mono in opposite directions and allow cooling. Store the tippets in aluminum or PVC tube(s) and cap both ends.

Remember, direct sunlight weakens monofilament, always store your monofilament line in a protective enclosure and in shaded areas.

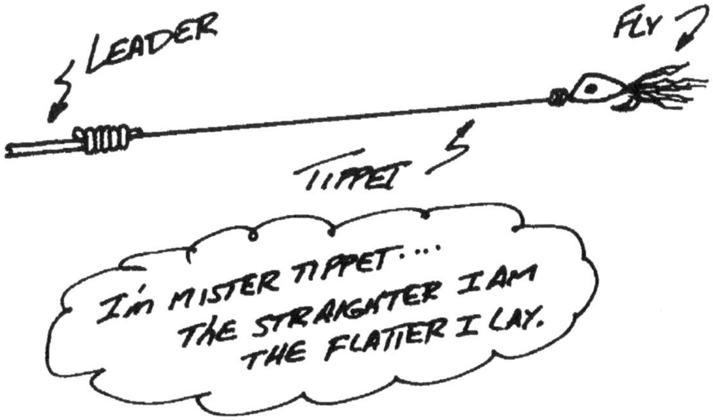

Class Tippet Pre-Test

Lefty Kreh recommended this simple test to determine the breaking strength of your leader to help meet IGFA class tippet rules.

1. Take about four feet of the tippet and make a Bimini Twist at both ends of the tippet material.
2. Soak this tippet in water for two hours.
3. Attach one Bimini Twist to the handle of a bucket filled with water.
4. Support the bucket off the floor with the other BiminiTwist.
5. Pour sand slowly into the bucket of water until the class tippet breaks. (Note: When the bucket hits the floor, water may splash out.)
6. Weight the bucket and sand on a certified scale. This weight will be the exact breaking strength of the tippet. This test will help you meet the IGFA rules.

Note: Scales used in grocery stores or meat markets are checked by state agencies and will be accurate for this pre-test.

Leaders and Tippets

The leader is the connection between the fly line to the fly.

Material

Monofilament: The most common leader material. Mono comes in a variety of sizes, stiffness and diameters.

Fluorocarbon: A synthetic material that claims to be nearly invisible under water by having the same refracting index as water. The down side is fluorocarbon is denser than nylon and sinks a little faster.

Braided Super Lines: A synthetic line made by weaving thin-diameter man-made materials. Advantages: No-stretch, low diameter and very strong line.

Taper Leader Sections

Butt Section: Heaviest portion of the leader, attached to the fly line end.

Mid Section: Section between the butt section and tippet.

Tippet: Section that attaches to the fly.

Leaders

Shorter Leaders: Powerful but less delicate, work well in windy conditions.

Long Leader: Made to turn over. Has less power but provide more delicacy and are appropriate for conditions which require delicate presentations and absolute dead-drifts.

Bite or Shock Tippet: A short, heavy section of a leader between the tippet and the fly. The material uses a large-diameter monofilament or wire (braided or a single strand). A bite tippet is ideal when fishing for sharp-toothed fish.

Shock Tippet

Large fish and sharp teeth require tippets of 80- to 120-pound-test mono, super braid and/or braided wire.

Pre-cut tippet to desired length and test prior to trip.

Store tippets in aluminum or PVC tube that is capped at one end, or both if possible.

Always inspect tippet for knicks, cracks, and abrasions.

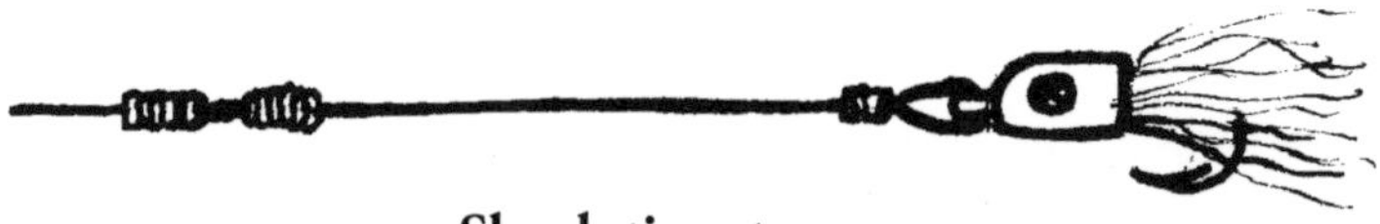

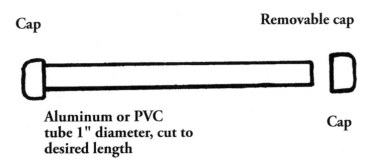

Fly-Casting System

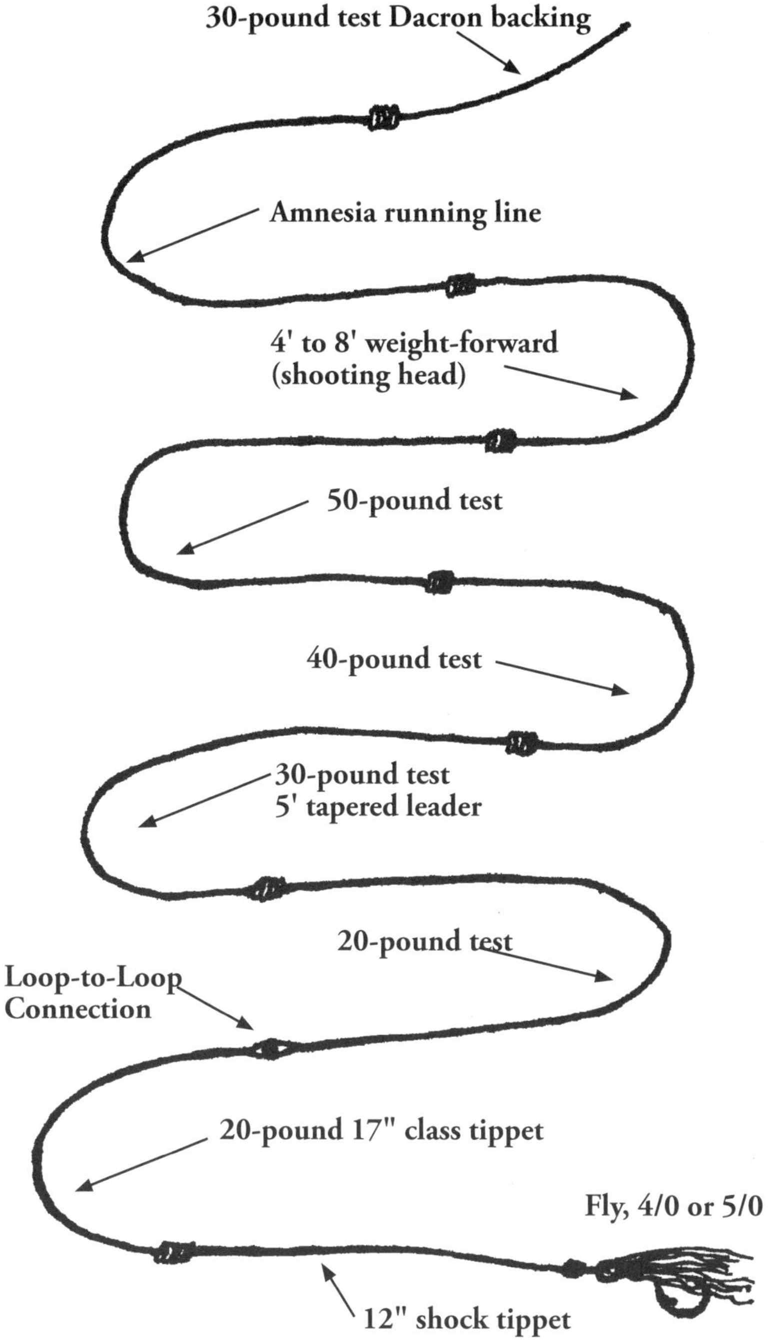
30-pound test Dacron backing
Amnesia running line
4' to 8' weight-forward
(shooting head)
50-pound test
40-pound test
30-pound test
5' tapered leader
20-pound test
Loop-to-Loop
Connection
20-pound 17" class tippet
Fly, 4/0 or 5/0
12" shock tippet

Lefty's Tapered-Leader Formula

Having tied these leaders for the coasts of Texas and Florida, Lefty has shown he is one of the smartest fishermen I've had the privilege to meet. These leaders unroll toward the target with ease because of the stiff butt section allowing the lighter sections to uncoil.

Length

Weight	10 ft	12 ft	14 ft	16 ft
50 lb	5 ft	6 ft	7 ft	8 ft
50 lb	1 ft	2 ft	3 ft	4 ft
30 lb	1 ft	1 ft	1 ft	1 ft
20 lb	1 ft	1 ft	1 ft	1 ft
10, 12 or 15 lb	2 ft	2 ft	2 ft	2 ft

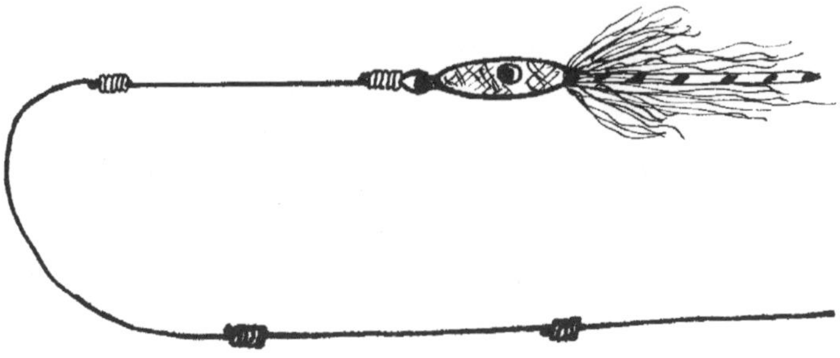

Saltwater Fly-Rig With Knots

A typical rig used for a variety of saltwater fishing. Knots may vary depending upon the application.

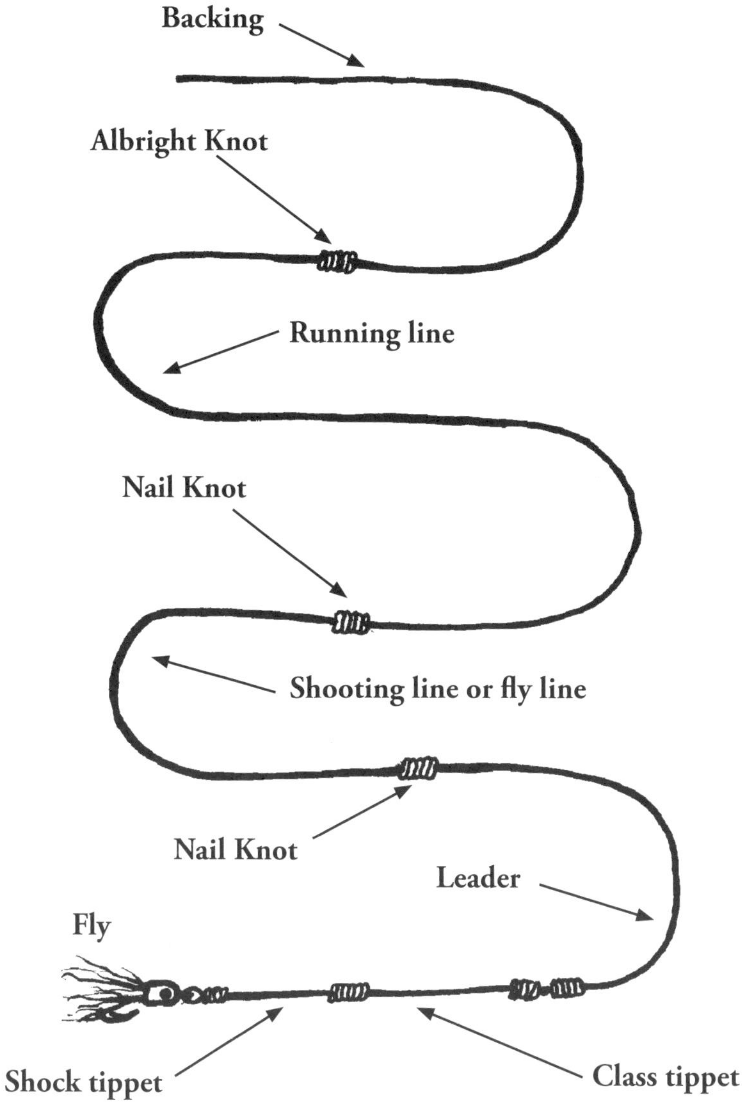

Saltwater Leader Rig

A typical saltwater rig. Leader, class tippet, and shock tippet are determined by fishing conditions and species of fish being sought.

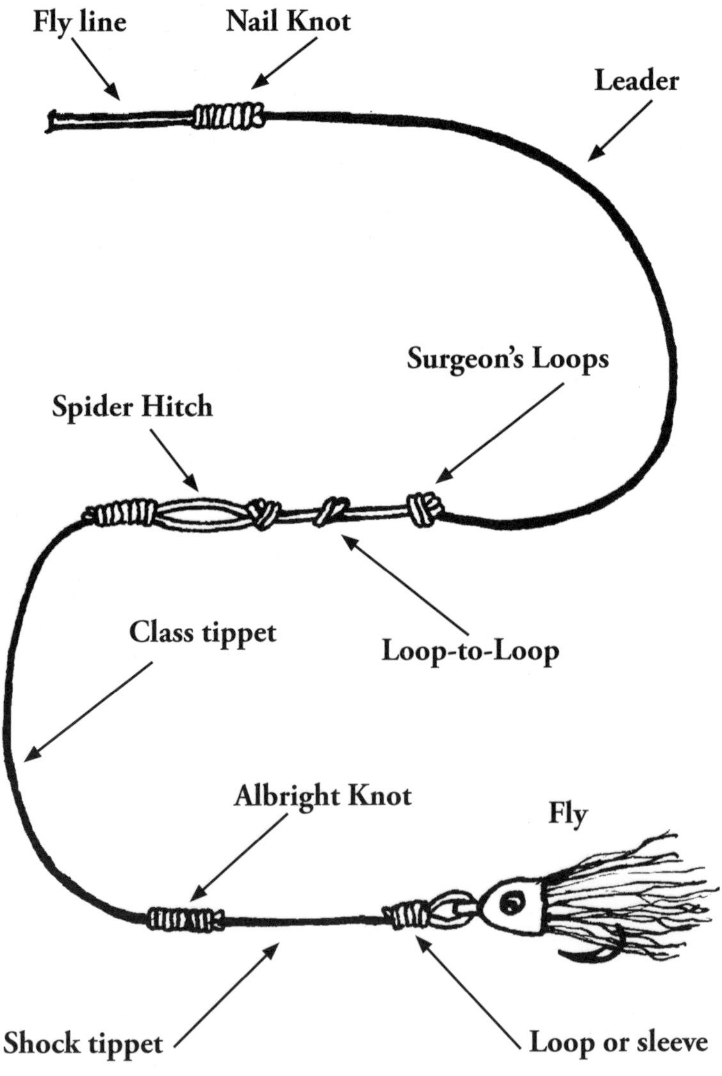

Basic Saltwater Tapered Leader

The basic saltwater tapered leader is ideal for starting in salt water. Test and adjust to the fish you are pursuing.

9' 6" Leader

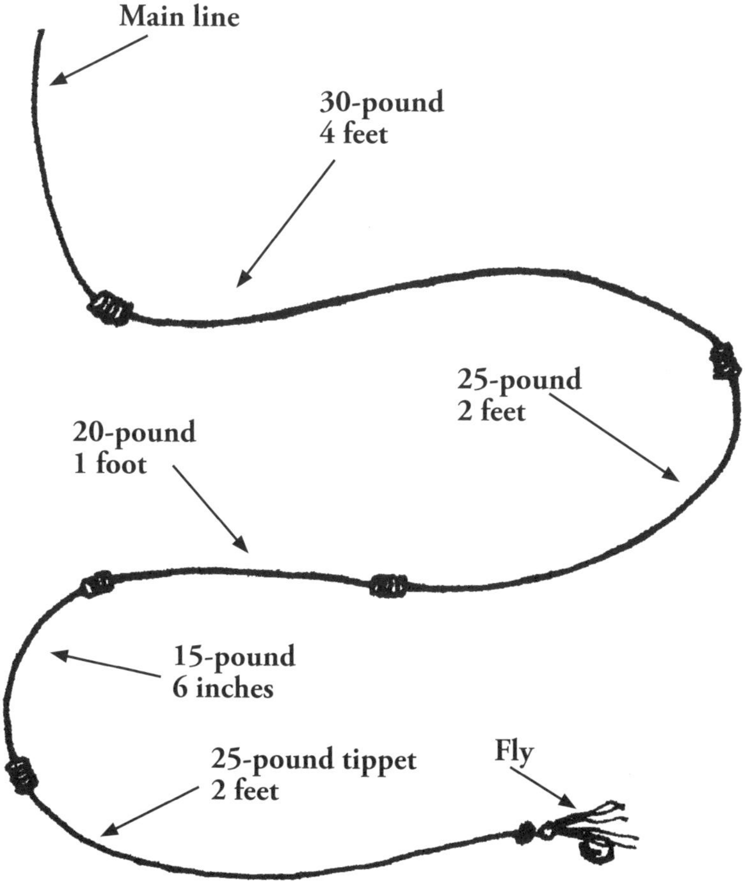

An all-monofilament construction makes the leader limp for easier turnover.

Saltwater Tapered Leader

This leader turns over well unless there is a strong wind. It's an all-purpose leader.

12'-13' Leader

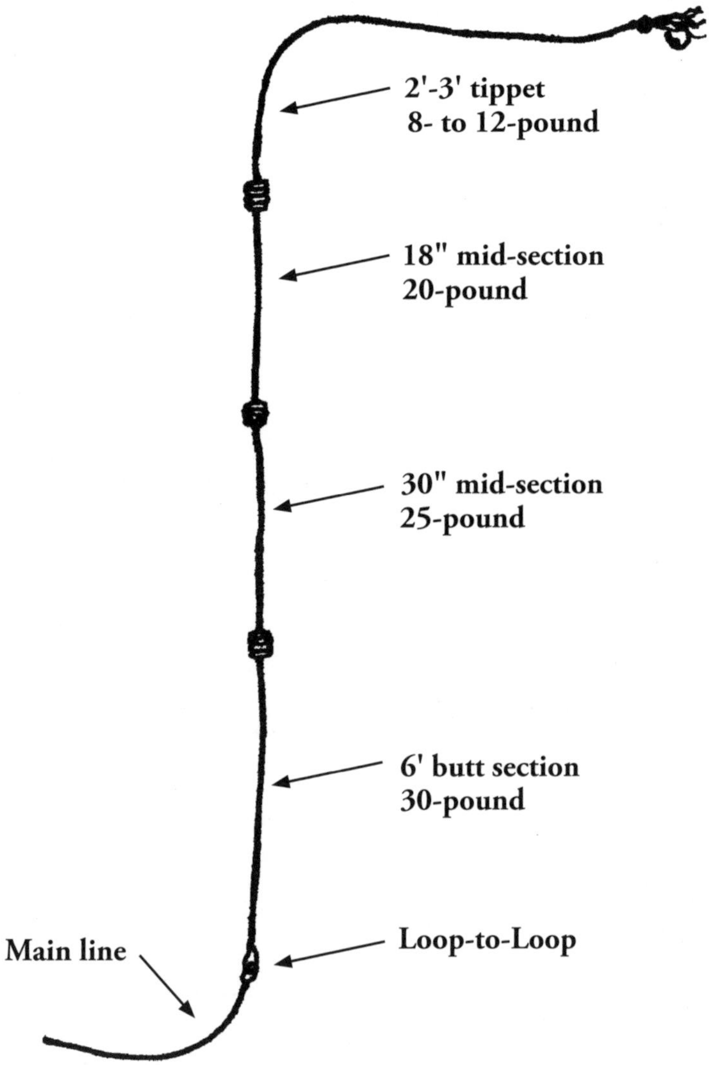

All-Around Saltwater Leader

These leaders have worked well when surf fishing in Florida, Texas and California. I recommend a loop-to-loop leader to fly line for quicker leader changes needed due to sharp-tooth fish and frayed tippets.

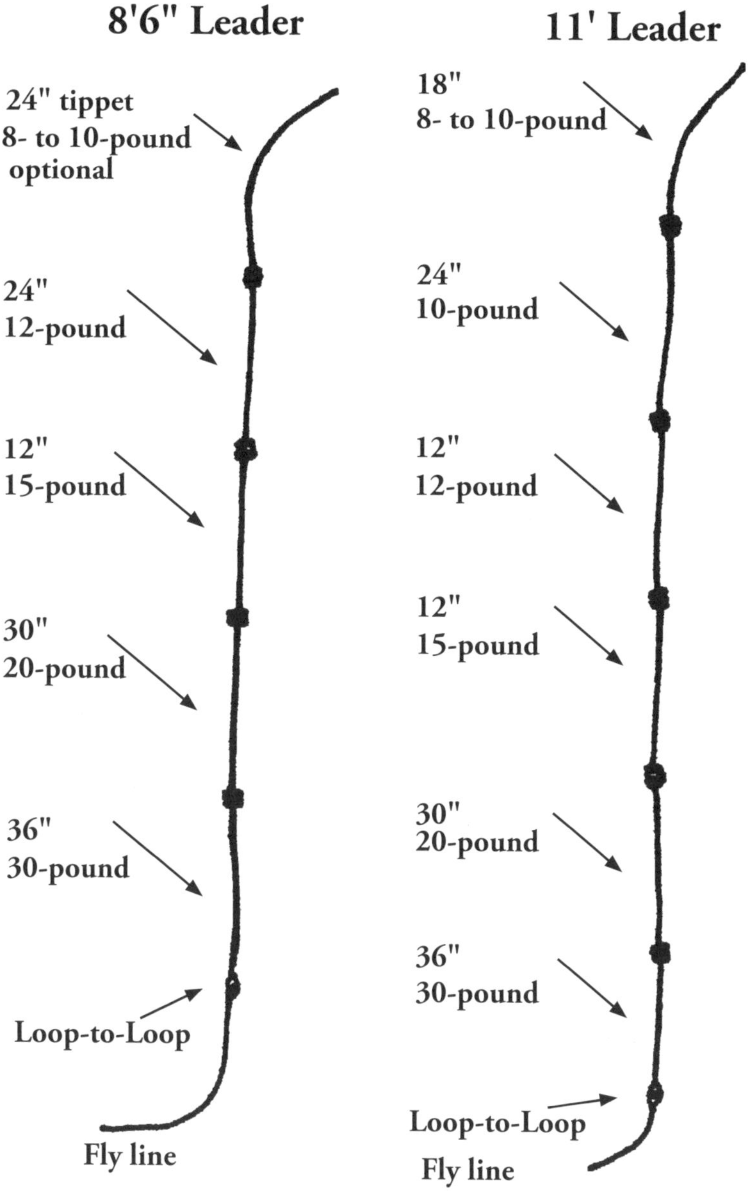

Heavy Saltwater Leader

A customer at Bob Marriott's Fly Fishing Fair in Fullerton, CA shared this leader with me. He told me that it would work well on all large fish: tarpon, shark, amberjack, tune, sails, etc.

9' Leader

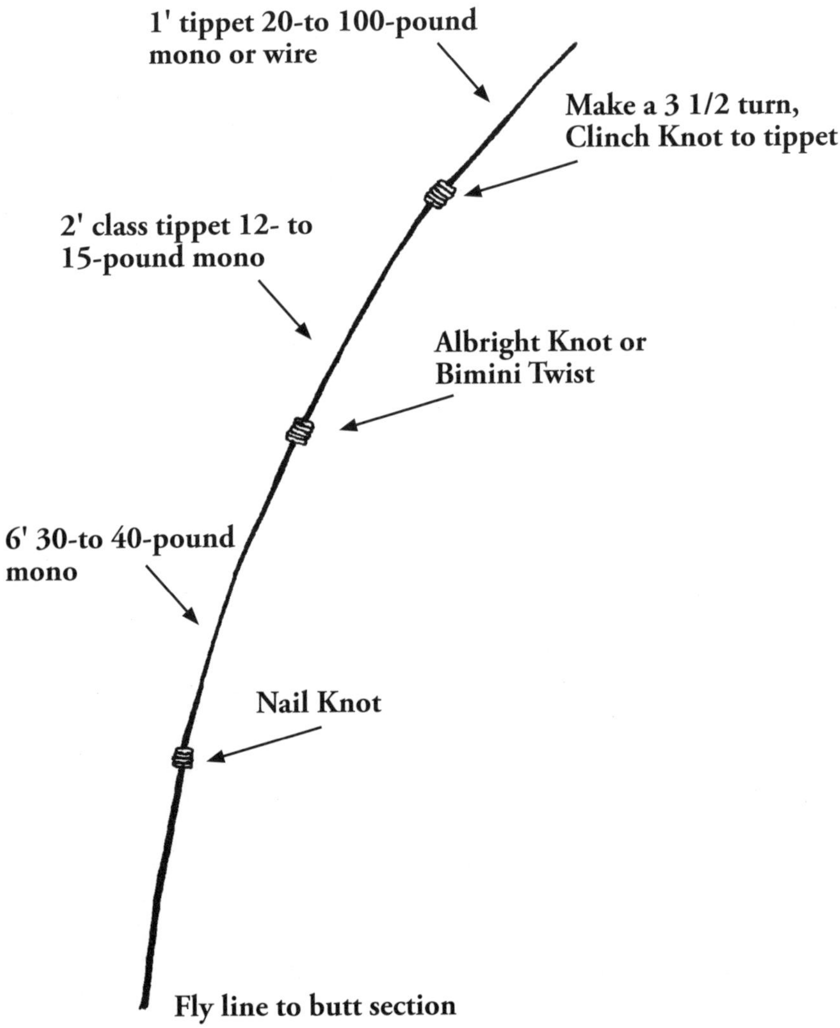

Billfish Leader

Class-tippet billfish leader.

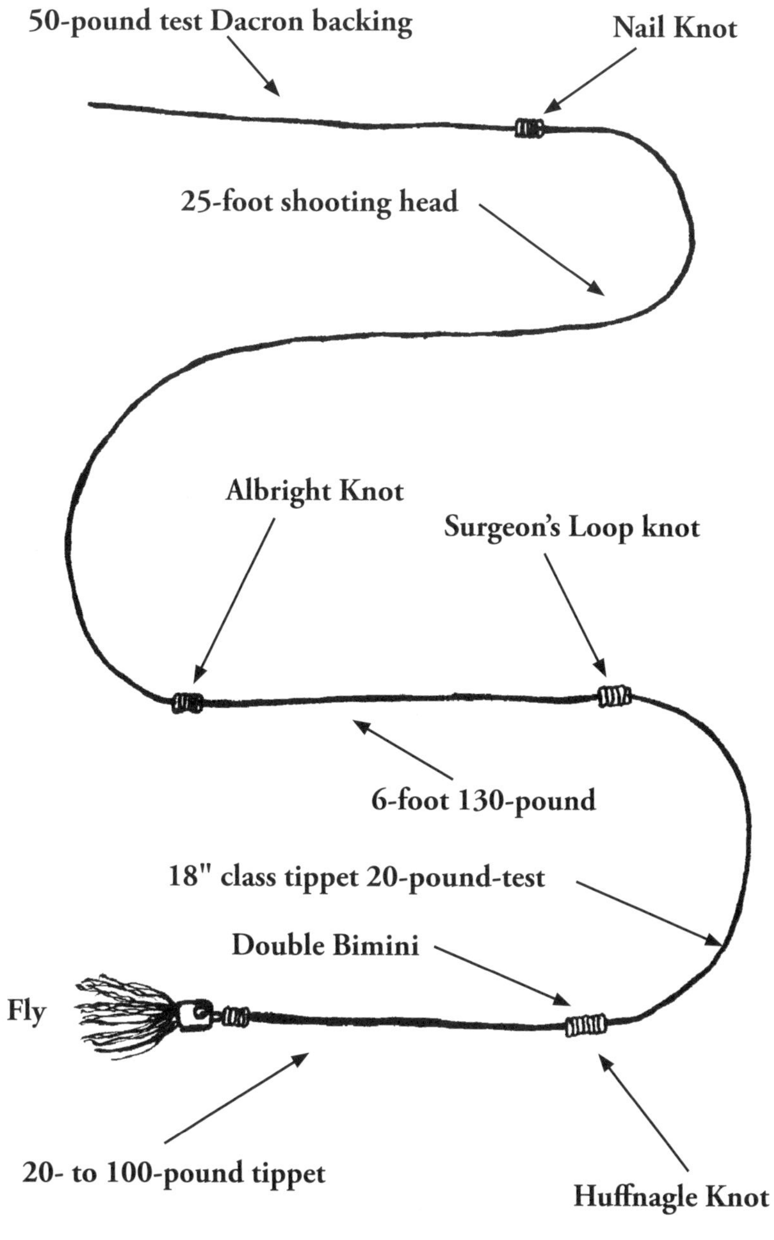

Bonefish Leader

This type of leader will turn over easily in windy conditions so use stiff mono in the butt section.

15 Foot Leaders

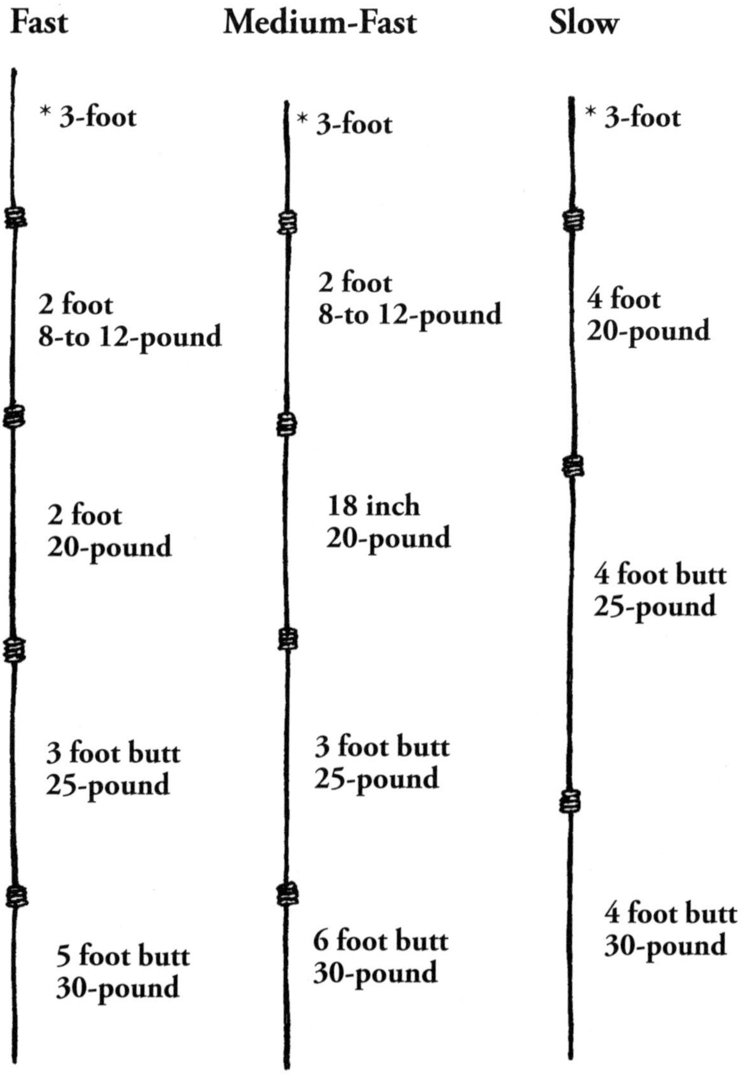

* Optional tippet

Bonefish Leader

(Continued)

Three different leaders that can be used, depending upon rod and/or wind conditions.

Fast	Medium-Fast	Slow
* 2 foot 8-to 12-pound	* 2 foot 8-to 12-pound	* 2 foot 6-pound
2 foot 20-pound	18 inch 20-pound	4 foot 8-to 12-pound
3 foot 25-pound	32 inch 25-pound	4 foot 20-pound
5 foot 30-pound	6 foot 30-pound	4 foot 30-pound

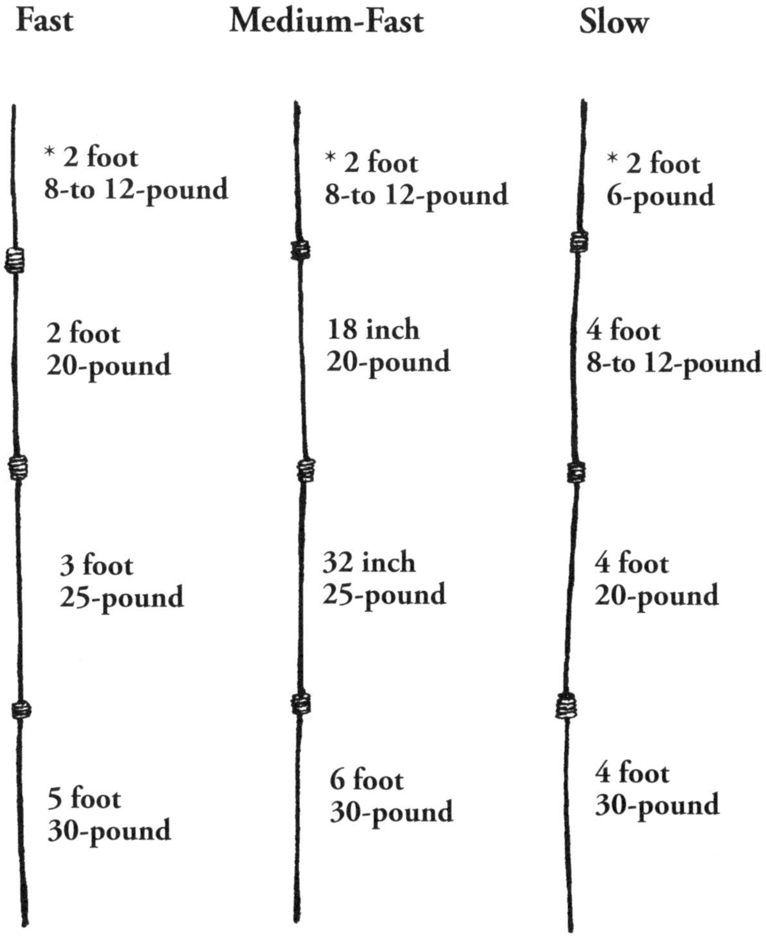

*** An additional tippet for IGFA records.**

Permit Leader

13' 6" Leader

All Purpose Permit Leader

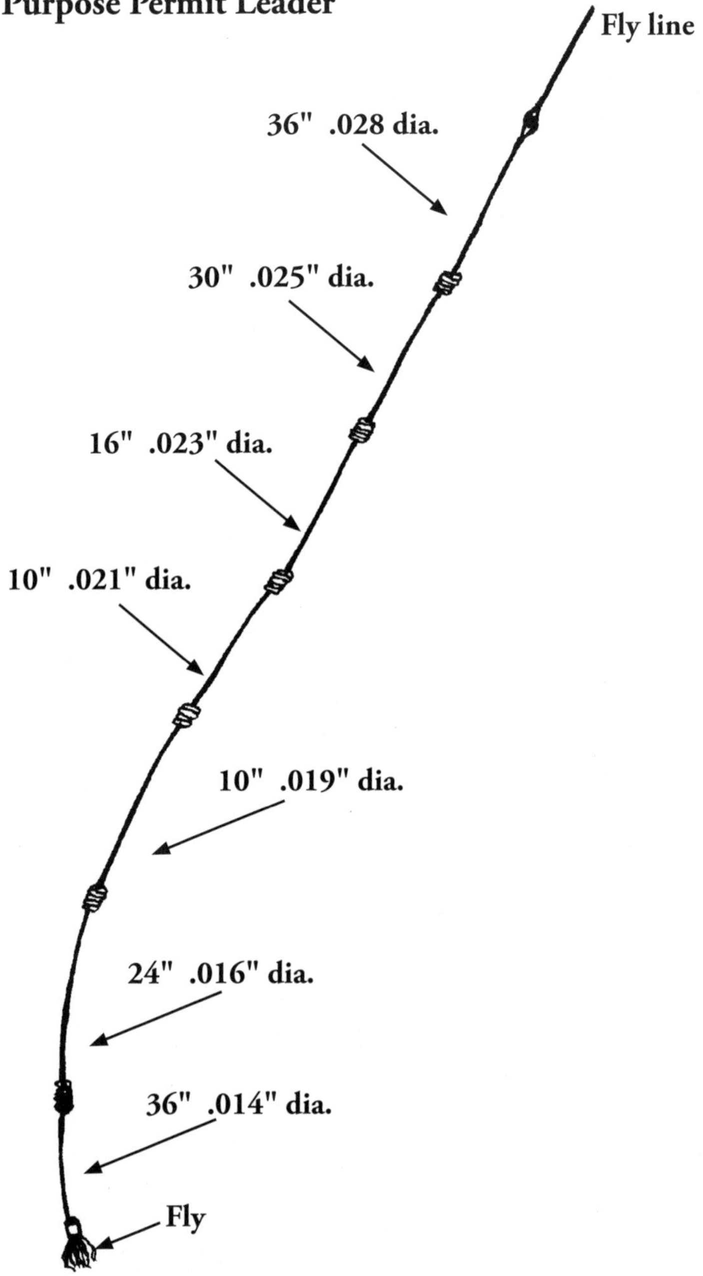

Redfish Leader

While fishing South Padre Island, Texas, I discovered that the fish required a soft presentation, as do bonefish. This 10' 6" leader worked well in windy conditions. (An additional tippet can be added.)

10' 6" Leader

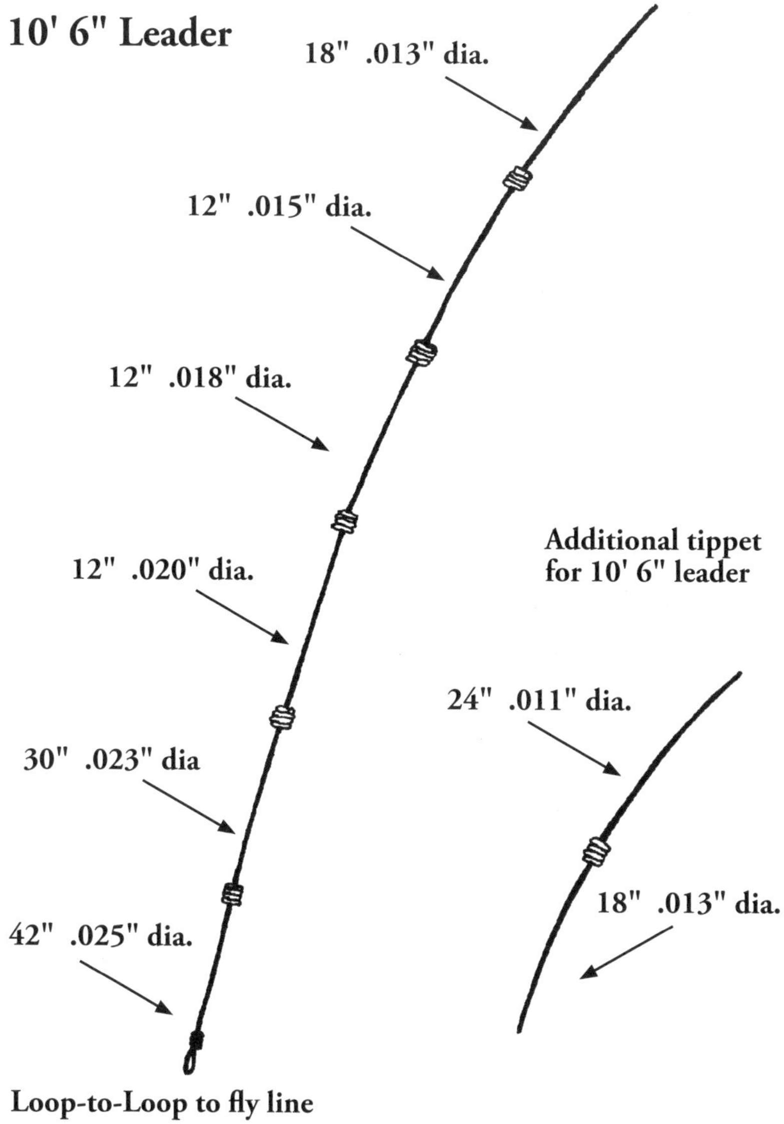

Sailfish Leader

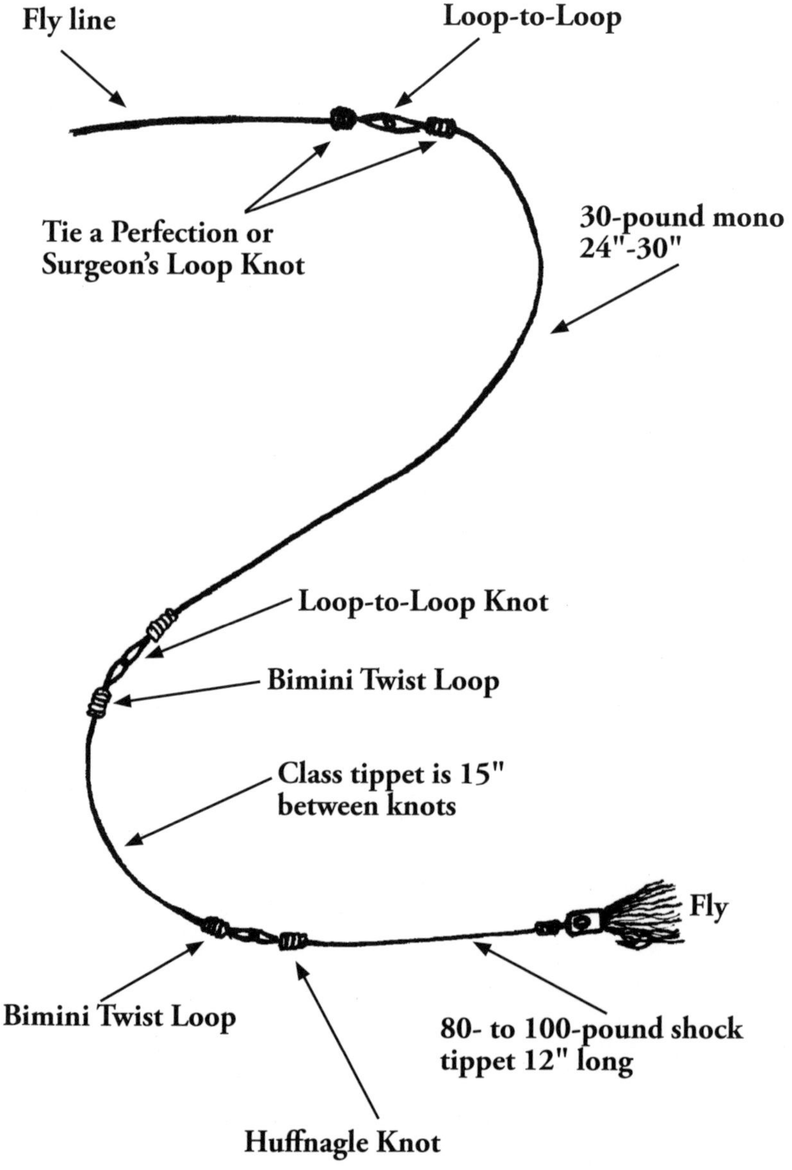
Fly line
Loop-to-Loop
Tie a Perfection or
Surgeon's Loop Knot
30-pound mono
24"-30"
Loop-to-Loop Knot
Bimini Twist Loop
Class tippet is 15"
between knots
Fly
Bimini Twist Loop
80- to 100-pound shock
tippet 12" long
Huffnagle Knot

Snook Leader

This leader is also excellent for barracuda. Simply change the shock leader. Note: If a shock leader is needed, use 30- to 120-pound tippet depending upon species of fish being sought.

12' Leader

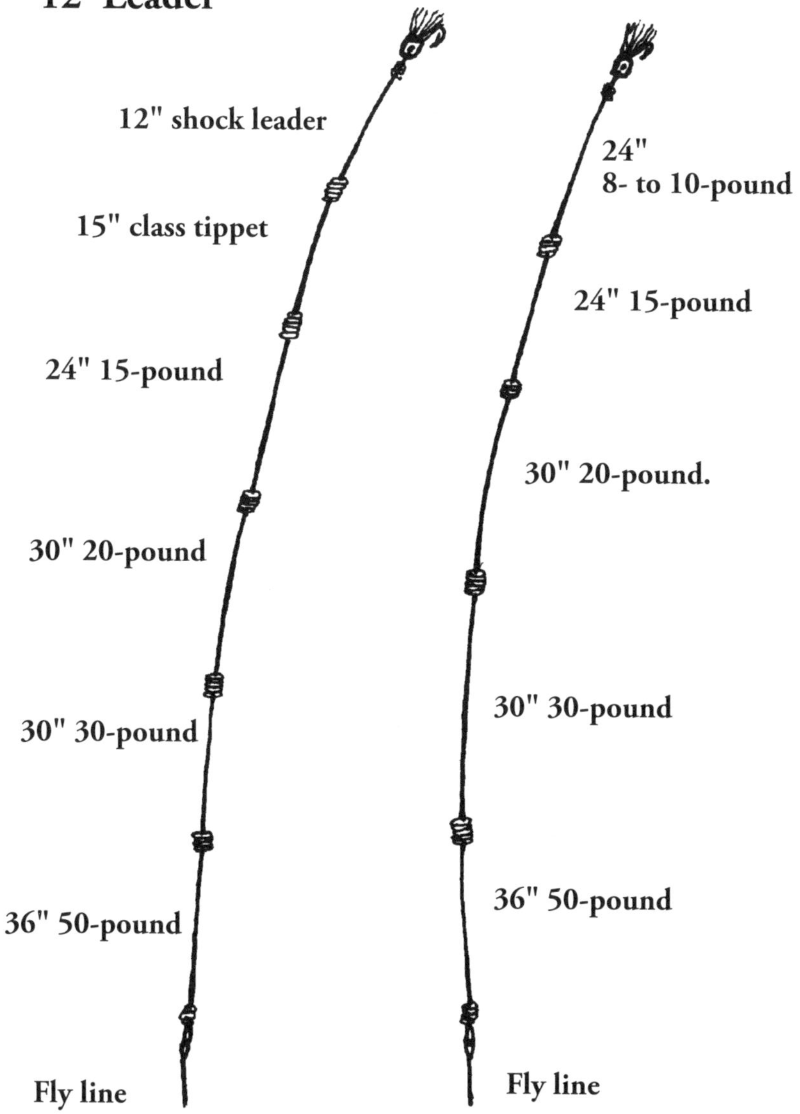

5' Leader for Steelhead

25-pound Butt section = 15"

15-pound Mid-section = 15"

10-pound Tippet = 30"

The length of this leader was chosen to give the fly maximum action and stealth. A five-foot-long leader hides the fly line tip from most bottom-feeding steelhead in water 4' to 5' visibility. The leader is short enough so that a heavy sinking tip line can hold a very lightweight fly close to the bottom. A leader this short will turn over a heavily weighted fly easily.

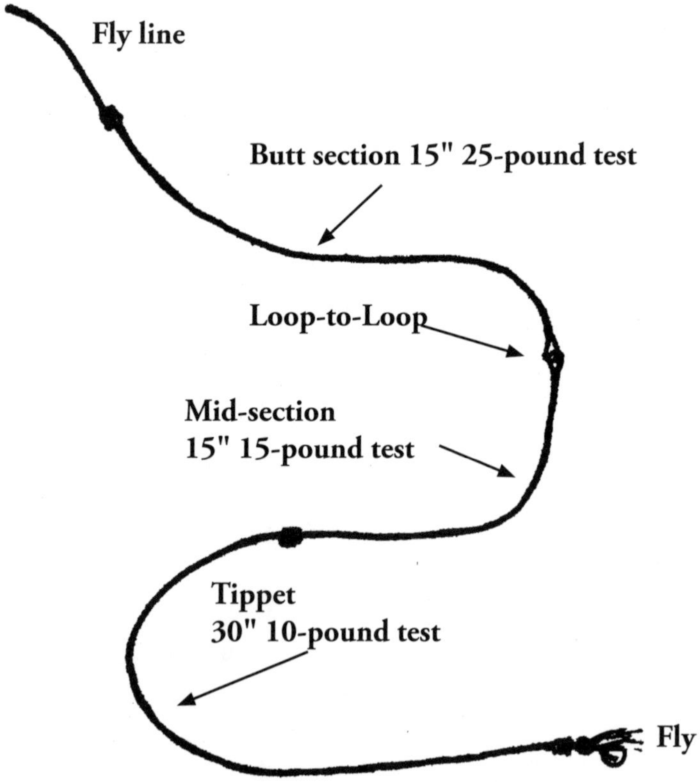

Experiment and make changes to fit your fishing style and water conditions.

Tarpon Leader

10' Leader

10- to 13-Weight
Floating Fly Line

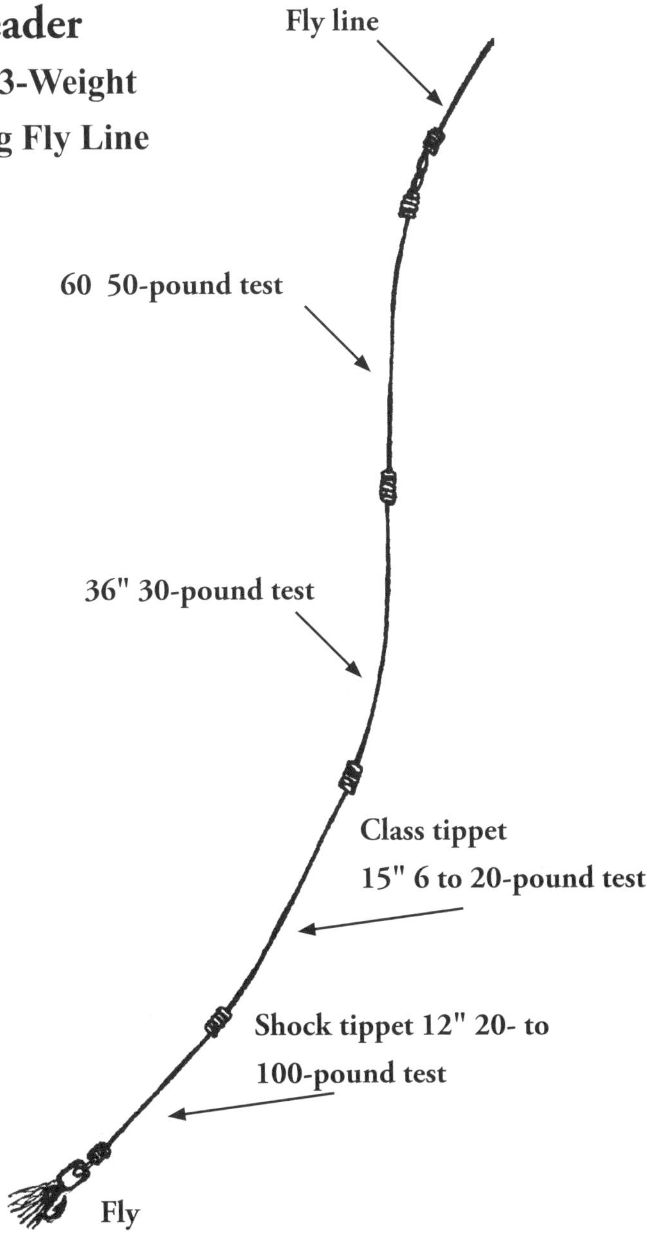

More Saltwater Books by Larry V. Notley

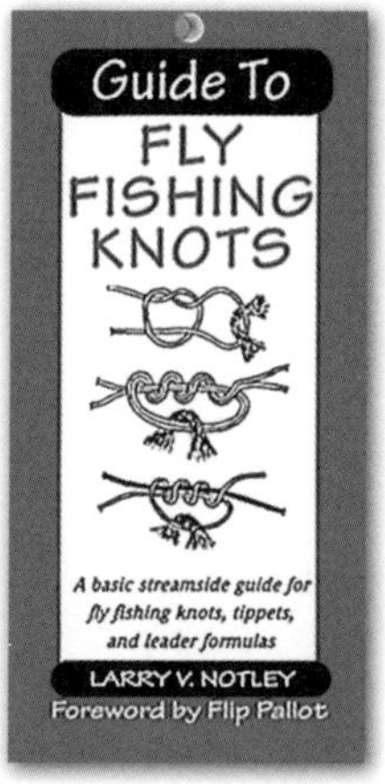

Guide to Fly Fishing Knots
by Larry V. Notley
Foreword by Flip Pallot
Larry includes: parts of your line; IGFA line test; tippet to fly size chart; knot-tying tips; terminology; knot applications; step-by-step instruction for joining lines, lines to flies, loop knots, dropper knots, and yarn indicator knots. Also, basic fresh- and saltwater leaders and trout and panfish leaders. Twenty knots are shared with text and illustrations showing each step. 3 1/2 x 7; 32 pages.
SB: $4.95
ISBN-13: 978-1-57188-183-0
UPC: 0-66066-00385-0

Guide to Saltwater Fishing Knots for Gear & Fly Fishing
by Larry V. Notley
In this book, Notley shares 47 knots sure to keep fish on your line. With clear illustrations and instructions Notley provides saltwater anglers with all the knots they need.
3 1/2 x 7 inches, 56 pages.
SB: $5.95
ISBN-13: 978-1-57188-273-8
UPC: 0-66066-00462-8

Fly Leaders & Knots
by Larry V. Notley
A comprehensive little book filled with leaders you need to catch a variety of fish—both fresh- and saltwater! This handy little guide is a must for all fly-anglers—there are knots and leaders for every kind of fish and every type of fishing situation you might encounter.
5 1/2 x 8 1/2 inches, 64 pages.
SB: $7.95
ISBN-13: 978-1-57188-121-2
UPC: 0-66066-00319-5

Ask for these books at your local fly/tackle shop or call toll-free to order:
1.800.541.9498 (8-5 p.s.t.) • www.amatobooks.com

Saltwater Fishing Books

Saltwater Flies of the Southeast & Gulf Coast

by Angelo Peluso

The year-round fly-fishing opportunities in the flats, in-shore, and off-shore waters of the Southeast and Gulf Coast are world-class. Game fish you will encounter: bonefish, tarpon, permit, pompano, sailfish and sharks, to name just a few. The hundreds of fly patterns in this book are proven fish-catchers.

8 1/2 x 11 inches, 160 pages, all-color.

SB: $32.95 (tentative price)

ISBN 13: 978-1-57188-478-7

UPC: 0-81127-00320-4

Tandem Streamers

by Donald A. Wilson

Streamers are incredibly effective on salmon and trout, but when trolling nothing beats a tandem streamer. Subjects included: dressing tandems; trolling techniques; important people in their development and use; and hundreds of streamer patterns. Hundreds of fly plates and historical photos.

8 1/2 x 11 inches, 188 pages, all-color.

SB: $29.95

ISBN-13: 978-1-57188-467-1

UPC: 0-81127-00307-5

Striper Moon

by Ken Abrames

This book is loaded with technical information, yet it is not a pure how-to book. Ken has put his heart, his soul, and his keen fishing mind into this effort. It is very enjoyable reading. But at the same time, the book is filled with information that can only be gained by spending innumerable hours not only fishing for striped bass, but thinking about them."

—Lefty Kreh

8 1/2 x 11 inches, 48 pages

SB: $19.95

ISBN-13: 978-1-57188-408-4

UPC: 0-81127-00242-9

Saltwater Flies: Over 700 of the Best

by Deke Meyer

An all-color fly dictionary of the very best saltwater flies for inshore and ocean use. Effective flies for all saltwater gamefish species. Photographed large, crisp and in true color by Jim Schollmeyer. Pattern recipes next to each fly. This is a magnificent book featuring the largest display of working saltwater fly patterns!

8 1/2 x 11 inches, 119 pages.

SB: $19.95

ISBN-13: 978-1-57188-020-8

UPC: 0-66066-00206-8

Tying Saltwater Flies: 12 of the Best

by Deke Meyer

SB: $9.95

ISBN-13: 978-1-57188-066-6

UPC: 0-66066-00257-0

Saltwater Flies of the Northeast

by Angelo Peluso

More than 100 fly-tiers, guides and captains—from the southern tip of New Jersey up through the rugged coastline of Maine—share their most productive saltwater flies. The fly photographs and artwork throughout this book are stunning! 11 1/4 x 8 3/4 inches, 191 pages, full-color.

HB: $29.95

ISBN-13: 978-1-57188-394-0

UPC: 0-81127-00228-3

Fly Fishing for Pacific Salmon II

by Les Johnson and Bruce Ferguson

Completely rewritten and updated, full-color follow-up to their popular 1985 book of the same name.

SB: $39.95

ISBN-13: 978-1-57188-434-3

UPC: 0-81127-00268-9

HB: $59.95

ISBN-13: 978-1-57188-422-0

UPC: 0-81127-00256-6

Ltd. HB: $130.00

ISBN-13: 978-1-57188-423-7

UPC: 0-81127-00257-3

Ask for these books at your local fly/tackle shop or call toll-free to order:

1.800.541.9498 (8-5 p.s.t.) • www.amatobooks.com

Absolutely Positively FREE!

Start your subscription to *Flyfishing & Tying Journal* with a FREE issue. Fill in the information below and we will send your first issue FREE. If you like it, send back the special renewal envelope that will arrive after the magazine. If you don't want a subscription, keep the issue and *do nothing*. No bills, no hassles, NO STRINGS ATTACHED.

We're confident you'll love *FTJ*. Each information-filled full-color issue will make your time on the water more successful, your time at the tying bench more enjoyable. Within our pages you'll find North America's hottest fly-fishing authors.

So go ahead, expect the best. *Flyfishing & Tying Journal* is your magazine!

To receive your FREE issue of FTJ send a copy of this coupon or call today!

Name:____

Address:______________________________________

City:____________________State:________Zip:____________

Flyfishing & Tying Journal
P.O. Box 82112, Portland, OR 97282
www.amatobooks.com • 800•541•9498 • FAX 503•653•2766
Offer available in U.S. only

0199